Cyberpsychology

Also by Ángel J. Gordo-López

Psicologías, Discursos y Poder (PDP)
Ángel J. Gordo-López and J.L. Linaza (eds)

Queer Andtherness
Ángel J. Gordo-López and Gill Aitken

Psychology Discourse Practice: From Regulation to Resistance
Erica Burman, Gill Aitken, Pam Alldred, Robin Allwood, Tom
Billington, Brenda Goldberg, Ángel Juan Gordo-López, Colleen
Heenan, Deborah Marks and Sam Warner

Also by Ian Parker

Deconstructuring Psychopathology
Ian Parker, Eugenie Georgaca, David Harper, Terence McLaughlin
and Mark Stowell-Smith

Psychoanalytic Culture: Psychoanalytic Discourse in Western Society
Ian Parker

Deconstructing Psychotherapy
Ian Parker (ed.)

Cyberpsychology

Edited by

Ángel J. Gordo-López and Ian Parker

First published 1999 by
MACMILLAN PRESS LTD
Houndmills, Basingstoke, Hampshire RG21 6XS
and London
Companies and representatives
throughout the world

ISBN 0–333–73576–5 hardcover
ISBN 0–333–73577–3 paperback

A catalogue record for this book is available
from the British Library.

This book is printed on paper suitable for recycling and
made from fully managed and sustained forest sources.

10 9 8 7 6 5 4 3 2 1
08 07 06 05 04 03 02 01 00 99

Editing and origination by
Aardvark Editorial, Mendham, Suffolk

Printed in Hong Kong

Abrazos Virtuales

For Rex Stainton Rogers (1942–99) who
encouraged and supported this project, and
many others besides

Contents

Notes on Contributors

Betty M. Bayer is Associate Professor of Social Psychology and teaches in women's studies at Hobart and William Smith Colleges, New York. She is co-editor of *Reconstructing the Psychological Subject: Bodies, Practices, and Technologies* (1998), and has published papers on feminist theory and questions of the body. She is currently engaged in research on the history of human–technology coordinations in scientific practices and identity, subjectivity and the body.

Steven D. Brown is a Lecturer in Social and Organizational Psychology at Keele University, and a member of the Centre for Social Theory and Technology. He is the author of *The Life of Stress* (forthcoming), and has published widely in the area of poststructuralism, technoscience and culture. Current research includes a project on groupware and mediation of memory as part of the ESRC's *Virtual Society?* programme.

Erica Burman is Professor of Psychology and Women's Studies in the Discourse Unit at The Manchester Metropolitan University. Her work is in the areas of feminist critiques of developmental psychology, subjectivity and discourse. Her books include *Deconstructing Developmental Psychology* (1994), *Psychological Theory and Feminist Practice* (ed.) (1990) and *Deconstructing Feminist Psychology* (ed.) (1998).

Nydza Correa De Jesús is Associate Professor in the Department of Psychology, Río Piedras Campus, University of Puerto Rico. She is also a Visiting Professor in the Social Psychology Department of the Faculty of Sociology and Politics at the Universidad Complutense de Madrid. Her field of interests range from epistemology and methodology in the human sciences, to consumption and the relationship between cities and subjectivity in current social theory.

John Cromby is in the Department of Interdisciplinary Human Studies at Bradford University. His interests include the social construction of subjectivity, and the development and evaluation of educational virtual environments for people with learning disabilities. Currently he has a P200MMX with 32mb of RAM, a 3D card and a copy of 'Quake 2' wherein he happily assassinates other cyborgs.

Heidi J. Figueroa-Sarriera is Associate Professor at the Department of Psychology, Río Piedras Campus, University of Puerto Rico. As a transdisciplinary social psychologist she is involved in research on cultural representations of high-tech designs and human–machine interfaces. She teaches social psychology at graduate and undergraduate level as well as graduate seminars on new technology and emerging subjectivities. She is assistant editor with Steven Mentor and Chris Hables Gray (editor) of *The Cyborg Handbook* (1995) and she co-edited with Madeline Román and María Milagros López (1994) *Más Allá de la Bella (In)diferencia: Revisión Postfeminista y otras Escrituras Posibles.*

Ángel Juan Gordo-López is Assistant Lecturer in the Department of Sociology IV at the Faculty of Political Sciences and Sociology at the Universidad Complutense de Madrid and a member of the Discourse Unit. He is the co-editor with J.L. Linaza of *Psicologías, Discursos y Poder* (PDP) (1996), co-author with Erica Burman *et al.* of *Psychology Discourse Practice* (1996) and currently working with Gill Aitken on *Queer Andtherness.*

Dan Heggs is a member of the Discourse Unit and his current research interests focus on discourse, narrative and representation strategies in comic books. His publications include the chapter on comics in *Critical Textwork: An Introduction to Varieties of Discourse and Analysis* (1999, Open University Press).

Steve Jones is a Professor and Head of Communication at the University of Illinois, Chicago. He is the author of five books, including *CyberSociety: Computer-Mediated Communication and Community, Virtual Culture: Identity and Community in Cyberspace,* and *Doing Internet Research* (Sage). His research focuses on the social consequences of communication technologies.

Jill Marsden lectures in philosophy at Bolton Institute. Recent publications on feminism and cyberculture include 'Virtual sexes and feminist futures: the philosophy of "cyberfeminism"' (*Radical Philosophy*, **78**), 'Reinventing nature' (*Women's Philosophy Review*, **13**), 'On the matter of sexual difference' (*Journal of the British Society for Phenomenology*, **27**), and 'Lines of flight: Freud, Schreber, Nietzsche' (*Journal of the British Society for Phenomenology*, **28**).

Virginia Nightingale writes about audience but is fascinated by human cultures of all times and types. Just before writing her response for *Cyberpsychology* she visited the neolithic sites in the Orkneys while on vacation. Some reading prompted by this visit mysteriously surfaces in her writing here. Virginia is Associate Professor in the School of Communication and Media at the University of Western Sydney, Nepean.

Ian Parker is Professor of Psychology in the Discourse Unit at Bolton Institute, where he directs the MSc Critical Psychology programme and is managing editor of the *Annual Review of Critical Psychology*. His books include *Psychoanalytic Culture: Psychoanalytic Discourse in Western Society* (1997, Sage).

James Sey is a Senior Lecturer in the English Department at Vista University (Soweto Campus), and teaches courses in popular culture in the Music School of the University of the Witwatersrand in Johannesburg. His PhD concerned the ways in which science fiction in various media can be read, through a psychoanalytic framework, as an implicit critique of technological culture, specifically the relationship between bodies and machines. He has recently co-edited and contributed to a special edition of the psychoanalysis and culture journal *American Imago*, on psychoanalysis in South Africa. He is currently interested in the confluence of digital technologies and conceptual art, and in the history of technology.

Carlos Soldevilla Pérez is Assistant Lecturer in the Department of Sociological Theory at the Faculty of Political Sciences and Sociology of the Universidad Complutense de Madrid. His research focuses on the analysis of personality and new contemporary styles of life. His doctoral thesis obtained the Doctoral Research Award in 1995 and his latest publication is

La Gènesis del Constructo Estilo de Vida en las Ciencias Sociales (The Genesis of the Style of Life Construct in Social Sciences) (1998).

Penny Standen is Reader in Health Psychology and Learning Disabilities at Nottingham University. After completing a PhD in ethology, she wasted too many years setting up a course to teach psychology to medical students at Nottingham and then delivering the teaching. During this time most of her research focused on psychological factors associated with health, illness and the delivery of healthcare. Her current appointment has allowed an indulgence in two of her interests: the place of disability in society, and computers and IT. These interests find expression in her research with John Cromby on the use of virtual environments with people with learning disabilities.

Francisco Javier Tirado is Assistant Lecturer in Social Psychology and Organizations in the Faculty of Psychology at the Universidad Autónoma de Barcelona (UAB). He completed his Masters in Social Psychology at UAB with a thesis 'Cyborgs and extitutions: new forms for the social', and he is now working on theoretical projects on the concept of the social and its relationship with the emergence of techno-aesthetics.

CHAPTER 1

Cyberpsychology: Postdisciplinary Contexts and Projects

ÁNGEL J. GORDO-LÓPEZ AND IAN PARKER

The activity of comparing the mind with different kinds of mechanical equipment has been common practice throughout the history of Western civilization. Greek philosophers and empiricist scholars depicted the human being as being no more than a tabula rasa, an image itself inspired by earlier ancient scribes' wax boards. Since then endless exemplars of thinking and machine analogies have been proposed to understand mental processes. Among these we can record the powerful impact of hydraulic systems, steam engines, assembly lines, calculation engines, electric circuits, computers, screen interfaces and, now, collective global environments epitomized by cyberspace.

These analogies have often rendered individuals and collectives into things that can be adapted to dominant economic and political requirements. Behaviourism in psychology – a tradition of research which developed against the background of phenomenology and the exploration of subjectivity in the Wundtian classical tradition in the discipline at the end of the eighteenth century, and as a reaction to that tradition – presented itself as the first thorough 'scientific psychology'. Then, in the 1950s the 'first cognitive revolution' in psychology broke the discipline from behaviourism as one powerful alienating tradition of research, and linked up with another no less alienating set of ideas about the self in popular culture, cognitive psychology. Although it promised a major transformation in the conceptual apparatus of the discipline, cognitive psychology succeeded in doing little more than 'filling in' the subject that behaviourist psychology had constituted.

The popular notion that the mind operates as if it were a machine (a 'black box' or, increasingly now, a computer) accompanied the cognitive revolution, and this popular notion operated both as a warrant for scientists involved and gained force as an effect of their work. The project of cognitive psychology, and then the even more grandiose ambition to develop a separate 'cognitive science' and 'cybernetic science' which claimed to be able to account for all psychological phenomena, appealed to popular notions of the self in Western culture. Here were profoundly ideological notions of the self as a container of private ideas and interiorized processes of thought that could, in principle, run completely independently of relationships with other people.

As Ashby (1956: 1, 3 – italics in original) put it, cybernetic science, 'treats not things but *ways of behaving*. It does not ask "what *is* this thing?" but *"what does it do?*... not "what individual act will it produce here and now?", but "what are *all* the possible behaviours that it can produce?".' But he also already raises a problem with the whole enterprise, 'What does happen when the system [for example the mind, the brain] is such that not all of it is accessible to direct observation?' (ibid.: 115). From this point on the irresolvable problem of 'unobservable systems' or 'black box theory' would have special importance in the field. The problem unleashed a fullblown programme of research and experiments in psychology. It was Boring (1944), as Galison (1994: 247) states, who first found 'Wiener's suggestion that all functions of the brain might be duplicated by electrical systems "very attractive"' and made a list of functions of the brain which put them in terms that could be translated into the terminology of 'input', 'output' and 'adjustment' (see Edwin G. Boring's letter to Wiener, 1994, cited in Galison, 1994). This body–machine tradition was also manifested in Turing's (1950) notion of the 'universal machine' (the computer), Tomkins' (1962) understanding of the brain as a homogeneous, differentiatable but not originally differentiated system with the potential for developing local qualitatively different forms of specialization, and von Neumann's work on computation and the brain (see Galison, 1994; Kosofsky Sedgwick and Frank, 1995). Overall, these projects worked on the premise that the human being is essentially an 'information-processor' (Simon, 1969; Mayer, 1981; Gardner, 1985).

But if cybernetics, as a science dedicated to the abstraction of formal properties of relations in systems, needed 'to isolate the systems of wider connection for the sake of formalisation and development of control processes' (Lerner, 1972: 2), cognitive psychology required machine analogies to secure the unstable relations which were being speculated to exist between inner information devices and outer social systems. These contradictory requirements helped set the stage for the ways cognitive psychology called for an account of wider networks of information, management and control to maintain its own various ambitious projects, which included, for example, design of education curricula in the USA (Noble, 1989). These projects are characterized by the way they perpetually shift in focus and rest on paradoxical epistemological foundations (Gordo-López, 1996).

Now psychology is leaping into the realm of new 'cyber' analogies to take cognitive systems approaches onward and upward. Leon James (1997), for example, argues that the internal structure of cyberspace is 'similar to and congruent with the mind'. Decision-making processes can be also seen as an internal form of 'clicking' virtual activities such as 'registering your vote on a Form, leaving an e-mail message of a Page, or copying and downloading an image' (ibid.). These kinds of analogies work hand in hand with ostensibly democratizing hopes for technology in which 'using and participating are the mechanisms by which virtual reality [and the cyberpersona] evolves'. In the age of cyberspace we are often told that one has the freedom to click on, access and participate in what these burgeoning cyberpsychological accounts refer to as 'communal mind'.

In sum, while the behavioural impetus in traditional psychological twentieth-century research continued to strengthen a conception of the human being as equivalent to a machine, cognitive reformulations of this behaviourist creed invited into psychology new machine metaphors, and one of the effects of this process was the reincorporation into the discipline of long-suppressed 'common sense' understandings of mental activities outside in the 'real world'. Of course, it has not only been the employment of such human–machine metaphors that has fuelled and prolonged the cognitive paradigm but also the enduring alliances between the academic apparatus of psychology and military-bureaucratic networks of information management and control (Haraway, 1991).

From the sciences of control to controlling sciences

Early cybernetic research focused on the design of anti-aircraft predictor devices able to make statistical forecasts of the operation of Nazi pilots' minds understood as embedded in a symbiotic relation with the performance of their aircraft. As Galison (1994: 235) notes, Wiener, a mathematician and physicist and founding figure of cybernetic sciences, 'came to see it [the anti-aircraft predictor] as the articulated prototype for a new understanding of the human–machine relation, one that made soldier, calculator, and the fire-power into a single integrated system'. The concept of information employed in this research reduced representations of decision-making processes to the activity of simple selection. Another key characteristic of this classic cybernetics often associated with Wiener's foundational research (1948, 1954), was the definition of control as 'a function for maintaining and preserving the conditions leading to concrete targets within a pregiven action scheme' (Navarro, 1990: 24 – our translation). The two main principles which governed this dominant understanding of the task of cybernetics were objectification processes which would turn the act of decision making into a calculable reified procedure, and the notion of control which could not function without a correlative objectification of the notion of a perceptual and cognitive target.

Meanwhile, a parallel track was being followed by those working away from classic cybernetics, in understandings of family systems, psychopathology and therapeutic work for example. A case in point is to be found in Bateson's (1972) definition of information as 'a difference which makes a difference'. This generative aspect of difference makes possible the emergence of new forms able to generate new objects and it thus avoids combining abstraction with the reductionism evident in classic cybernetics. However, even that more humanist tradition was also marked by 'the objectification of action as a process of difference rather than as a selective process' (Navarro, 1990: 24 – our translation). Nydza Correa de Jesús in her chapter amplifies our understanding of these technocultural conditions for cyberpsychology by deepening the ways the 'subject occupies positions already destabilized by the subversion of reality'. It is in those very forms of closure, however, that Correa de Jesús envisions possibilities, not in subverting or abolishing rules but in the construction of new rules in new realms. In short, it is in the 'leap from lineal to complex thought, where knowledge generates from thinking the thought that thinks about the systems of observation' that Correa de Jesús places cyberpsychology.

The science of servomechanism and control was not restricted to the behaviour of fighter pilots or psychological applications in the wider military–industrial complex. As Sadie Plant (1995: 25) comments, 'If cybernetic systems can be seen to develop out of the histories of technologies and tools, they also emerge on complex lines of immanent activity which constitute the undersides of the histories of science, the arts, and technology.' It is with this in mind that we can now better comprehend some of the other navigational aid connotations of the term 'cybernetics' derived from the Greek *kubernetes* and *kybernetike*, which means the 'art of steermanship'. As Guilbaud (cited in Jang, 1994: 21–2) notes, the concept

> 'Cybernetics' is the root of various words to do with sailing including Latin words such as *gubernaculum* (a helm), and *gubernator* (a helmsman); and the French word *gouvernail* (a rudder)… The derivates of the term have different metaphorical meanings; for instance, govern, governor, government are also political metaphors.

These etymological considerations also help us to understand the ways the broad compass of cybernetics in Western culture, and cognitive psychology as a crucial orientation to human behaviour within it, progressively moved from being the science of prediction and control to being one of the important controlling sciences. Our vision of the possibilities and dangers of cyberpsychology here, then, must navigate tendencies towards control and disorder, predicted and unexpected outcomes, and regularities of movement and transgressive differences. Cyberpsychology thus exists in a field of tense relationships between classic and alternative cybernetics, and between the histories of art, science and technology. The dense productive natures of these tensions have themselves provided the conditions of possibility for this book, and have enabled us to bring together the work of psychologists, cultural theorists and feminist philosophers working in the sphere of technology and subjectivity to explore links between psychological culture and cyberculture, and between technoscience and politics.

A first common concern running through the book, and picked up by each contributor in turn with slightly different inflections to the argument, is the way cyberneologisms and practices have come to permeate psychology and related disciplines at various degrees of complexity and levels of awareness. A second common concern is the way cyberspace, and the different forms of subjectivity that inhabit it, poses a challenge, or not, to technologies of surveillance and control which comprise the modern 'psy-techno complex', which we define as the dense network of virtual and material technologies and practices to do with the 'mind' and 'behaviour' that comprise academic and professional work and psychology inside and outside the classroom and the clinic in popular culture.

The range of ideas introduced and explored so lucidly and radically by our contributors and an explicit opposition to 'meta-narratives' in some of the chapters would seem to encourage us to resist any kind of introductory framing, for that framing would always do some violence to the specific arguments. However, we still feel it necessary to reflect on the wider conditions of possibility for cyberpsychological phenomena and its possible trajectories. As Joanne Hodge (1995: 34) argues, 'It is in response to questions within the existing discipline of psychology that the neologism *cyberpsychology* presents itself.' This means that we need to take care to focus both upon the way the questions are asked in psychology as a particular disciplinary apparatus and domain of work and upon the way psychology is embedded in an interdisciplinary network where different kinds of question can be asked. For sociological perspectives, for example, there are real dangers of losing sight of critiques of power. Such dynamics can be already seen in some 'critical' psychological research that focuses on subjectivity *per se* to such an extent that it abandons the crucial subject matter of any critical approach to the discipline, *viz.* subjectification processes and our location in wider dynamics of oppression and resistance. There are also dangers in the way we might be tempted to stay within the orbit of the discipline and engage in a psychologizing reframing of, for instance, ecofeminist and cyberfeminist critiques of the relations between science and gender. Such anxieties underpin the following reflections on the technocultural conditions of possibility for cyberpsychology and then the broader postdisciplinary context for this project.

Technocultural conditions of possibility for cyberpsychology

Lewis Mumford's (1934: 12) definition of technological developments as a set of complex relations which embrace 'the knowledge and skills and arts derived from industry or implicated in the new technics, and which include various forms of tools, instruments, apparatus and utility' as well as social structure, disciplinary coordinations or regimentation, is helpful here to understand the conditions of possibility, or technocultural preparation for cyberpsychology.

Mumford (1934: 42) identifies examples of the cultural preparation of early industrial technologies in 'the slaves and peasants who hauled the stones for the pyramids, pulling in the rhythm to the crack of the whip, the slaves working in the Roman galley, each man chained to his seat and unable to perform any other motion than the limited mechanical one'. Similarly, Gigerenzer (1997: 33) recalls how the computer was 'originally modeled after the new social organization of work, and, after an individualistic incarnation, the social organization of work is now being modeled after the computer'.

While Mumford developed a relational account of the development of technology in order to understand, for example, the way processes of individuation and regimentation are intimately bound up with the way they were culturally prepared (for example, in clock theory), Michel Foucault, for his part, has shown a correlative, although limited, engagement with technological complexity. Foucault (1988: 18) illustrates the way that dynamics of regulation and control and the self-knowledge of the modern subject comprises four different types of interrelated technologies:

> Production, which permits us to produce, transform, or manipulate things.
>
> Sign systems, which permits us to use signs, meaning, symbols, or signification.
>
> Power, which determines the conduct of individuals and submits them to certain ends of domination, and objectivizing of the subject.
>
> The self, which permits individuals to effect by their own means or with the help of others a certain number of operations on their own bodies and souls, thoughts, conduct, and way of being, so as to transform themselves in order to attain a certain state of happiness, purity, wisdom, perfection or immortality. (Foucault, 1988: 18)

Although he acknowledges that these different technologies 'hardly ever function separately, although each one of them is associated with a certain type of domination' (ibid.: 18), Foucault was more interested in 'the interaction between oneself and others and in the technologies of individual domination, the history of how an individual acts upon himself, in the technology of the self' (ibid.: 19).

Exploring the conditions of possibility for cyberpsychology now entails thinking strategically about these kinds of accounts, including the possibility they may themselves operate as forms of technology (cf. Stone, 1995; Gray, 1996). It also entails thinking of strategies whereby we may trespass against the different gradients of resistance in the discipline of psychology in order to recognize its own part in the different psy-techno complexes that comprise Western culture (Burman *et al.*, 1996; Gordo-López, forthcoming).

Recently there has been a revival of interest in theoretical psychology which addresses relations between technology and subjectivity (Schraube, 1997), technologies in the history of the discipline (Edwards, 1996), networks of power (Michael, 1996), technologies of the body (Bayer and Shotter, 1998), the productive work of technical objects in psychoanalytic culture (Parker, 1997), the composition of selves in information society (Barglow, 1994) and the updating of a recurrent concern in the discipline with techniques of government and self-government (Rose, 1996). Nevertheless, most of this work still often seems to be a little too much preoccupied with catching up and leaping aboard the technoculture wagon, and fails to address contemporary forms of regulation that it feeds upon and maintains. This fixation with technology, evident on occasion even on the 'critical' margins of the discipline often also results in the colonization of new spaces with old languages. Still worse, these kinds of study – and we include this collection of writings too – threaten, albeit unwittingly, to play their part in the taming, incorporation and dissolving of disruptive subversive transgressive cybercultural monsters into the discipline.

The very activity of focusing our critique on the very real *centripetal* forces in psychology that attempt to draw each and every phenomenon in culture into its embrace might itself bring about the selfsame unintended effects. It might also drive our analysis of cyberpsychology into the mistaken endeavour of trying to know more fully and authentically our own disciplinary real 'selves', an endeavour that would all the more thoroughly mask the *centrifugal* forces of the discipline, the way it repeatedly throws out ideological conceptions of the self into psychological culture.

It is with these dangers in mind that we want to reconsider, from a cyberpsychological angle, other points of reference and ways of delimiting the activity of critique which resists any such drive toward a complete self-sufficient picture of ourselves as (critical) psychological, well-disciplined creatures. This reconsideration might then afford along the way a different understanding of the way social constructionism – ostensibly one of the most critical approaches in psychology at the moment – works in cyberspace as loyal court critic and reluctant celebrant. Social constructionism participates in what Castel (1984) refers to as a 'postdisciplinary' mode of being. Social constructionism also participates to varying degrees and with various kinds of different effects in psychological culture and the engorgement of contemporary psychologism. The social constructionist incorporation and purification of machine culture, the re-enchantment of the plasticity and lightness of being must itself be problematized.

Francisco Tirado takes up these themes in his chapter, and argues that the 'cyborg' is a metaphor. Representing cyborgs means to dissolve their subversive potential and to turn them into 'a unique, identifiable species'. But, he asks, 'If "cyborg" has broken beyond the limits of metaphor, what is it now? What shall we call it? How do we understand it?' It is from the possibility of thinking metaphorically that Tirado revisits social constructionism. Thinking of the social from the cyborg angle entails thinking it from the angle of cartography from where the social often emerges as an *effect* rather than a temporally fixed ontology of distributed relationships and actions. With mesmerizing style Tirado maps and imagines cyberpsychological events and trajectories as part of 'a project that is always open, without doctrinal or methodological limits'.

Shifting attitudes toward technological issues in psychology – be it mainstream, theoretical or critical – coincides, as we have already indicated, with the increasing power of psychological culture, and this wider culture goes well beyond, and then returns to condition, academic and professional psychology. Analytical concepts such as the 'psy-complex' and now the notion of 'psy-techno complex' are often still too preoccupied and entertained by the activity of simply denouncing processes of regulation, and they tend to omit or, worse, obscure the disciplinary function of other imaginary spheres in which psychological selves are fabricated and in which deep ideological psychologism is rooted. If we were to focus only on explicitly psychological places and spend all our energies directing our critiques to the terrible things the discipline is overtly doing to people, we could well contribute to the constitution of other kinds of imaginary places in culture along the way which, just as efficiently manufacture real psychological 'subjects'.

Another way of highlighting why we need to include an understanding of the cultural preparation of cyberpsychology in wider psychological culture is to show how archaic scientific traditions and religion shared a common pattern of work and underlying interests when they were most powerful in attributing certain qualities to things, purifying things of the kind of dirty matter which did not fit those attributions, individualizing ways of thinking and behaving, and reappropriating community knowledge represented in such practices as alchemy. Scientific judgement has historically and contemporaneously attributed knowledge and supernatural 'techniques' to particular individuals – wise women, witches, cyberfeminists – rather than to the community to which they belong and which made it possible for them to interpret and change things.

Such dynamics of individuation and individualization contribute to the view that, as Dan Heggs' chapter notes, 'individual solutions are preferred over societal problems'. Heggs suggests that the origin story in superhero comics 'serves to protect, not the society in which it appears, but the individual against threats to a past fantasy state found in the "family"'. These are fantasies, Heggs notes, that fit comfortably into the mould of US society. Discourses and practices surrounding witches, superheros, and cyborgs, among others, illustrate how the legitimation of scientific techniques is often actually rooted in people's own activities and forms of knowledge. What scientific strategies of legitimation in the service of technological power do is to engage in the disappropriation of local community knowledge, the re-presentation of the knowledge in expert discourse and the delegitimation of people's links with their communities (Jordanova, 1989; Alvarez-Uría, 1993).

To collude with the view that there are clear and necessary lines of demarcation between local everyday and universalizable expertise without reflecting on the conditions of possibility for those forms of demarcation and the functions of specific defining technologies is to end up incorporating challenges to power at different points in history into whatever sociopolitical conditions obtain. The way in which representations of bodies, emotions, odours, or styles of language acquisition often work is also to engage in such collusive strategies, and such considerations are pertinent with respect to cyberpsychological research. This is evident, of course, in the Taylorist demand for the workforce to be adaptable to measurement and control, as James Sey points out in his contribution. Sey reviews the correspondence between different forms of subjectivity and management in contemporary technoculture and emphasizes the way that, in the passage from modes of production in early modern society to modes of information governed by digital technologies of consumption, the body has only apparently been liberated from, and has actually been swallowed by, technological systems. We also need to reflect upon the way representations of virtuality can themselves call upon notions of subjective plasticity and flexibility in the development of identities that are actually disturbingly desirable to workplace managers in new conditions of flexible knowledge production.

The postdisciplinary context of cyberpsychology

According to Giddens (1991, 1992), one of the most striking transformations in modern society recently has been in the growing sense of *autonomy* as a crucial characteristic of the reflexive self. Autonomy is portrayed as a condition for the self to be able to relate to other social beings on equal terms and as a requirement for people to be able to safeguard the democratic projects of public life. The most important factor here, according to Giddens (1991), lies in a complex understanding by 'ordinary' people of *psychological* literature. Giddens then turns back to an analysis of cultural production to understand the ongoing transformation of the field of intimacy by examining sources which promote people's reflexive practices and knowledge in modern society. As Varela and Alvarez-Uría (1997: 18 – our translation) indicate, 'The influence of psychological culture – or a suspicious psychologism – subsumes Giddens's sociology.'

Similar relational patterns can be noted in recent transformations in the intimate relation between psychology and technoculture. The way in which psychology is now coming out of its technoscientific closet should be treated with care. This process of acknowledging deep connections with technoscience – and military agendas in the case of cognitive science – is useful, but it could also become part of a wider performance of democratization that, by imposing new notions of fitness, health and information processing, participates all the more in a psychologizing culture of unification and the suppression of critique, conflict and resistance. Psychological cultural politics is well able to incorporate small doses of awareness of technoscience which are around in popular cyberculture in images of monstrosity and transhumanity. This is something that Steve Brown deals with in his chapter.

Brown emphasizes the distinguished role of cognitive psychology in 'the recovery of the quotidian from the uncanny'. It is in this preparation, as part of the wider umbrella of the new world order "where life itself becomes a problem of coding"; that cognitive psychology looks with interest to the emerging strategies of transhumanist coding, such as the 'extropian movement'. This movement sees in 'the fluidity of humans, and their alliances with biotechnics... a passage for salvation in a pure state of complete disorganization or entropy'. These new visions fit neatly into a new evolutionary stage of virtual reality and cyberpsychology. It is precisely by addressing technoscience in small manageable quantities that psychology is able to tame and represent images of cyberspace and virtual reality in order to facilitate the transition to greater democratization, to visions of interactivity and participation in new global villages.

In this way, disenchantment with the modern world on the part of many people can be handled and progressively smoothed out in comforting images of technological progress (Castel, in Friedman, 1986). Meanwhile, these strategies of inoculation and immunization against a sense of risk also have the effect of bloating further the individualized self and the institutionalization of humanist images of the person. As Gigerenzer (1997: 33 – in conference guide) states, the relations between the computer and psychology 'became institutionalized as an indispensable research tool in the psychological laboratories in the 1970s, it became widely accepted as a model (or at least a useful metaphor) for the individual mind' (see also Gigerenzer, 1991). In other words, the relations between cybernetics and psychology have been incorporated and institutionalized as another psychological shift coherent with humanist premises while putting forward the view that the computer was incorporated as a metaphor for the understanding and simulation of the human mind's faculties.

Such fake democratization of psychology and technoculture contributes to the very dangers it claims to ameliorate. Just as Foucault (1992: 136 – our translation) once argued that peaceful civil society, a camouflage for warfare, 'should be understood as the continuation of war and, therefore, decoded as episodes, fragments, displacements of war itself', so Castel, (in Tabares, 1986: 25) for his part, now cogently points out that a problematization of this state of affairs also demands an acknowledgement of the complex tasks and risks that face us as we try to deal with such issues. Cyberpsychological risk-taking also has, therefore, to be aware that it may be endorsing wider processes of inoculation and immunization.

Reflection on the postdisciplinary context of cyberpsychology here has included an emphasis on the individualizing potential of the project. In addition, it has led us to consider cyberpsychology as part of wider psychological culture with respect to images of risk and the way it promotes democratizing fictions of opening access for all to the means of production, to information technology, and the vision of computer-mediated communication (CMC) as a transparent medium for communities.

Psychological immersion in technoculture and technohistory should be understood in a context where complex relations of production and information require complex strategies to problematize existing ideological positions. Now, cyberpsychology has to live with the even more complex and horrifying risk of populating psychological culture. This could result in more amplified and plastic forms of the self that are happy to draw upon 'technochic' transhumanism or extropianism in small doses. These new forms of humanism play the trick of aesthetisizing technological experience, as if subjectivity in technoculture has not already been asthetisized enough. In this way cyberpsychology might become even more compatible with liberal democratic visions of the history of subjectivity and possibilities for its enlargement (for example, Renaut, 1997).

Cyberpsychological 'missives'

Cyberwork in psychology, then, faces specific dangers, and, we believe, confronts specific tasks. In a manner quite different from developments in other disciplines such as cultural studies, communication studies or even 'cyborgology' itself (Gray *et al.*, 1995), cyberpsychology is not presented here as something to be 'incorporated'.

First, psychology is rooted in technoculture as one of the key technosciences and technologies of the self, and for this reason it finds it difficult to strike a distance from cyberculture, to see it as alien, monstrous or as its unacknowledged repressed other. Psychology is so used to assimilating what is different to it into something which is the same, particularly with respect to technological rhetorics and practices, that critical work has to struggle to make the difference evident. In some senses 'cyberpsychology' and 'cyborg body politics' is immanent to the psychological discipline and to psychological culture, as Betty Bayer points out in her chapter. Bayer shows a grounded awareness of the different correspondences between distinct forms of theorizing subjectivity and management styles. The focus of her contribution is on the ways in which the psychological apparatus, its history of cyborg body politics, naturalizes relations while making engendering boundaries. Bayer argues that querying normalizing and naturalizing practices is a key strategy to 'unseat epistemic sovereignty'. So, if a danger is that the radical transgressive nature of cyberpsychology is almost, as it were, too close to be seen, one rationale for this book is to render visible this omnipresent yet peculiarly hidden thing.

Second, we need to be careful not simply to endorse fantasies of liberation that surround new technologies in the mass media and popular culture (see Penley and Ross, 1991). The cyberpsychological arguments collected in this book do not, then, limit themselves either to identifying new critical spaces that cyberspace opens up or possibilities for developing critiques of psychology. They are sensitive to the ways in which cyberpsychology itself may operate in the service of power and become a willing accomplice of the 'psy-techno complex', as Erica Burman points out with respect to developmental psychology. Burman indentifies 'the tense and contested moment of cyberpsychology always vulnerable to recuperation into the individualism of both dominant psychology and of the market for technological consumption'. The analysis which Burman derives from comparing motifs of development in the child and the cyborg is with a view to identifying their individualizing, and engendering potential in cyberculture.

Third, our vision of critical cyberpsychology is of it as a strategy which is able to resist the alchemy of 'saturated selves' as much as it resists the promise of false democratization. If there is any form of identification at work in the arguments in the chapters in this book with cyberpsychology it is in the manner of identification in 'queer theory' (Jagose, 1996), one in which it plays with the misunderstanding of those who try to incorporate it and attempt to 'know' it better than it knows itself. Heidi Figueroa-Sarriera's chapter on identity and selfhood is signal in this regard. She questions essences by attending to the relations between different forms of identities across 'real' and 'virtual' spaces. Putting identity at centre stage, Figueroa-Sarriera insists on the inadequacy of imposing debates and argument from those theories which maintain a continuity, 'essence' or identity of the self upon performative models which assume identification always operates in situated contexts. Research in computer-mediated communication, for example, supports the view that forms of identity and processes of identification are constructed in CMCs in *synchronic* time. This calls for an understanding informed by metaphors of territorialization, which produces enclosed spaces in conjunction with nomadic perspectives that break and subvert boundaries.

Fourth, we propose that perhaps it is in the domain of the queer sexual drive and its transgressive and transfigurative work on identity that cyberpsychology may revel best in its monstrosity and perform its most progressive role (Parker, 1996, Gordo-López and Aitken, in prep.). It is surely its very conspicuous promiscuity which defines it as a satisfactory partner to couple with in order to address the intimate but transformative relations between management-information-control networks and discipline. Jill Marsden reveals in her chapter part of the discursive machinery that fixes, for instance, the feminizing bodiless experiences of Freud's patient, Judge Schreber, with feminized predispositions and a contemporary cultural receptiveness to images and experiences of the postbiological body. Freud's analysis of Schreber's transsexualizing delusions, serves as evidence, for Marsden, to confirm the prejudices of traditional psychology and the ways these prejudices inform a voluptuous and disembodied feminized psyche. Varela (1997, 1998) has identified similar processes which she refers to as 'feminising devices', something which finds a genealogical referent in the work of Georg Simmel (Oakes, 1984) and a resonance in ongoing cyber-feminists (Plant, 1995, 1997).

Fifth, we want to emphasize again that it would be mistaken to conceive of cyberpsychology as something which is destined to improve modern psychology. Cyberpsychology 'itself', whatever it is, is not interested in bringing psychology up to date and stretching the boundaries of psychological culture to make it all the more accessible to information management. John Cromby and Penny Standen in their chapter explore the limits of cyberspace and its dilemmas in 'hands-on' research to assess the potential of virtual environment devices for critiques of mainstream psychology. We take Cromby and Standen's concerns seriously, and there is evidence that cyberpsychology's incorporative nemesis is already on the scene.

Take, for instance, a new US journal like *CyberPsychology & Behavior* (1988) which aims to cover 'how these technologies are changing the way we live, work, play, and interact with each other' (publisher's leaflet). Among the topics it promises to include are:

Demographics of Internet users... long distance learning... social isolation... delivery of mental health services over the Internet... neuropsychological effects of multimedia… virtual reality support systems in medicine… the debate over restrictions on Internet content… the question of universal access to the Internet… Internet addiction… computer phobia… and many other major issues of the day.

In contrast, cyberpsychology in this book is neither a way of knowing ourselves better in the information society nor a way of discovering the real essence of psychology, let alone how to create better relationships with 'psychologists, psychiatrists, sociologists, educators, computer scientists, business executives, and opinion makers' (publisher's leaflet, *CyberPsychology & Behavior*).

To avoid such psychological enframing of cyberpsychology, then, we have to be able devise ways of articulating its own death. That is, cyberpsychology needs to embed within itself a self-annihilating device, a certain kind of critical and self-critical narrative which both helps it to resist incorporation into the discipline and, at that moment it is incorporated, to go critical and explode inside the discipline causing the maximum amount of damage. Think of it as containing a highly sensitive critical clock mechanism which is triggered when it finds itself being published in mainstream books and journals and becoming part of the social scientific and psychological spectacle. You are reading this already. Is this the time? We want to insist that it is only in its *ephemeral* use that the potential of cyberpsychological critique can function, that it will be able to be the deconstructive spanner in the machinery of the psy-techno complex.

Ephemeral and self-annihilating methodological gravity

The discipline of psychology enjoys great flexibility within networks of power, and cyberpsychology must also be flexible to avoid being adapted and simply plugged into those networks. Not only must cyberpsychology be ephemeral, then, it must also, when need be, demand the weight of gravity, and, rather like the virtual guerillas in Chiapas, find a way of finding the means of resistance to power not only in the 'meaning' of the message but in the frequency, size, and direction the message takes towards its target. We are referring here to the way the message can be articulated through pre-analytical programming much in the way macros which crash computer systems could be addressed to Mexican banks and multinationals supporting an oppressive regime

(Domínguez, 1998). But 'gravity' should not only be understood in terms of the gravity of the communication.

Cyberpsychology could even find, in the thorough assimilative process that the Situationists used to call 'recuperation' (Debord, 1977) (see Parker, 1996), or 'reification', resourceful ways to confer gravity on its own postdisciplinary technocultural context of possibility. This option enables cyberpsychology to become slightly more a disciplinary 'object'. From this perspective, the essential function of cyberpsychological drives, according to Carlos Soldevilla Pérez in his contribution, is to assure its 'objectificatory function'. Soldevilla Pérez traces the psychogenesis of the first technical device (or 'proto-object') and moves on to note relations between social construction-ist identities, Toyotism and cyberspace. This psychogenesis of the techniques and surrounding vertiginous sensations it evokes puts cyberpsychology in touch with a pagan mysticism, for Soldevilla Pérez, which resonates with Haraway's (1992) reading of biblical stories. In Haraway's case, 'what makes these (Judeo-Christian) figures so evocative and compelling is precisely their resistance to being represented as fully human... "trickster figures"' (Prins, 1993: 11). If one thinks of Jesus as a hu-man, father, spirit... or anorexic cyborg, with respect to Soldevilla Pérez's argument, might not the cyborg trickster even become a kind of *hallucinogenic toreador*.

In order to explore the margins of its *fetishistic* nature and devia-tions, cyberpsychology might:

- Let 'itself' be syncretized or negentropically assembled while generating a self-identity crash, a terminal fetishizing crisis of psychology, the self.
- Let 'itself' be incorporated by disciplinary orders and participate in disciplinary implanted memories, trajectories and management technologies performed through the psychological terminals where the circuits of corporate interests intersect.
- Let 'itself' be vanquished or dis/appropriated precisely in order to provoke generative frictions and the bringing to the surface of the underside of Promethean relations between technology and subjectivity.

Such strategies require:

- Highly sensitive devices to register the way cyberpsychology is being instrumentalized by technocultural networks of information management and control which define cyborg body politics and practices.

■ Complex awareness of the current postdisciplinary contexts and trajectories of cyberpsychology within them in order to stress the individualizing and accommodating potentials of cyberpsychology as well as ways to subvert them by means of collective ambiguity and spatialization.

Will this work? The book traces the development, history and contradictory understandings of cyberpsychology in four main parts. The first part, *Conditions of Possibility for the Psy-Techno Complex*, traces historical and contemporary lines of argument around the fascination between different forms of psychological and machine culture. The chapters in this section lay out the conditions of possibility for cyberpsychology within the psy-techno complex. The second part, *Body Politics, Ethics and Research Practice*, provides more contemporary lines of arguments around the relationship between psychology and cyberculture. Each of the chapters in this section draws attention to notions of embodiment and relational presence as well as to the ethical and political issues surrounding them. This part provides instances of the way cyberculture has been played out in psychological research and practice. The third part, *Trajectories, Identities and Events*, situates cyberpsychology in the interplay between the mobility and constraints of information networks. The chapters in this section attend to the way in which cyberpsychology might itself accomplish aspects of control and discipline that were starting to escape the discipline of psychology.

The final *Commentaries* section includes brief responses to the arguments by Steve Jones and Virginia Nightingale. We invited them to reflect on some of the issues raised in the book from their own very different perspectives. This part of the book is motivated by the wish to promote debate and 'cyberpsychological' reflections among researchers in communication studies, cultural theory, sociology, and, of course, psychology.

References

Alvarez-Uría, F. (1993) 'El historiador y el inquisidor. Ciencia, brujería y naturaleza en la génesis de la modernidad', *Archipiélago*, **15**: 43–60.
Ashby, W.R. (1956) *An Introduction to Cybernetics*. London: Fontana.
Barglow, R. (1994) *The Crisis of the Self in the Age of Information: Computers, Dolphins and Dreams*. London: Routledge.

Bateson, G. (1972) *Steps to an Ecology of Mind*. London: Paladin.

Bayer, B.M. and Shotter, J. (eds) (1998) *Reconstructing the Psychological Subject: Bodies, Practices, and Technologies*. London: Sage.

Boring, E.G. (1944) Letter to Wiener, 13 Nov., box 2, folder 66, Norbert Wiener Papers, collection MC-22, Institute Archives and Special Collections, Massachussetts Institute of Technology, Archives, Cambridge, MA.

Burman, E., Aitken, G., Alldred, P., Alwood, R., Billington, T., Goldberg, B., Gordo-López, A.J., Heenan, C., Marks, D. and Warner, S. (1996) 'Postscripts', in Burman *et al*. (co-authors) *Psychology Discourse Practice: From Regulation to Resistance*. London: Taylor & Francis.

Castel, R. (1984) *La Gestión de los Riesgos*. Barcelona: Anagrama.

Debord, G. ([1977] 1983) *Society of the Spectacle*. Detroit: Black & Red.

Domínguez, R. (1998) 'The Zapatista electronic movement: clogging up the pipelines of power', *Crash Media*, **1**: 5.

Edwards, P.N. (1996) *The Closed World: Computers and the Politics of Discourse in Cold War America*. Cambridge, MA: MIT Press.

Foucault, M. (1988) 'Technologies of the self', in Martin, L.H., Gutman, H. and Hutton, P.H. (eds) *Technologies of the Self: A Seminar with Michel Foucault*. Amherst: The University of Massachusetts Press.

Foucault, M. (1992) 'Curso del 7 de enero de 1976' [at the College de France], in *Microfísica del Poder*, 3rd edn (Varela, J. and Alvarez-Uría, F. eds and trans.). Madrid: La Piqueta.

Friedman, D. (1986) 'Homo psicológicus' [Interview to Castel] (F. Alvarez-Uría trans.), *Revista de la Asociación Española de Neuropsiquiatría*, **VI**(18): 454–62.

Galison, P. (1994) 'The ontology of the enemy: Norbert Wiener and the cybernetic vision', *Critical Inquiry*, **21**: 228–66.

Gardner, H. (1985) *The Mind's New Science: A History of the Cognitive Revolution*. New York: Basic Books.

Giddens, A. (1991) *Modernity and Self-Identity: Self and Society in the Late Modern Age*. Oxford: Polity Press.

Giddens, A. (1992) *The Transformation of Intimacy: Sexuality, Love and Eroticism in Modern Societies*. Oxford: Polity Press.

Gigerenzer, G. (1991) 'From tools to theories: a heuristic of discovery in cognitive psychology', *Psychological Review*, **98**: 254–67.

Gigerenzer, G. (1997) 'Social computers'. Paper delivered in the International Society for Theoretical Psychology Conference, Berlin, April/May 1997.

Gordo-López, A.J. (1996) 'The authority of cognitive psychology: deformation versus outright critique', *Acheronta 3*, at http://www.psiconet.com/acheronta/acheronta3/The%20authority%20of%20Cogntive%20psychology.html

Gordo-López, A.J. (forthcoming) 'Lifting technosexual bans: crafting psychology', in Bayer, B., Duarte Esgalhado, B., Jorna, R., Schraube, E. and Maiers, W. (eds) Volume of Proceedings of the 7th International Society for Theoretical Psychology (title to be announced). North York, Ontario: Captus University Press.

Gordo-López, A.J. and Aitken, G. (in prep.) *Queer Andtherness* (provisional title). Oxford: Polity Press.

Gray, C.H. (1996) 'Afterword: rethinking technohistory', in Gray, C.H. (ed.) *Technohistory: Using the History of American Technology in Interdisciplinary Research*. Malabar, FL: Krieger.

Gray, C.H., Mentor, S. and Figueroa-Sarriera, H.J. (1995) 'Cyborgology: constructing the knowledge of cybernetic organisms', in Gray, C.H., Figueroa-Sarriera, H.J. and Mentor, S. (eds) *The Cyborg Handbook*. London: Routledge.

Haraway, D. (1991) *Simians, Cyborgs, and Women: The Reinvention of Nature*. London: Free Association Books.

Haraway, D. (1992) 'Ecce Homo, ain't (ar'n't) I a woman, and inappropriate/d others: the human in a post-humanist landscape', in Butler, J. and Scott, J.W. (eds) *Feminists Theorize the Political*. London and New York: Routledge.

Hodge, J. (1995) 'Fashion, film and filosophy: reflections on cyberpsychology', in Burman, E., Gordo-López, A.J., Macauley, W.R. and Parker, I. (eds) *Cyberpsychology: Conference, Interventions and Reflections*. Manchester: Discourse Unit, Manchester Metropolitan University.

Jagose, A.M. (1996) *Queer Theory*. Melbourne: Melbourne University Press.

James, L. (1997) 'Cyberpsychology: principles of creating virtual presence' at http://www.soc.hawaii.edu/~leonj/leonj/leonpsy/cyber.html

Jang, S. (1994) *Information and Programming: Strong and Weak Thinking in Information Technology*. Unpublished PhD thesis, Lancaster University: Lancaster.

Jordanova, L. (1989) *Sexual Visions*. Hemel Hempstead: Harvester.

Kosofsky Sedgwick, E. and Frank, A. (1995) 'Shame in the cybernetic fold: reading Silvan Tomkins', *Critical Inquiry*, **21**: 486–522.

Lerner, A.Y. (1972) *Fundamentals of Cybernetics* (Gros, E., trans.), George, F.H. (ed.). London: Chapman & Hall.

Mayer, R.E. (1981) *The Promise of Cognitive Psychology*. San Francisco: W.H. Freeman.

Michael, M. (1996) *Constructing Identities*. London: Sage.

Mumford, L. (1934) *Technics and Civilization*. London: George Routledge & Sons.

Navarro, P. (1990) 'Ciencia y cibernética. Aspectos teóricos', in *Nuevos Avances en La Investigación Social. La Investigación Social de Segundo Orden*, special issue of *Suplementos: Textos de la Historia Social y del Pensamiento*, **22**: 23–31.

Noble, D.D. (1989) 'Mental material: the militarization of learning and intelligence in US education', in Levidow, L. and Robins, K. (eds) *Cyborg Worlds: The Military Information Society*. Worcester: Free Association Books.

Oakes, G. (ed. and trans.) (1984) 'Introduction', in *Georg Simmel: On Women, Sexuality, and Love*. New Haven and London: Yale University Press.

Parker, I. (1992) 'Psicoanálisis y sociedad, subjetividad y psicología social', in Correa De Jesús, N., Figueroa-Sarriera, H.J. and López, M.M. (eds) *Coloquio Internacional sobre el Imaginario Social Contemporáneo (Proceedings)*. Cayey: Universidad de Puerto Rico.

Parker, I. (1996) 'Theoretical discourse, subjectivity and critical psychology'. Inaugural Professorial Lecture at Bolton Institute, 3 October.

Parker, I. (1997) *Psychoanalytic Culture: Psychoanalytic Discourse in Western Society*. London: Sage.

Penley, C. and Ross, A. (1991) 'Introduction', in Penley, C. and Ross, A. (eds) *Technoculture*. Minneapolis: University of Minneapolis Press.

Plant, S. (1995) 'The Virtual, the Tactile and a Female Touch', in Burman, E., Gordo-López, A.J., Macauley, W.R. and Parker, I. (eds) *Cyberpsychology: Conference, Interventions and Reflections*. Manchester: Discourse Unit Manchester Metropolitan University.

Plant, S. (1997) *Zeros + Ones: Digital Women and the New Technoculture*. New York: Doubleday.

Prins, B. (1993) 'The ethics of hybrid subjects: feminist constructivism according to Donna Haraway', in *Collection of Papers for the Centre for Research into Innovation, Culture and Technology on: European Theoretical Perspectives on New Technology: Feminism, Constructivism and Utility*. London: Brunel University.

Rose, N. (1996) *Inventing Our Selves: Psychology, Power, and Personhood*. Cambridge: Cambridge University Press.

Renaut, A. (1997) *The Era of the Individual: A Contribution to a History of Subjectivity* (DeBevoise, M.B. and Philip, F., trans.). Princeton, NJ: Princeton University Press.

Schraube, E. (1997) 'Towards the things themselves. Reflections on a critical psychology of technology'. Paper delivered in the International Society for Theoretical Psychology Conference. Berlin, April/May.

Simon, H.A. (1969) *The Sciences of the Artificial*. Cambridge, MA: MIT Press.

Stone, A.R. (1995) *The War of Desire and Technology at the Close of the Mechanical Age*. Cambridge, MA: MIT Press.

Tabares, J. (1986) 'Entrevista a Robert Castel', *El Criticón*, **2**: 21–8.

Tomkins, S. (1962) *Affect, Imagery, Consciousness*, 4 vols. New York: Springer.

Turing, A.M. (1950) 'Computing machinery and intelligence', *Mind*, **59**: 433–60.

Varela, J. (1997) 'El dispositivo de feminización', in Alvarez-Uría, F. (ed.) *Jesús Ibáñez. Teoría y Práctica*. Madrid: Editorial Endymion.

Varela, J. (1998) *El Nacimiento de la Mujer Burguesa*. Madrid: La Piqueta.

Varela, J. and Alvarez-Uría, F. (1997) 'Sociología del género. Algunos modelos de análisis', *Archipiélago*, **30**: 11–21.

Wiener, N. ([1948] 1961) *Cybernetics or Control and Communication in the Animal and the Machine*, 2nd edn. Cambridge, MA: MIT Press.

Wiener, N. (1954) *The Human Use of Human Beings: Cybernetics and Society*, New York: Anchor.

PART ONE

Conditions of Possibility for the Psy-techno Complex

The chapters in this first part of the book lay out the context, or 'conditions of possibility' for the emergence of cyberpsychology, and they do so by widening the focus to the domain of the 'psy-complex' in its contemporary technological forms in order to situate cyber-psychological modes of corporeality and subjectivity. The 'psy-techno complex' is itself, of course, woven into cultural mutations and the governance of the body and soul.

James Sey describes the production of body technologies in production processes of Taylorism and Fordism and in forms of representation of the body in movement epitomized by chronopho-tography. The 'secret ontology of technology' and fantasies of the labouring body and posthuman modes of being open up the road to two temptations, that we might now be liberated by cyberculture or further emiserated by it. A close attention to new spaces of control and resistance, however, should lead us to beware either simple reaction and, instead, to trace how we might move through these new 'conditions of possibility' rather than celebrating or bewailing them.

Carlos Soldevilla presents a quite different take on the question, and combines a profoundly pessimistic account of the development of the 'technical proto-object' emerging through narcissistic fantasies of fusion and separation and the 'drive for domination' first exercised through the infant's control of its own muscular apparatus with a redemptive vision of how we might retrieve possibilities of salvation and connection and the return to an innocent engagement with others in the world. Psychoanalysis is a key resource for the grim side of Soldevilla's account and Castilian spiritual texts a driving force behind his hopes for escape.

Psychoanalysis also figures in Jill Marsden's chapter which revolves around a detailed reading of the case of Schreber, which for Freud was a crucial expression of psychotic breakdown and is now interpreted by Marsden as providing an uncanny anticipation of connections between the feminization and technologization of the body. Freud's own interpretation of Schreber's 'cyberpsychosis', Marsden argues, 'condenses the ceaseless multiplicity of the unconscious affects to the formal unity of the signifier'. Against this, an adequate understanding of the intensely gendered postbiological body needs to draw upon accounts of 'cyborg' subjectivity.

Freud fixes accounts of subjectivity through the process of interpretation, and this modern activity of the freezing of signification is very much what Nydza Correa de Jesús indicts in her account of the way modern psychology as a whole participates in the production of 'rational representation' and 'closed systems'. Cyberpsychology may be able to counter this by opening a multiplicity of areas for the experience of space and time, and Correa de Jesús gives the example of the 'performative action of opening windows' in cyberculture as recognizing changes in context and changes within specific contexts.

The chapters intensify the critical gaze of cyberpsychology upon the discipline of psychology – for example, in Sey's account of the collusion of the discipline with practices of regulation, or in Correa de Jesús's critique of rational representative closure in its discursive apparatus. And they turn around to interrogate cyberpsychology itself – for example in Soldevilla's scathing account of the complicity of social constructionism with motifs of plasticity and adaptability in industrial society, or in Marsden's demonstration that psychoanalytic modes of argument open and then block an understanding of the place of the body in networks of relationships. An understanding of the conditions of possibility for cyberpsychology in the psy-techno complex thus necessitates increasingly sceptical readings of its claim to deliver us from old twentieth-century psychology *and* of attempts to employ old psychology to rescue us from cyberculture.

CHAPTER 2

The Labouring Body and the Posthuman

JAMES SEY

The idea has taken hold in recent times, in both academic and popular contexts, that human beings are in the process of somehow losing control of their own culture, that the functions and parameters of society, far from being an expression of subjective individual or collective concerns, are in fact being given to us by the various forms of information technologies that have proliferated over the last 30 years, most emblematically in the shape of the home computer. From this picture of an information-saturated, thoroughly mediated and technologized planet, it is a short step to the bleak and millennial idea that history is moving, as Foucault (1970) famously predicted, towards an era where the figure of man will be washed from the sands of history by the waves of a self-regulating technoculture. Machines, after all, particularly those circulating information in abstract forms, are not prone to the ills of the flesh – sickness, fatigue, mortality, contingency and unreliability. In the human and social sciences this type of apocalyptic pronouncement of an imminent posthuman culture has become a growth industry.

In this chapter I would like to revisit some of the antecedents and epistemological underpinnings of these claims for contemporary technoculture, particularly, as my title indicates, in the key areas of labour and the body. I will be concerned to take issue with an overly enthusiastic heralding of a posthuman technocratic social order, and will present a partial and contingent alternative argument asserting a different trajectory for technology, and information technology in particular, in human culture.

Central to the arguments that follow will be an understanding of human subjectivity, especially in our technological modernity, as a partial, polymorphous and adaptable phenomenon. Such an understanding is inseparable from a consideration of the forms of *embodiment* of the human relation to technology – the relationship, in short, between bodies and machines in their most characteristic field of activity and interaction – at work. Correlatively, changes in the form and function of technology will be considered, primarily the move from earlier 'modernist' industrial technologies of production, where the body is a crucial component of machine culture's productivity, to the contemporary 'postmodernist' digital technologies of consumption, where a cultural and political economy of image-based representations apparently liberates the body from a subservient relation to technological systems.

Methodologically, then, the argument requires a historical detour; in this case, a measure of comparison between modernist attitudes to the human relation to technology in the late nineteenth and early twentieth centuries, and the ostensibly very different relation, as just outlined, of our own fin-de-siècle postmodernity. What I will argue is that the move from modernist industrial technologies of work, typified by ergonomics, Taylorism and Fordism, to the postindustrial 'disappearance' of the work-centred society and the corresponding rise of consumption and leisure technologies, has in fact produced remarkably similar psychological effects and reactions which suggest a certain historical continuity in our relationship with technology that militates against the idea of a posthuman society.

Industrial technology and life

The fascination with the relationship of humans to technology might be characterized as ontological, since it so fundamentally reflects our general ambivalence emerging from the sense (given shape by psychoanalysis and ethnology) of a negotiation between natural versus cultural elements, our instinctual life versus our 'civilization'. The prehistory of this fascination need not concern us here, but with the rise of industrial culture in the West in the nineteenth century, an important inflection is given to the relationship between the human and the technological which receives its apotheosis in the principles of 'scientific management' of F.W. Taylor which revolutionized industrial production in the early twentieth century. As Georges Canguilhem (1992: 63) points out, Taylorism established a mode of working life premised on the subjection of the body to the order of industrial machinery:

> With Frederick Taylor and the first technicians to make scientific studies of work-task movements, the human body was measured as if it functioned like a machine. If we see their aim as the elimination of all unnecessary movement and their view of output as... mathematically determined factors, then rationalization was... a mechanization of the body. But the realization that technologically superfluous movements were biologically necessary movements was the first stumbling block to be encountered by those who insisted on viewing the problem of the human-body-as-machine in exclusively technological terms.

Canguilhem elegantly describes here the essence of the modernist order of industrial technology – that is, that human bodies must behave like machines, must *identify* with a machinic system. He also subtly poses the converse problem of the intransigence of the biological for the purposes of production and industrial work, one to which we shall return.

This regime of identification with technology in the industrial order imposes a fear of the prosthetic, dehumanizing effects of technology which produces certain typical 'pathological' reactions, most typically a fear of work. Yet, some of the visions of the captains of Taylorist industry might themselves be viewed as pathological. In his recently published book *Serial Killers*, Mark Seltzer (1998: 69) recounts a fantasy revealed by Henry Ford, one of the patriarchs of industrial capitalism and pioneer of the Taylorist assembly line means of production:

> The production of the Model T required 7,882 distinct work operations, but, Ford observed, only twelve percent of these tasks... required 'able-bodied men'. Of the remainder – and this is clearly what Ford saw as the central achievement of his method of production – 'we found that 670 could be filled by legless men, 2,637 by one-legged men, two by armless men, 715 by one-armed men and ten by blind men'. If from one point of view such a fantasy projects a violent dismemberment of the human body and an *emptying out of human agency*, from another it projects a transcendence of the natural body and the *extension of human agency through the forms of technology that supplement it*.

Seltzer here succinctly specifies the characteristic ambivalence which lies deeply buried in the bedrock of contemporary technoculture – that regarding the nature of technological prosthesis. What he calls the 'double-logic of prosthesis' (1998: 37) marks both the inseparability of human culture – and thus subjective identity – from the technologies which shape it, but also the attendant fear of human obsolescence and even destruction – often, interestingly, in the brutal and violent form here imagined by Ford – brought about by those same technologies.

In the context of the general epistemological question of the double role played by technology in human agency posed here by Seltzer, the specific history of human agency in the development of large technological systems of production such as the factory system takes on a symptomatic importance. As Canguilhem implies, the question of agency must be differently posed when the body is enjoined not only by a technological system – that of the factory – but by an ideological system – that of industrial capitalism – to behave as if it were non-living, that is, as if it were a machine. As such a technological and ideological system, Taylorism (and its most famous realization, Fordism) was subject to contestation and opposition, both epistemological and sociological. It did not arise in a vacuum, but came to be identified with the successful operation of the factory system in the early twentieth century.

Prior to the success of the Taylorist system of the scientific management of working bodies, the integration of the human body with industrial technology in a manner which would optimize productivity was a central concern of nineteenth-century science in the USA and Europe. This fascinating history of the rise of the science of work and pre-Taylorist ergonomics is the subject of Anson Rabinbach's book *The Human Motor: Energy, Fatigue and the Origins of Modernity* (1992). He argues that the Taylorist idea that humans could be identified with machines in the industrial order to further productivity arises from the dominant scientific paradigms of the nineteenth-century, those of thermodynamics and 'labour power'. In this 'transcendental materialist' conception, humans were simply one of the many organisms and machines giving productive expression to the irreducible amount of energy circulating in the universe, as per the dictates of the first law of thermodynamics. The second law, that motion implies entropy, however, presented a crucial problem to efficient productivity, and Rabinbach's book is a detailed account of these modernist attempts to explain and deal with the most characteristic physical and psychological response of humans to the demands of the system of industrial productivism – that is, physical and psychopathological fatigue.

A vast array of scientific methods and new inventions proliferated at this time designed to explain and eradicate the obstinate tendency of the human organism to become fatigued and inefficient in performing industrial work-task movements. We will discuss the most important of these in the next section, but crucial to this scientific enterprise, apart from the notion that the actions of the body in work-tasks should aspire to the regularity and indefatigability of the factory machine, was the attempt to properly domesticate fatigue to a productive industrial social order. The new sciences of work in the last fin-de-siècle, such as ergonomics or the chronophotography of Etienne-Jules Marey, were designed to explain fatigue within a social context which was not only productivist in line with the idea of a thermodynamic theory of 'labour power', but also within the context of bourgeois social reform.

Explanations of fatigue thus became refined, not only along class lines, but along moral ones, and took on the character of an ideological explanation of non-productivism, as in the case of the scandalized disapproval of aristocratic ennui. Intriguingly, these scientific explanations of non-productive fatigue began to concentrate on possible *psychological* explanations of such obstructive behaviour. Rabinbach convincingly traces the origins of a psychopathological response to the imposition of industrialized work regimes in the form of 'neurasthenia' or 'psychasthenia', a deeply unproductive form of generalized and paralysing fatigue which became something of an epidemic in the Europe at the close of the nineteenth century.

For the scientists of work, as well as for psychiatrists and physiologists, such a response to the progress of the industrial technological order had to be thoroughly investigated, explained, and, if possible, removed, for ostensibly humanitarian reasons – concern for the physical well-being of the proletariat – as much as in the interests of economic and political progress (Rabinbach cites the impulse to social reform as the major difference between ergonomics in the European sciences of work and the more openly capitalist and productivist American Taylorism, although they are commonly conflated). What is interesting for our purposes is that this scientific project was an attempt to account for a broad-based social phenomenon from more than a utilitarian or technicist, that is, 'productivist' foundation. Perhaps for the first time, in the form of the concept of 'neurasthenia' (defined by Rabinbach as a kind of fatigue reaction to the demands of modernity), we have a symptomatic psychological reaction to technology. Also highly significant, however, in the context of current debates about the cultural and psychological role of technology, is the mobilizing of an entire technological arsenal and scientific epistemology to explain and deal with a subjective and psychopathological phenomenon. As Rabinbach puts it, in the attempt to account for fatigue as a psychological reaction to the imposition of a technological regime of work, nineteenth-century science was 'attributing an objective basis to highly subjective states', but was also 'creating a framework for knowledge, for norms, and for models of human nature that redefined the body and its external limits' (1992: 44). At this point we can begin to trace an extension of the body–machine relation; the scientific refinement of the notion that humans have a psychological imbrication with technology.

Time, motion and the 'unknown language' of the body

For nineteenth-century scientists, the problem of body fatigue for productivism rapidly became posed in materialist and thus techno-logical terms. A vast array of machines and techniques was developed in order to elaborate a physiological technics – in Foucauldian terms a sophisticated disciplinary apparatus for productive techno-logical bodies – which were all designed to inscribe the body in a new nexus of *technographic* knowledge. The most important of these new graphic technologies were developed to record previously unrecordable physical processes such as heart rate, muscular contraction, and, most importantly, movement.

The motion of the body was an area of concern ostensibly to further refine techniques to combat the urgent problem of the fatigue and inefficiency of working bodies. However, we can also understand the concern of fin-de-siècle science to more closely understand human motion in terms of the 'double-logic' of technological pros-thesis. That is, the invention of technologies to facilitate a closer examination and graphic recording of motion meant both a 'decom-position' (Rabinbach) of movement into its constituent elements in order to fit into an industrial technological paradigm, but also meant an understanding of the ways in which human motion was uniquely non-technological, an understanding approaching metaphysics.

Rabinbach devotes an extensive discussion in *The Human Motor* (Chapter 4) to the various physiographic technologies of the French scientist Etienne-Jules Marey, whose work in inventing machines to record human physiological activity is credited with influencing such disparate figures as Marcel Duchamp, the Futurists and Eadweard Muybridge. Marey is best known for his work in 'chronophotography', a technique said to have anticipated cinematography (see Doane, 1996). The technique involved the attempt to accurately record, through multiple exposure, single plate photography, a full range of human and animal motion through time. Through the use of such techniques Marey was able to discover what he called an 'unknown language' of the body; that is, the decomposition of motion revealed the 'successive instants' which made up the duration of human movements, and also the various forms of extension through space (conoid, hyperboloid and so on), which defied Euclidean geometry. It was a graphic visual technology which aspired to the ever increasing refinement of the record of successive instants, frozen in time, rather than the recording of continuity of movement which would form the basis of cinema technology, the chief leisure technology of the twentieth century (for an account of Marey's relation to nascent cinema technologies, see Doane, 1996).

While such discoveries were scientifically surprising, they also had important philosophical and aesthetic consequences which stemmed from their reconfiguration of the body and subjectivity. The work of Marey and others at this time was not a disinterested scientific enquiry, but was designed in the first instance to produce a more efficient relation between industrial machines and working bodies. This became the major application of industrial ergonomics, and Marey's insights were indeed applied to these and other such areas as military training. Rabinbach uses the examples of Bergson and Valery, however, to indicate the impact of these graphic technologies in aesthetic and philosophical areas. In short, the chronophotographic decomposition of human movement showed how a technological intervention might alter or add to not only a knowledge form (the 'unknown language' of the body) but also knowledge about the subject itself. That is, the graphic technologies revealed that the role of human consciousness itself, and not its technological analogues, was to perceive movement 'erroneously', that is, in a way that made it possible for cultures to exist in synchronous time. Consciousness imposed a structure of coherent perception of duration and extension on the non-Euclidean trajectories of human motion.

This consequence of Marey's experiments also had the aesthetic result of providing the avant-gardes of European modernism with a scientific *raison d'être* where representation could be replaced by the idea of a technology that revealed the illusion of realism at the heart of conscious perception itself. Institutional science and the aesthetic avant-gardes were thus united by a fascination with the ways in which new technologies could revise the relation of the body to the constituent conditions of its consciousness – extension and duration, space and time. At the heart of this modernist technological endeavour was, we have seen, the attempt to improve productivity in labour contexts, but the attempt to isolate and decompose the body's extension and duration meant the technology began to manifest itself as an attempt to *reduce distance and time* to the condition of instantaneity and presence. Such aspirations inscribe such technophysiographic machines as Marey's in a general logic of modernity – the beginning of the era of information overload, of 'speed and dynamism' as the Futurists had it. This linked Marey's apparently objective, and obsessive, scientific pursuit of pure representations of human extension and duration with a far more metaphysical and aesthetic modernist Zeitgeist:

> Marey... diligently searched for the most... self-effacing link between the body and the recording instrument, tending ultimately to privilege air pressure. Photography was, in this respect, ideal since its means of connecting object and representation – light waves – were literally intangible and greatly reduced the potentially corruptive effects of mediation... Marey consistently contrasted the graphic method [that is, his own] favourably to phonetic language and statistics, heavily mediated forms of representation that were potentially obscure... (as well as slow – instantaneity was an aspiration). (Doane, 1996: 326–7)

Marey's project to isolate and objectify the extension and duration of human motion thus stands at an epistemological crossroads: on one hand he typifies the commitment of technological disciplinarity in nineteenth-century science to give an objective and materialist account of the instrumentality of the human body and how it could be adapted to technicist and productivist ends; on the other, he provides us with what might be called a secret ontology of technology – that is, his techniques for the recording of human movement aspire to the extension and duration of human movement itself, to the erasure, as Doane's point implies, of the distance between the body and the technology which extends its agency, to the erasure of the trace of the technology itself. The paradox of the double register of the body–technology relation is here most evident: a technology which enables a greater knowledge of the human being, which must be like air, or like light, rather than the reduction of the human to an identification with the technological state implicit in ergonomics and Taylorism. The ambivalent position of the technology in this thickening of human self-knowledge is remarked on by Benjamin (1970: 238–9), specifically referring to the quintessential modernism of photography and cinema:

> A different nature opens itself to the camera than opens to the naked eye – if only because an unconsciously penetrated space is substituted for a space consciously explored… Even if one has a general knowledge of the way people walk, one knows nothing of a person's posture during the fractional second of a stride… The camera introduces us to unconscious optics as does psychoanalysis to unconscious impulses.

It is no accident that both the major problem for productivist technology and the aesthetic response to the body–technology relation should take shape as a psychological symptomatology – in the realm of science and work translating as neurasthenic fatigue (an aetiology often imbricated with aesthetics in the form of the obsessive writing out of symptoms, or the refusal of industrial work by many aesthetes, for instance the so-called 'decadent' movement), and in the realm of aesthetics and philosophy the newly revealed possibilities which science presented for the refining of human consciousness beyond the limitations of perception.

We might distil from the exemplar of Marey's objective materialist attempts at the graphic inscription and chronophotographing of the 'unknown language' of the body the fundamental ambivalence around the possible conflicts between human and technological agencies in establishing and developing new scientific knowledge. We might also see an interesting connection between the attempt to erase the trace of technology, or, more accurately, the attempt to close the gap between instrument and object of knowledge – body and machine – and the rise of *post*modernist 'invisible technologies', the digital technocultural infosphere of our contemporary fin-de-siècle. The historical continuities between the ends of the two centuries occupy the rest of this argument.

The technological body in the postindustrial era

Walter Benjamin's auratic theory of art in 'The work of art in the age of mechanical reproduction' devolves crucially on the question of distance:

> The definition of the aura as 'a unique phenomenon of a distance however close it may be' represents nothing but the cult value of the work of art in categories of space and time perception. Distance is the opposite of closeness. The essentially distant object is the unapproachable one. Unapproachability is indeed a major quality of the cult image. (1970: 245)

We began by discussing the erasure of what appears to be a very different kind of distance, that between machines and humans, in the era of industrial ergonomics. The concept of distance invoked here by Benjamin seems to maintain a distinction between the aesthetic and the technological inasmuch as the latter, as we have seen in the case of Marey's physiological technologies, seeks to erase the distance between itself and its subject, the human body. This tendency of certain forms of technology to the state of invisibility, or 'absent prosthesis', represents a certain reversal of the trajectory of the technological imperative of the industrial era, seen in Ford's dismemberment fantasy, where the body and psyche are enjoined to become machinic, to identify with the machine in the workplace.

However, the identification with the machine in either trajectory – that of the 'reduction' of human being to a machine-like state or that of the disappearance of technology in the service of knowledge of the human – might be seen to be present in the realm of the aesthetic from the beginning. Although the project of industrial technology in modernity was to domesticate an often intransigent human psyche to a productivist regime, these same technologies were being used to develop new forms of art and mass entertainment, photography and cinema being the most important. We have already touched on the avant-garde's ambivalent and metaphysical acceptance of technology, but it was in the field of mass entertainment that the impact of the new 'vision machines' was most keenly felt.

Especially in the nascent form of cinema, the psychic potency of the technologically mediated illusion of reality could hardly be underestimated. Films such as Chaplin's *Modern Times* and Lang's *Metropolis* were ironic reflections on the impact of technology on human life, in the language of those vision machines. Although he was opposed to the cinema's use as a tool to foster a mass entertainment illusion, Marey could only have admired the technology which enabled it – pure light and direct mediation of the image, even though the medium could be manipulated. Cinema was the first technology to convincingly erase the time of representation (it seemed to be in real time) and the distance between technology and object (since it comprised light, and later sound waves). Now, technology could disappear into its object, the human could re-emerge from the identification with the machine which marked the industrial order, into a new era where subjectivity could be reasserted and technologies would become less ambivalently prosthetic.

This apparent disappearance of technology into the landscape, into the service of the subject, has marked the technological trajectory of this century. As the base of primary industry has become eroded, and multinational corporations have replaced the national character of science and technology of the late nineteenth century, so the inversion of the body–machine relation has continued. But this apparent shift from identification with the machine in the industrial order to the rise of 'service technologies' conceals another development. Rather than a disappearance of technology in the postmodern era, as Seltzer (1998: 33) points out, what develops is the 'naturalization of machine culture':

> The incorporations of the technological process and the life process have by now become a thoroughly naturalized component of machine culture. One rediscovers here the familiar intersections between natural bodies and technologies, somatic and machinal systems of circulation… [O]ne rediscovers… a precise co-ordination of bodies and spaces. This involves not merely the spectacle of stilled bodies in moving machines… in the relentless… commuting 'homeward'… The nominal division between public and private has in effect given way.

Once more the focus here is on the distance between technology and its object, the technological erasure this time of the division between public and private, emblematized by transport systems. These come to replace private human intimacy with an abstraction of the relation with others; a deindividuation and 'hypertypicality' of experience produced by our common interaction within a large technological system, for instance, the feeling of alienating and ambivalent intimacy shared by strangers on a train or plane. Thus, with the vast proliferation of technological systems beyond the initially crucial confines of the industrial relation between body and machine, we can discern that the ostensible disappearance of technology from the body which might seem to mark a move into postmodernity in fact emerges as the disappearance of the body into technology. Technological systems, that is, have extended to form the context of our experience of time and space, duration and extension.

In postmodernity thus the distinction between the subject and its extension and duration (which implies, it goes without saying, the human relation to mortality) which so preoccupied Marey and the modernist avant-garde might itself be superseded by the relation of the subject to the telecommunicative instant, what Paul Virilio (1993) calls 'the third interval' (that is, light – the first two intervals being space and time). The triumph of technology over extension and duration by instantaneous telecommunication was highly prized, as we have seen, by the physiologists of the later nineteenth century, but only insofar as such technology enabled them better to understand and control the 'human motor'. Now that such a technological order is a reality, it is represented rather differently. Two examples will suffice, which also indicate how much of the sociocultural effects of contemporary technology play out in the arena of visual representation.

Paradoxically, one of the major areas of contemporary human endeavour which has been radically affected by the telecommunicative technologies of the third interval – television itself in this case – is sport. This is paradoxical of course because of the increased possibilities presented by TV to distinguish participation from spectation. The refinement of the technology to enable the watching of sport seems in many ways a direct descendant of Marey's chronophotographic techniques. The 'action replay' and super slow motion photography enable the viewer to minutely trace the arc of the throwing arm, the trajectory of the ball, the contact in the tackle, and so on, enabling the sedentary and distanced viewer to become either a wishful voyeur or a postmodern technographic scientist *manqué*.

The second example is that of David Cronenberg's 1982 remake of the 1950s sci-fi B movie *The Fly*. In this film a scientist invents a device called a teleporter, a science fiction staple which enables the instantaneous transport of an object for any distance, from telepod to telepod. When he perfects the device and enters the womb-like pod for his first test, a housefly slips in unnoticed. In the teleportation the genetic material of both creatures is mingled by the technology, which thus stays faithful to its operational technique. A horrific new species results and the biohorror fun begins. This example is instructive in showing the obstinacy, even in popular entertainment contexts, of the aspiration of the technological to eradicate extension and duration, the 'unique phenomenon' of distance which marks the aesthetic; but also in pointing out the affinity between the aesthetic and the contingent – in this case the unforeseen presence of the housefly – which is anathema to the ontology of technology. That is, technology retains an operational commitment to predictable cause and effect relations and replicability which cannot account for contingency (since the contingent defines life) or aesthetic principles.

Virilio (1993: 4) presents a new model of the body–technology relation emerging from the telecommunicative instantaneity of postmodern technology:

> These... technologies (based on the digital signal, the video signal and the radio signal) will soon overturn... the nature of human environment and its animal body, since the development of territorial space by means of heavy material machinery is giving way to an almost immaterial control of the environment... that is connected to the terminal body of men and women.

Virilio's metaphor of a 'terminal' existence in the postmodern era of telecommunicative life, that is, one with the double sense of being at an end and also connected to the computer terminal and TV screen is an increasingly common metaphor in premillennial accounts of the posthuman direction contemporary technology is leading culture. We now turn to the psychical effects of and alternatives to such a vision.

The posthuman and the abject

Virilio (1993: 11) continues these observations on the nature of telecommunicative culture with an account of its effects on the human body and psyche, which is quotable here for its representative apocalyptic take (shared by theorists like Baudrillard and Arthur Kroker) on the concept of a posthuman culture as much as for its intrinsic interest:

> Where motorized transportation and information had prompted a
> general mobilization of populations swept up in the exodus of labour
> (and then of leisure), modes of instantaneous transmission prompt the
> inverse, that of a growing inertia... [T]eleaction no longer requires
> human mobility, but merely a local motility... The shift is ultimately
> felt in the body of every city dweller, as a terminal citizen... We have
> before us the catastrophic figure of an individual who has lost, along
> with his or her natural mobility, any immediate means of intervening
> in the environment.

We remarked in the earlier account of the rise of neurasthenia as an
oppositional subjective response to the technological regime of
industrial work that the psychological consequences of the identification of the human with the machinic tends to be posed in symptomatic or psychopathological terms. Such states escape or refuse the
ideological consequences of that regime so that the technological
order – which is, we have implied, still representative of a disciplinary modernity, whether it manifests itself as industrial or digital –
must continue to develop and refine techniques for the recuperation
of the unruly psychological subject into a technological order, or a
'body-machine complex', as Seltzer (1998) has it.

In contrast, apocalyptic millennial accounts of the advent of
'posthumanity', represented here by Virilio, work within the binary
structure of an ideological opposition between the human and the
technological, where the ontological category of the human must be
reasserted in the face of the threat arising from its own technoculture – thus Virilio's characteristic mourning of the demise of
human agency and mobility quoted earlier.

Two opposing views of cyberpsychology in a posthuman culture
thus emerge. On one hand is a subject rendered productively pathological – or one 'liberated', depending on one's ideological stand-
point – by the notion that cyberspace and information networks
enable a system of symbolic exchange without the body, the paradox
of a metaphysical anthropology. In this conception human psychology and our disciplinary understanding of it are ostensibly freed
from the necessity of repression and are at liberty to adopt and
discard different identities in subjective interaction, thus loosening
the determining roles played by somatic factors like sex. Psychology
adopting a posthuman, or extreme constructionist, view of such
shifts in the basis of symbolic exchange and identity constitution,
then need to adapt to the implication, surely unintended, that the

basic polymorphous character of human identity would be given free expression. Perhaps the discipline has done so in rather more of an anti-constructionist vein, yet one which retains the identity of psychology as a human science discipline, through an ever increasing refinement of diagnostic categories of pathology, a representative case in point being False Memory Syndrome.

In direct opposition to this utopian and radical–liberal view of cyberpsychology is the more conservative lament for the passing of the human which the information era might imply, emblematized by Virilio's view of the telematic person given earlier. What both views have in common is a tendency to ignore altogether the *a priori* conditions of possibility which enable the theorizing of a posthuman society as the next stage in a technologically driven evolutionary continuum. As Foucault pointed out, the positivity, or actualization, of power/knowledge in modernity is such that one must see these utopian and dystopian responses to the body–machine complex as being representative rather than radical. The preservation, and even refinement, for example, of categories of abnormality and pathology within psychology as a discipline (and the correlative reassertion of the somatic basis and neurological treatment of much 'postmodern' mental illness) point to a maintenance of the subject within these constituent conditions of power/knowledge, rather than a superseding and recasting of them.

There seems to be a more productive avenue of enquiry, however, in reviewing these different responses to the 'pathologizing' of the human body and psyche. The picture painted by both the utopian and dystopian versions of cyberpsychology are in any case reminiscent of the Fordist dismemberment fantasy, and thus fail to move the understanding of the body-psyche-technology relation out of the modernist paradigm into the postmodern one it espouses. We should in this regard recall the foundational ambivalence of this relation and accept, as Seltzer does, the *a priori* status of a completely imbricated human and technological culture. Certainly this is not to deny that there are ethical and ideological responses to our contemporary technoculture which must be made, but what form can these take?

Seltzer (1998) is concerned with an extreme pathology of identity in technoculture – that of serial killing – which, he asserts, occurs within a 'pathological public sphere', an arena of the contemporary mediascape which encourages the absolute identification with technology and the consequent erasure of subjective identity in its normative forms.

It is possible, however, to delineate a less overtly pathologized form of resistance to the elision of the human from technoculture which it is possible to read as analogous to the manifestation of neurasthenia, the pathological fatigue of the nineteenth century, as itself a form of ethical and ideological resistance – that is, a symptom as defence. This resistance manifests itself as an affirmation of the abject or corporeal status of the body in physical terms or in aesthetic versions.

By this reassertion of the corporeality of the body we do not intend a disavowal of the imbrication of the human and the technological. Rather, it is an attempt to read an alternative set of cultural symptoms against the backdrop of the dominant discourses of either technophilia about the digital era, the 'second industrial revolution', or a reactive apocalyptic technophobia. It seems clear that something of the character of Foucault's 'repressive hypothesis' is at work in the proliferation of thought around the posthuman condition, where the eruption of discourse and critical attention paid to a phenomenon marks its recuperation into the cultural landscape in a delimited and controllable form, and it is certainly possible to assert an often parallel proliferation, or at least, renewal of interest, in the body itself as the degree zero of thought and experience.

In what Foucault termed the 'Unthought' (1970) and in the recent renewal of interest in forms of physical and psychological abjection abounding in sociopsychological forms in everything from body modification, alternative sexuality and serial killing to popular cultural forms like so-called 'scuzz cinema' (*Pulp Fiction, Trainspotting*) and the corporeal art of Damien Hirst, Cindy Sherman or Andrès Serrano, we can continue to see how the body provides the limit not only to experience, but to knowledge and power also. In understanding the impact of cyberpsychology, and assessing the prospects of the reconfiguration of psychology in an era of postcorporeal identity, we should not be overly hasty in removing the question of the corporeal body from the agenda of psychology in a technological culture.

References

Benjamin, W. (1970) 'The work of art in the age of mechanical reproduction', in Benjamin, W. *Illuminations*. London: Fontana.
Canguilhem, G. (1992) 'Machine and organism', in Crary, J. and Kwinter, S. (eds) *Incorporations*. New York: Zone Press.

Doane, M. (1996) 'Temporality, storage, legibility: Freud, Marey and the cinema', *Critical Inquiry*, **22**: 313–43.

Foucault, M. (1970) *The Order of Things*. London: Tavistock.

Rabinbach, A. (1992) *The Human Motor: Energy, Fatigue and the Origins of Modernity*. Berkeley: University of California Press.

Seltzer, M. (1998) *Serial Killers*. London: Routledge.

Virilio, P. (1993) 'The third interval: a critical transition', in Conley, V.A. (ed.) *Rethinking Technologies*. Minneapolis: University of Minnesota Press.

CHAPTER 3

Vertiginous Technology: Towards a Psychoanalytic Genealogy of Technique

CARLOS SOLDEVILLA PÉREZ
(TRANSLATION BY ÁNGEL J. GORDO-LÓPEZ
AND IAN PARKER)

A Klee painting named 'Angelus Novus' shows an angel looking as though he is about to move away from something he is fixedly contemplating. His eyes are staring, his mouth is open, his wings are spread. This is how one pictures the angel of history. His face is turned towards the past. Where we perceive a chain of events, he sees one single catastrophe which keeps piling wreckage upon wreckage and hurls it in front of his feet. The angel would like to stay, awaken the dead, and make whole what has been smashed. But a storm is blowing from Paradise; it has got caught in his wings with such violence that the angel can no longer close them. This storm irresistibly propels him into the future to which his back is turned, while the pile of debris before him grows skyward. This storm is what we call progress. (Benjamin, 1991: 249)

As the twenty-first century dawns, when the seemingly unshakeable certainties that maintained the legitimacy of modernity are starting to dissolve, to read and revise a substantial chapter of our lifetimes seems appropriate. I am referring in particular to the penultimate meta-account of modernity that, after hoisting discourses pertaining to electronic and digital information technologies to the top rank of the cultural superstructure, now presents itself under the rubric of 'cyberculture'.

Although cyberculture has been mostly analysed from the perspective of sociology and cultural studies (for example, Benedikt, 1991; Penley and Ross, 1991; Featherstone and Burrows, 1995; Jones, 1997), its thematics and functions can be also dealt with critically from within the realm of psychology (Burman *et al.*, 1995; Gordo-López and Macauley, 1995; Parker, 1996). The purpose of this chapter is to present a cyberpsychological critique of 'technique' and its symbolic expansion as 'cyberculture'. I draw on psychoanalytic inter-pretation to account for the psychogenesis of the first technical device (or 'proto-object') and on genealogical and deconstructive attempts to resist and challenge positivist and empiricist tendencies in modern psychology (Varela and Alvarez-Uría, 1988; Parker and Shotter, 1990; Alvarez-Uría, 1991; Parker, 1997). I then move on to identify ideolog-ical and psycho-social functions of 'social constructionism' as played out in the discipline of psychology and their compatibility with ongoing cybercultural projects. The final section explores possibilities of a non-nihilist cyberpsychology and emphasizes ontotheological undercurrents which inform my cyberpsychological reading (Trías, 1995, 1997; Gárate Martínez and Marinas, 1996; Moya, 1997).

Preliminary assumptions for the psychogenetic study of technique

A common practice in the psychoanalytic tradition, as in the other social sciences, is to work along the tracks of a parallel discourse: that of psychoanalysis on the one hand, and the rest of the social discourses on the other. Drawing on the work of psychoanalysts and social psychologists who oppose this parallel discourse (Ibáñez, 1985, 1994a; Gárate Martínez, 1990; Gárate Martínez and Marinas, 1996; Marinas, 1997), and Freud's own study of psychogenesis, I shall start by identifying structural connections between the psychogenesis of different technologies (destruction, production, information and communication). This conjunction informs my understanding of historical relations between the production of knowledge, forms of power and processes of subjectivation (Soldevilla Pérez 1991, 1994).

The reflections offered here, nevertheless, contrary to categorical and assertive modes of argument, re-present their assumptions from an *ironic* and *distant* point of view. This rhetorical strategy of doubting what has been stated, while simultaneously being in discord with what is said, also reflects on the way that the original statements were perfectly understandable within a certain logic and picture of the world (Rorty, 1989, 1991). Another qualification is that, although psychoanalytic theory informs my analysis of the psychogenesis of technique, I do not pretend to explain technological development by postulating its exclusive origin in a drive or an instinct as the final and sufficient cause (Ricoeur, 1969; Rorty, 1989).

According to Basalla (1988: 16), a theorist of technological evolution, 'artefact is the analytical unit for the study of technology'. This definition helps us to relate and utilize a psychoanalytic understanding of technique as a *proto-object* (or technical proto-artefact) or as an effect of the irrepressible unfolding of human desire of omnipotence. In short, it expresses a perverse narcissism (Brown, 1959, 1972). This definition obeys the psychoanalytical premise that the individual is forever seeking for a loving sexual adjustment, longing for an ideal of completeness within a relation with another. But this ideal suffers from a serious difficulty at the time of materializing itself in reality. The object of love and the object of desire never get to couple with each other in the sphere of affective-erotic relations.

The adequacy of psychoanalysis for the study of the technological proto-object formation

Freud identifies two types of drives in his early formulation of the libido theory: the ego drive, directed towards itself and seeking satisfaction of needs (for example, through fantasies of hunger, in dreams), and the sexual drives, directed towards the other and seeking enjoyment and reproduction. Nevertheless, following clinical observations, Freud (1914) starts to argue that key psychical conflict is not so much contingent upon tensions between self-conservation or personal needs (*Ananké*) on the one hand, and sexuality (*Eros*) on the other, as between contradictory *unconscious* sexual desires.

Freud's (1914) exploration of narcissism, his studies of perverse sexuality, and his meditation on war and death (Freud, 1915a), led him to reformulate libidinal theory (Freud, 1920a). Narcissistic omnipotence, insatiable and unsatisfied, moves in a twofold path: towards regression (a masochistic drift into the achievement of a degree zero of tension – or *Nirvana*); and towards developing aggressive and destructive tendencies (a sadistic drift into reification, aggression and domination of the other, whose ultimate object would be that which best arrives at its sadomasochistic target – or *Thanatos*).

In what follows I suggest that we need to attend to the infancy of the technological event (or development of the technological proto-object), which are intimately connected with other childhood events (or the determined choice of pulsional object). It is on this set of complex relations that I base my understanding of the psychogenetic development of technique.

Omnipotence and trajectories of narcissism

Introducing the subject of narcissism entails facing one of the most important theoretical discrepancies between different psychoanalytic schools, expressed in the controversy around the genesis of the 'ego'. What impels Freud to introduce the concept of 'narcissism' (Freud, 1914) is a mythical assumption or original momentous attempt to decode the complex beginning of psychical life, when the incipient 'ego' become the structuring apparatus of the personality (Green, 1986).

Freud is initially interested in clinical observations of auto-erotism, psychotic perversion and megalomania. In *Three Essays on the Theory of Sexuality*, Freud (1905) argues that the sexual instinct in childhood is not unified. It initially lacks an object, and this lack defines it as auto-erotic. In the Schreber case, narcissism appears as an indispensable libidinal stage in which, before selecting the outer object, the individual takes its own body as a loving object:

> Recent investigations have directed our attention to a stage in the development of the libido which it passes through on the way from auto-erotism to object love. This stage has been given the name of narcissism. What happens is this. There comes a time in the development of the individual at which he unifies his sexual instincts (which have hitherto been engaged in auto-erotic activities) in order to obtain a love-object; and he begins by taking himself, his own body, as his love-object, and only subsequently proceeds from this to the choice of some person other than himself as his object. This half-way phase between auto-erotism and object-love may perhaps be indispensable normally. (Freud, 1911: 197–8)

Later, in *Totem and Taboo*, Freud ([1912]1913) establishes a functional equivalence between the megalomania of the child's own narcissism, and omnipotent thinking observed in 'primitive' civilizations. Later still, Freud postulates the existence of individual characteristics of extreme narcissism, which he claims are also clinically observable. This is evident, for example, in his accounts of the selection of homosexual object as a form of narcissism (Freud, 1910) and this kind of account is taken further in his descriptions of narcissism in 'The psychogenesis of a case of homosexuality in a woman' (Freud, 1920b). It will be apparent that Freud unfortunately plays out this kind of analysis in the domain of 'homosexuality' as if that were itself equivalent to perversion, but the lesson of psychoanalysis is that narcissistic perversion operates just as much in the domain of 'normal' heterosexuality in contemporary culture.

For Freud, the ego at this point tends to do without the other as an erotic-affective object, and relies instead on primary narcissism. This kind of narcissism has a threefold trajectory – and the notion of the ego here could be seen as equivalent to the archaic ego of Klein ([1921]1945); the false self of Winnicott (for example, 1971); and the pre-ego of Dolto (1984):

- One oriented towards a 'progressive narcissism', that moves gradually from auto-erotism to object-libido.
- Consisting of a drive towards a 'regressive narcissism', whose pulsional horizon tends to reach a tension degree zero in which there is an insistence and repetition which drives it towards a return to the inanimate thing, because the drive always seeks for complete satisfaction (Freud, 1920a).
- With a tendency towards a 'perverse-fetishistic narcissism' whose trajectory is determined by the drive to possess the fetish object.

In *Instincts and Their Vicissitudes* we are already put on the track of relations between narcissism (auto-erotism), sadism and subsequent action displayed by the function of muscular activity (Freud, 1915b). Three moments constitute a perverse narcissistic structure: as experience of muscular activity, as transitional object, and later as constitution of a (phallic) fetish of omnipotence. But, how can the move towards the constitution of the *technical object* be understood?

My answer is that the satisfying experiences of the 'power drive' or the drive to domination is gradually focused upon an object, corporeal muscular activity, which becomes as auto-erotically satisfactory. This muscular activity becomes the first and internal fetish-object that makes possible a certain experience of omnipotent completeness. This constitution of musculature as the first technical object (that is a technical proto-object), becomes, metaphorically, the germ of the machine. As Ramonet (1997: 33) puts it:

> [I]n the same way the industrial revolution entailed the substitution of muscle by machine, the computer revolution supposes the replacement of the brain by the computer. (our translation)

The transitional object: second object of the empowering drive

Up to now we have seen how the empowering drive requires a corporeal object. Once this object is obtained by means of the experience of muscular activity, it operates as a resource for the unfolding of aggression and domination in the service of perverse narcissistic subjectivity. Winnicott (1971: 17) defined the concept of 'transitional object' as 'the infant's transition from a state of being merged with the mother to a state of being in relation to the mother as something outside and separate'. The object is called 'transitional' because it is an external object to which the child has attributed qualities of the primary object, the mother, but it also initiates the first intimations of identity:

> Attention is drawn to the rich field for observation provided by the earliest experiences of the healthy infant as expressed principally in the relationship to the first possession. This first possession is related backwards in time to auto-erotic phenomena... Transitional objects and transitional phenomena belong to the realm of illusion which is at the basis of initiation of experience... This intermediate area of experience, unchallenged in respect of its belonging to inner or external (shared) reality, constitutes the greater part of the infant's experience, and throughout life is retained in the intense experiencing that belongs to the arts and to religion and to imaginative living, and to creative scientific work. (Winnicott, 1971: 16)

The transitional object, therefore, is the symbolic substitute that constitutes the basis for more complex symbolic activities, including science, technique and art. It also facilitates the attainment of 'the capacity to be alone' through the restoration and internalization of object relations and symbolic competencies. These accord the ego support and allow it to tolerate solitude without anguish while developing exploratory epiphanies of autonomy and creativity. The notion of transitional objects paves the way to an understanding of the symbolic function and technical creativity, both in its playful and artistic dimensions. It also, of course, paves the way to fetishistic relations, which enable the child to distinguish between fantasies and factual reality, between inner and outer things, between subjectivity and objectivity (Winnicott, 1971: 64).

In this way, Winnicott argues that art, science and technique, originally transitional objects and phenomena, are outcomes of a primary competence to engage in play, to explore and to create, and are intimately related to sublimation and symbolic capacities. Drawing upon Winnicottian theorization on transitional objects, I propose that the essential function of the drives, and in our case the empowering drive, is to assure an 'objectificatory function', a term coined by Green (1986). For the infant's own investment of perverse narcissism, its objectificatory function is a *fetishistic* one.

The 'technical proto-object' as the final object of the empowering drive

Perhaps this is a good place to raise the following questions: What is the technical object, in its origin, but a fetish of power and what is its value? Freud (1927) notes that the fetish has an ambivalent value. On the one hand, 'it' recognises constituent ontological lack, and, on the other, it denies such a lack by replacing it with the (phallic) object.

Freud is thus compelled to conceptualize the denial of reality, castration and the splitting of the ego in order to provide an adequate account of their key role in perversion. According to our argument so far, then, perverse narcissistic positioning also constitutes the psychotype of the technologists, ever willing to organize complicity with each of the mass consumers, eager consumers of their own perverse artefacts and devices (including high-technological ones). This perverse narcissistic positioning of the technologist also needs to define an enemy as target of their rivalry.

For that reason perverse narcissism is content neither with the development of warfare nor with its wider political and economic effects. It has to innovate and elaborate these technological developments permanently in order to provide us all with our object of completeness (the technical object as a device of power), while making us revolve around its conquests, formerly as warfare and lately as productive, informational and communication systems.

I have located these twisted imbrications between technique, violence, socialization and technologically mediated communication in the psychogenesis of the libidinal economy of perverse narcissism, and the way these economies are invested by dominant powers, in which the economy, politics and the militia are essentially subsumed under technological and media devices. Such an assembly leads the cultural anthropologist París (1991: xvii-xviii) to state that:

> The relation between technology and violence continues to mark the course of inhuman development. This course shifts from the seeking of a destructive increase in a first stage to the conquest of precision as destiny. But it would be erroneous to overemphasise the importance of recent technological developments in warfare and forget the importance of political, psychosociological, informative strategies that have acted as key factors. (our translation)

Consequently, *technique* is not so much the outcome of a series of conscious experiences generated, accumulated and selectively directed by a certain cognitive strategy, as a proto-object whose constitution responds to erotic-affective demands (libidinal investment) of a concrete pulsional dynamic. It is also a perverse narcissistic one (sado-fetishistic) whose ultimate function is to sustain the longing for completeness. Later, this omnipotent wish functions as a motivation for the constitution of the first technical proto-object, weapon or warfare development.

In this light the disturbing characterizations of our time postulated by Heidegger in *The Question Concerning Technology* ([1954] 1962) now seem not so strange. According to Heidegger, the vertiginous and sinister character of technique represents a double danger. It masks the magnetism of the natural and unravels the mystery that always safeguards the sacred. This Janus-faced nature of the technical entails significant risks. Technique is tied to the secular and anthropomorphic adventure that, when radicalizing itself in modernity, unfolds a technological titanism that foments and develops the inner and intersubjective aggressiveness of the human condition. This technological titanism returns as a narcissistic and perverse omnipotence which is nowadays processed and expressed through the symbolism of cyberculture and the ideological function of social constructionism within it.

The cybercultural construction of light subjectivity

Within the broad area of the social sciences, and in the psychological realm in particular, social constructionism postulates a ductile subjectivity adaptable to contemporary economic and political demands. Whereas the hegemony of 'behaviorism' obeyed the necessities of an industrializing phase in culture in which the order of the day was the disciplining of the workforce as if it were a machine as part of a Taylorist chain of production (see Sey in this volume), social constructionism is now the psychosocial paradigm which best responds to the demands, first of Fordism and, at present, of Toyotism (for example, Gergen, 1991). It does so by rendering available while theorizing anonymous, impersonal and light subjectivity types, ever ready to act out in multiple functional codes, without any sort of attachment.

Social constructionism satisfies the demands of (late) capitalism which needs 'light', plastic and dispossessed subjectivities. Social constructionist subjectivities which cohabit in cyberculture are adjustable to precarious work contracts, extensive times of unemployment, and happy to reinforce dominant assumptions of highly functional geographical mobility. These kinds of subject are the best, most adaptable types to conform to high-tech trial and error procedures, experimentation, and attitude questionnaires which rest upon relations of ruling that demand flexible measurement concerned with predicting the capacities of individual malleability. The socially constructed subject is the best consumer of plastic and light identities (whether extra-curricular, professional, sexual, transsexual, real or imaginary) (Ibáñez, 1994a, 1994b).

Cushman (1990) suggests that what is needed is an empty subjectivity without historical memory, root or community in order to optimize processes of adaptation to frenetic production–consumption rhythms compatible with new devices in high-technological supply, and for a consumer attracted to organic and aesthetic surgery, to forms of biotechnology to enhance their plasticity and adaptability to the market. As Paul and Noller point out, borrowing Turkle's (1997) arguments, such experiments hold out a future of unlimited omnipotence, in which everyone can imagine themself as they would dream themselves to be, even at the moment when they suffer in an empty solitude:

> Hysteria, based on sexual repression was the neurosis in Freud's time. Today we don't suffer it less, but we do so in a different manner. In our panic about aloneness, combined with a fear of intimacy, we experience a sensation of emptiness, dislocation and unreality of the self. And there the computer, a companion without feelings, is able to effect a compromise. One is able to communicate without being vulnerable. The necessity for being with another person is substituted by the computer as a kind of second self. (Paul and Noller, 1997: 48) (our translation)

This latest extension of new technologies has therefore resulted in a precarious subject, with 'adaptive and non-critical identity', an excessively vicarious one, which satisfies demands of an over-technologized socialization. These transformations indicate the end of a self-identity understood as a permanent reflective project upon itself and of interactions with its own 'sector of life style' (Giddens, 1991, 1992). The counterpoint of this subjectivity fed by omnipotent self-fascination is a 'technomaniac delirium' shadowed by 'the twilight of duty and responsibility' (Lipovetsky, 1994: 11).

Technique puts into work narcissistic fascination by the self-simulated other (Girad, 1986). This double or replicant thus satisfies omnipotent yearnings at the cost of amputating Eros, so creating a double wreckage of the self. This is captured already in the literature which opened modernity (but which had already spoken against modernity itself) and epitomized, for example, in Shakespeare, when Richard III says: 'Since I cannot be a lover, I am fated to being an evil-doer', in the work of Mary Shelley on Dr Frankenstein and his monster; and Stevenson's Dr Jekyll and Mr Hyde. Such visions are also present in cybercultural fiction, in representations of the human being and the cyborg, and the revolt of the replicant in films such as *Blade Runner*.

Technology compensates for powerful feelings of inferiority in which the present-day personality is immersed in, modelled upon and socialized by technologies of adaptation. This, in the Internet era, facilitates the emergence of an ontology of impersonality, or a deficit of personality as expressed by the director of the McLuhan Program at the University of Toronto, Derrick de Kerkhove in the statement that 'In cyberspace we are nobody.'

The condition of being no one is representative of the novel personality of the petit cyberplanetary bourgeoisie which denies all forms of identity and belonging save for the one to be 'hacked' into. We approach, therefore, diagnoses which suggest that we are living in a time of 'consummated nihilism' and the maximization of immediate personal profit, or, according to Gil Calvo (1990), in a time of 'emancipated automata'. This era obeys Max Weber's grimmest diagnoses of the mechanical automatization of instrumental reason, and is now confirmed by the emergence of a new caste of expert systems bureaucrats and their government of and through the megamachine (Moya, 1992). For that reason the logical consequence of the modernization process, following the Weberian argument, is the social construction of 'an empty' personality (Cushman, 1990) 'put off centre' by the loss of sense and value (Sampson, 1985) and 'decentred' by the splitting of its spheres of action into opposed spheres of value (Gárate Martínez and Marinas (1996), preventing its users ever developing a sense of agentic subjectivity and community with any form of self-development as its emerging outcome.

This omnipotent excess of technoscience leads to disorder, to *hybris*, by rendering excessive admiration of technologists and their exclusive God-like right to transform nature. This is excess of technological titanism where the avidity of phallic enjoyment is revealed in its full force. This excess precipitates moments of crisis and the return of the hidden revolt of the repressed at the very moment cyberculture becomes anchored in techniques with a potential for mass destruction. This mass destruction is expressed in atomic armaments, and narcissism, violence and perversion which together severely threaten the existence of life through contamination and destruction of finite natural resources, an increasing division between the growth of wealth for a few and conditions of scarcity for more than half of humanity, moral sequestration of experience, the complete hegemony of competitiveness and the reification of intersubjective relations, profound distress in everyday life, struggles for community and decolonization, the growth of sado-masochistic tendencies which make manifest the deepest primitive destructive instincts, and generalized cases of pederasty, child pornography, and snuff movies.

Cyberculture versus the age of the spirit

As opposed to such a modernity which is contingent upon the autonomy of technique which intends to also dispossess psychology of its function as a conscious reflection of cultural, social and political events, I have opted for a psychoanalytic theory upon which to ground a psychogenetic reading of technique. From this approach it has followed that the technical object in cyberculture, with the cyborg as paradigm and ideological referent of contemporary personality, can be read as an ontological culmination of a psychological perverse narcissistic type. Cybercultural discourse has thus become the last foundational chapter of modernity, the contemporary mega-account of hypermodernity.

Consequently, I argue that postmodern social science must now turn towards the ontotheological horizon to confront a society and culture based on the incredible power of technique and its machines, and whose ultimate expression is reached in forms of life in late capitalism. Against this we need to turn to a vision from 'critical postmodernity' that, in line with the work of Jünger (1951), is able to recover a vision of ontology as the only power that can resist the world of machines, and retrieve the immutable and timeless essence of human nature. Its implicit constituents are a *pathos* adjusted by knowledge of the zenith of perverse narcissism and an *ethos* freely assumed as an individual reaching for the raising of a civilizing, ecological and shared awareness. Only by connecting with an ethical and religious viewpoint can we provide not only theoretical legitimacy, but also rituals of compassionate work that may facilitate a substantive interlinking of individual and collective life, a connection between presences and absences; between life, disease and death, and between the memory of cultural legacy and its transmission to future generations.

I believe it important to recognize that the origin of the technical object lies in the conflictual nature of the human psyche. This assumption equips us to avoid the devilish processes which accompany the inexorability of technocrat reason. It also enables us to engage in the exploration of the complexity of technological forms of expression while making possible a renunciation of the naïve idea of constructing a technological order independently of conflicts of the personality, of atomic confrontation or, in ecological terms, of environmental pollution.

Uncontrolled technological development threatens to become the corollary of an omnipotent destiny of the drive for power and domination, and of phallic enjoyment which is now omnipresent in cyberculture. Against such phallic enjoyment I counterpose an ethical/religious vision and pious fellow feeling and I believe that this, as Gárate Martínez and Marinas (1996: 4) argue, can articulate our own symbolic tradition with the *opus nigrum* of psychoanalytic experience, without entailing the ascription to any institutional scholastic:

> In this cultural lineage the expression of the Castilian poetic mystic '*a knowledge not knowing/all science transcended*' can well fit the impulse and the track of the analytical journey that tries to think itself from our language. However, to our understanding, with two conditions: mysticism should not be mistaken for instituted theology, nor for prescriptions of karmas for consumption. (our translation)

A discourse welcoming the sacred must be understood as the symbolic experience of an encounter which bears witness to the spirit and maker of community cohesion. This would be a variety of experience able to translate into psychodynamic vocabulary as something not too distant from the prototypical self-knowledge and care of the self conceptualized, for example, by Bion (1974, 1996) as the 'mother with the capacity for reverie'; by Winnicott (1971, 1984) as the provision of 'good enough mothering'; or by Lacan (1938, 1966) as an ethical imperative epitomized as 'love that is conducive to enjoyment in desire'.

This ethical/religious ethos supports the 'true age of the spirit' as initiated by Joaquín de Fiore, a Calabrian abbot of the twelfth century, a teacher of Saint Francisco de Asís and Saint Buenaventura. Mannheim (1936) identifies de Fiore as the generating agent of social utopism, while Moya (1997: 62), for his part, identifies him as a figure who:

> Animates the secret history of the western spirit in this Joaquinist tradition of holy and heresies, missionaries and revolutionaries, poets and thinkers. Dante, Tail of Rienzo, Tomás Müntzer, Jacob Böhme, Lessing, Kant, Hörderlin, Fichte, Novalis, Schelling, Hegel, Saint-Simon, Comte, are some of the decisive names in this tradition.

This tradition has been exhaustively studied by De Lubac (1981a, b), and it now flourishes once more in works of Trías (1995) and Moya (1997). For that reason, I shall conclude that, as against 'active nihilism' which replaces experience by experiment, that elevates technological toys and special effects as alternatives to art, that turns the useful and the ingenious into a commercial fetish, and that replaces any common project with the sum of prevailing onanisms, there exists an ethics of ethical/religious discourse syntonic with the 'age of the spirit'.

The age of the spirit renders possible a more proportionate and civilized relationship with nature, with the natural satisfaction of things in life. It is thus able to come to grips with the fact that life is fragile and terrible, but also beautiful and prodigious. Life always attempts to obtain an encounter with the natural thing, that is to say, an encounter with the Trinitarian key of truth, beauty and beatitude as the ultimate justification of being on the earth, and holds open the possibility of recovering our original innocence.

References

Álvarez-Uría, F. (1991) 'La caja de Pandora: sociología del conocimiento y psicología clínica', *Clínica y Salud*, **2**(1): 51–6.

Basalla, G. (1988) *La Evolución De La Tecnología*. Barcelona: Editorial Crítica.

Benedikt, M. (1991) *Cyberspace: First Steps*. Cambridge, MA: MIT Press.

Benjamin, W. (1971) *Angelus Novus*. Barcelona: Edhasa.

Benjamin, W. (1991) 'Theses on the philosophy of history', in Arendt, H. (ed.) *Illuminations* (trans. Harry Zohn). London: Fontana Press.

Bion, W.R. (1974) *Seminarios de Psicoanálisis*. Barcelona (1991): Paidós.

Bion, W.R. (1996) *Memorias del futuro*. Madrid: Julián Yébenes Ed.

Brown, N. ([1959]1967) *Eros y Tanatos (El Sentido Psicoanalítico De La Historia)*. México: Joaquín Mortiz.

Brown, N. (1972) *El Cuerpo Del Amor*. México: Joaquín Mortiz.

Burman, E., Gordo-López, A.J., Macauley, W.R., and Parker, I. (eds) (1995) *Cyberpsychology: Conference, Interventions and Reflections*. Manchester Metropolitan University: Discourse Unit.

Cushman, P. (1990) 'Why the self is empty?', *American Psychologist*, **45**(5): 599–611.

De Lubac, H. (1981a) *La Posteridad Espiritual de Joaquín de Fiore, De Joaquín a Schelling*. Madrid: Ediciones Encuentro.

De Lubac, H. (1981b) *La Posteridad Espiritual de Joaquín de Fiore, De Saint-Simon a Nuestros Días*. Madrid: Ediciones Encuentro.

Dolto, F. ([1984]1986) *La Imagen Inconsciente del Cuerpo*. Barcelona: Paidós.

Featherstone, M. and Burrows, R. (1995) *Cyberspace/Cyberbodies/Cyberpunk: Cultures of Technological Embodiment*. London: Sage.

Freud, S. (1905) 'Three essays on the theory of sexuality', in Richards, A. (ed.) (1977) *On Sexuality, Pelican Freud Library*, Vol. 7. Harmondsworth: Pelican.

Freud, S. (1910) 'A special type of choice of object made by men', in Richards, A. (ed.) (1977) *On Sexuality, Pelican Freud Library*, Vol. 7. Harmondsworth: Pelican.

Freud, S. (1911) 'Psychoanalytic notes on an autobiographical account of a case of paranoia (dementia paranoides)', in Richards, A. (ed.) (1979) *Case Histories II: 'Rat Man', Schreber, 'Wolf Man', Female Homosexuality, Pelican Freud Library*, Vol. 9. Harmondsworth: Pelican.

Freud, S. ([1912]1913) 'Totem and taboo: some points of agreement between the mental lives of savages and neurotics' in Richards, A. (ed.) (1985) *The Origins of Religion, Pelican Freud Library*, Vol. 13. Harmondsworth: Pelican.

Freud, S. (1914) 'On narcissism', in Richards, A. (ed.) (1984) *On Metapsychology: The Theory of Psychoanalysis, Pelican Freud Library*, Vol. 11. Harmondsworth: Pelican.

Freud, S. (1915a) 'Thoughts for the times on war and death', in Richards, A. (ed.) (1985) *Civilization, Society and Religion: Group Psychology, Civilization and its Discontents and Other Works, Pelican Freud Library*, Vol. 12. Harmondsworth: Pelican.

Freud, S. (1915b) 'Instincts and their vicissitudes', in Richards, A. (ed.) (1984) *On Metapsychology: The Theory of Psychoanalysis, Pelican Freud Library*, Vol. 11. Harmondsworth: Pelican.

Freud, S. (1920a) 'Beyond the pleasure principle', in Richards, A. (ed.) (1984) *On Metapsychology: The Theory of Psychoanalysis, Pelican Freud Library*, Vol. 11. Harmondsworth: Pelican.

Freud, S. (1920b) 'The psychogenesis of a case of homosexuality in a woman', in Richards, A. (ed.) (1979) *Case Histories II: 'Rat Man', Schreber, 'Wolf Man', Female Homosexuality, Pelican Freud Library*, Vol. 9. Harmondsworth: Pelican.

Freud, S. (1927) 'Fetishism', in Richards, A. (ed.) (1977) *On Sexuality, Pelican Freud Library*, Vol. 7. Harmondsworth: Pelican.

Gárate Martínez, I. (1990) *Clínica Psicoanalítica. De la Clínica a la Cura, del Grupo a la Ética del Sujeto*. Bordeaux: Ed. IGM.

Gárate Martínez, I. and Marinas, J.M. (1996) *Lacan en Castellano*. Madrid: Quipú Ediciones.

Gergen, K.J. (1991) *El Yo Saturado*. Barcelona: Paidós.

Giddens, A. (1991) *Modernidad e Identidad del Yo: El Yo y la Sociedad en la Época Contemporánea*. Barcelona: Península.

Giddens, A. (1992) *La Transformación de la intimidad. Sexualidad, amor y erotismo en las sociedades modernas*. Madrid: Cátedra.

Gil Calvo, E. (1990) 'El autómata emancipado', *Claves de Razón Práctica*, 2: 46–52.

Girard, R. (1986) *El Chivo Expiatorio*. Barcelona: Anagrama.

Gordo-López, A.J. and Macauley, W.R. (1995) 'From cognitive psychologies to mythologies: advancing cyborg textualities for a narrative of resistance, in Gray, C.H., Figueroa-Sarriera, H.J. and Mentor, S. (eds) *The Cyborg Handbook*, New York/London: Routledge.

Green, A. (1986) 'Pulsión de muerte, narcisismo negativo, función desobjetalizante', in Green, A., Ikonen, P., Laplanche, J., Rechardt, E., Segal, H., Widlöcher, D. and Yorke, C. (1991) *La Pulsión de Muerte*, pp. 65–78. Barcelona: Amorrortu.

Heidegger, M. ([1954]1962) *La Pregunta por la Técnica*. Barcelona: Época de Filosofía.

Ibáñez, J. (1985) *Del Algoritmo al Sujeto*. Madrid: Siglo XXI de España editores.

Ibáñez, J. (1994a) *El Regreso del Sujeto*. Madrid: Siglo XXI de España editores.

Ibáñez, J. (1994b) *Por una Sociología de la Vida Cotidiana*. Madrid: Siglo XXI de España editores.

Jones. S. (ed.) (1997) *Virtual Culture: Identity and Communication in Cybersociety*. London: Sage.

Jünger, E. (1951) *La Emboscadura*. Barcelona: Tusquets.

Klein, M. ([1921]1945) *Love, Guilt and Reparation and Other Works*. London: Hogarth Press.

Lacan, J. (1938) *La familia*. Buenos Aires (1978): Ed. Argonauta.

Lacan, J. (1966) *Escritos I y II*. Mexico (1984): Siglo XXI.

Lipovetsky, G. (1994) *El Crepúsculo del Deber*. Barcelona: Anagrama.

Mannheim, K. (1936) *Ideología y Utopía*. FCE. México.

Marinas, J.M. (1997). 'Por qué dicen ciencia cuando es tecnología?: notas sobre el contexto social de la ciencia', *Cuadernos de Realidades Sociales*, 49–50.

Moya, C. (1992) *Repensando Weber*. VVAA. (1992). Madrid: Escritos de Teoría Sociológica.

Moya, C. (1997) 'Releyendo ahora a Jesús Ibáñez', in Álvarez-Uría, F. (ed.) *Jésus Ibáñez. Teoría y Práctica*. Endymion. Madrid.

París, C. (1991) *Crítica de la Civilización Nuclear: Tecnología y Violencia*. Libertarias. Madrid.

Parker, I. (1996) 'Psychology, science fiction and postmodern space', *South African Journal of Psychology*, **26**(3): 1–7.

Parker, I. (1997) *Psychoanalytic Culture: Psychoanalytic Discourse in Western Society*. London: Sage.

Parker, I. and Shotter, J. (eds) (1990) *Deconstructing Social Psychology*. London: Routledge.

Paul, G. and Noller, P. (1997) 'Jóvenes fans del ordenador', *Letra Internacional*, **49**: 43–51.

Penley, C. and Ross, A. (eds) (1991) *Technoculture*. Minneapolis: University of Minneapolis Press.

Ramonet, I. (1997) *Un Mundo sin Rumbo*. Madrid: Debate.

Ricoeur, P. (1969) *Hermenéutica y Psicoanálisis*. Buenos Aires: Ediciones Megápolis.

Rorty, R. (1989) *Contingencia, Ironía y Solidaridad*. Barcelona: Paidós.

Rorty, R. (1991) 'Freud y la reflexión moral', in Rorty, R. (1993) *Ensayos sobre Heidegger y otros pensadores contemporáneos*. Barcelona: Paidós.

Sampson, E.E. (1985) 'The decentralization of identity: towards a revised concept of personal and social orders', *American Psychologist*, **40**: 1203–11.

Soldevilla Pérez, C. (1991) 'El espacio postmoderno en la psicolog'a social española'. *Interacción Social*, **2**: 175–81, Madrid: Universidad Complutense de Madrid.

Soldevilla Pérez, C. (1994) 'Reflexión y/o especularidad ante el paso del noroeste de la psicología social española', **4**: 227–38. Madrid: Universidad Complutense de Madrid.

Trías, E. (1995) *La Edad del Espíritu*. Barcelona: Destino.
Trías, E. (1997) *Pensar la Religión*. Barcelona: Destino.
Turkle, S. (1997) 'Multiple subjectivity and virtual community at the end of the Freudian century', *Sociological Inquiry*, **67**(1): 72–84.
Varela, J. and Álvarez-Uría, F. (1988) *Las Redes de la Psicología*. Libertarias. Madrid.
Winnicott, D.W. (1971) *Playing and Reality*. Harmondsworth: Penguin. *Realidad y juego*. Buenos Aires (1972): Granica (ed.). *Realidad y juego*. Barcelona (1996): Gedisa.
Winnicott, D.W. (1984) *Deprivación y delincuencia*. Barcelona (1990): Paidós.

CHAPTER 4

Cyberpsychosis: The Feminization of the Postbiological Body

JILL MARSDEN

[Sexuality] is badly explained by the binary organisation of the sexes, and just as badly by a bisexual organisation within each sex. Sexuality brings into play too great a diversity of conjugated becomings... Sexuality is the production of a thousand sexes, which are so many uncontrollable becomings. *Sexuality proceeds by way of the becoming-woman of the man and the becoming-animal of the human*: an emission of particles. (Deleuze and Guattari, 1980: 278)

Despite the celebrated revolutionary potential of postmodernist approaches to gender, the spectre of biological fundamentalism continues to haunt any genuine attempt to deconstruct the binary organization of the sexes. From 'strategic essentialism' to 'écriture féminine' feminist theory has persistently sought to denature the patriarchal ideology that social roles are physiologically ordained, indicating how both men and women may access and live out the cultural behaviour deemed appropriate to the 'opposite' sex. Yet as a principle of social control the power of gender is tacitly reinforced rather than subverted by these symbolic reversals. This is because the 'natural attitude' to gender is never realistically challenged by semiotic philosophies which regard bodily sex as the essential *sign* of gender even when lived at odds with itself. Indeed, identities are postulated as fluid precisely to the extent that bodies are *discursively* positioned as immutable such that even tampering with the 'natural order' has the tendency to leave this dogma intact. As is well known, the candidate for sex-change surgery has to 'perform' their prospective gender more zealously than any so-called member of the 'biological' sex, thus securing the power knowledge of psycho-biologism in the very moment of its defiance. But what might it mean to *change* sex if there is no longer any certainty about *the* sexes? This is not a question of transsexualism (itself the literal inscription of the natural attitude) but of modifying the socio-political status of sexual *reality*, a possibility already glimpsed in the new forms of subjectivity emerging from the interface between humans and cybernetic technology – a material transformation which has consequences far exceeding the idealist philosophy of representation.

This chapter will address the interrelation of psyche, body and gender in cyberculture, asking what becomes of gender within the virtual environment. The locus for this discussion will be Daniel Paul Schreber's (1903) *Memoirs of My Nervous Illness* in which the question of *sexing* materiality will be explored. After briefly outlining the salient framework of the *Memoirs* I shall show how Freud's analysis of Schreber's *feminization* confirms the prejudices of traditional psychology and how a cyberpsychological reading of the *Memoirs* produces very different resources for critical practice. I then go on to address the political issue of viewing the postbiological body as *feminized* and ask what this means for feminism. Is the feminization of the cybersubject another fetish of French high theory – a titillating substitute for genuine empowerment – or does the biopolitical materialism of cyberpsychology dramatically reconfigure the lived reality of sex?

The 'Order of Things'

In 1911 Freud published his paper *Psychoanalytic Notes on an Autobiographical Account of a Case of Paranoia (Dementia Paranoides)* based on Daniel Paul Schreber's book *Memoirs of My Nervous Illness* (1903). Unlike Freud's other famous case histories, 'the Schreber Case' was based entirely on Freud's analysis of written testimony and, as such, constitutes a strikingly insightful exercise in literary interpretation. It is not difficult to see why Schreber's *Memoirs* exerted such a fascination on Freud. The subject of Freud's study suffered twice from nervous illness, the second of which generated an intricate and complex hallucinatory system in which sexual transformation is conditioned by profound changes in modes of communication. In 1884 Schreber was admitted to the Psychiatric Clinic of the University of Leipzig where he was successfully treated by its Director, Professor Paul Emil Flechsig. Discharged after six months, he resumed his position as Judge at the County Court in Leipzig and continued to excel in the legal profession, rising to the rank of President of the Court of Appeal at Dresden in 1893. However, in this year Schreber suffered his second and more prolonged period of illness and it is of this time that the *Memoirs* speak.

The psychiatric adviser to the court at which Schreber appealed for rescission of his tutelage summarized Schreber's world view as follows:

> The patient's delusional system amounts to this: he is called to redeem the world and to bring back to mankind the lost state of Blessedness. He maintains he has been given this task by direct divine inspiration, similar to that taught by the prophets; he maintains that nerves in a state of excitation, as his have been for a long time, have the property of attracting God, but it is a question of things which are either not at all expressible in human language or only with great difficulty, because he maintains they lie outside all human experience and have only been revealed to him. The most essential part of his mission of redemption is that it is necessary for him first of all to be *transformed into a woman*... He has the feeling that already masses of 'female nerves' have been transferred into his body, from which through immediate fertilization by God new human beings would come forth. Only then would he be able to die a natural death and have gained for himself as for all other human beings the state of Blessedness. (Schreber, 1903: 272–3)

In a narrative which prefigures McLuhan's (1964: 3) typification of electric technology, the *Memoirs* expound a philosophy of communication which extends the boundaries of Schreber's body into a vast network of connection beyond all familiar spatio-temporal coordinates and species boundaries. Schreber informs his readers that in the normal course of things regular contact between God and human beings occurs only after death, although in special circumstances He engages in 'nerve contact' with highly gifted individuals. However, 'such "nerve contact" was not allowed to become the rule' because the nerves of living human beings have such power of attraction for God, 'particularly when in a state of *high-grade excita-*

tion' that He would not be able to free Himself from them again, and would endanger his own existence (Schreber, [1903] 1955: 48). In the 'Order of Things' God approaches corpses to draw up their nerves to 'the forecourts of heaven' (ibid.: 49) where souls enter a state of Blessedness and become one with Him. Ascension to grace takes this unusual form because, according to Schreber, 'the human soul is contained in the nerves of the body' (ibid.: 45) and God 'is only nerve, not body, and akin therefore to the human soul' (ibid.: 46). Nerves from corpses have to be purified by God 'according to the variable condition of the respective human souls' hence there are 'various *grades* of Blessedness' which determine the longevity of contact with the divine. However, *'not even the soul is purely spiritual, but rests on a material substrate, the nerves'* (ibid.: 244) so while disembodied, God is a fully material presence. It thus emerges that Schreber's deity is not a transcendent being, extrinsically presiding over the system, but a fluctuating assemblage of immanent components, reflecting the current state of the migration of souls.

As an indirect consequence of Schreber's nervous illness, a 'crisis' ensues in the Order of Things. Irresistibly attracted to Schreber's overcharged nervous system, God is drawn into a dangerous neural alliance with him which inhibits souls from attaining Blessedness via their usual route. Unable to understand the needs of the living and in a bid to free Himself, God inadvertently torments Schreber by straining to 'draw up' his nerves. Schreber reasons that appeasement for God can only be won by providing what is relinquished through their unfortunate fusion, namely the state of Blessedness for nerve souls. He explains that as part of everlasting Blessedness 'voluptuousness' is granted to souls in perpetuity and as an end in itself but to human beings solely as a means for the preservation of the species. However, as a result of Schreber's unique position within the Order of Things he is obliged to prostitute his body as a magnet for the nerves of God, to enable departed souls to engage in sexual pleasure at his expense. Explaining that he must 'cultivate voluptuousness' as much as possible in order to please God, Schreber sees it as his destiny to tirelessly indulge in the kind of corporeal excitation he assumes to be the sole preserve of *women*, the rationale for this being that female bliss, unlike male bliss, consists 'mainly in an uninterrupted feeling of voluptuousness' (ibid.: 52).

A final point worth mentioning before proceeding to Freud's analysis is the precise catalyst for Schreber's unprecedented neural link up with God. On Schreber's interpretation, difficulties *only* began to occur when his doctor, Professor Flechsig, effectively hacked into his nervous system during psychiatric treatment. In the 'Open Letter to Professor Flechsig' which prefaces the *Memoirs* Schreber dates the onset of his hallucinations to the time at which his physician came on-line:

> I have not the least doubt that the *first impetus* to what my doctors always considered mere 'hallucinations' but which to me signified communication with supernatural powers, consisted of *influences on my nervous system emanating from your nervous system*. How could this be explained? I think it is possible that you – at first as I am quite prepared to believe only for therapeutic purposes – carried on some hypnotic, suggestive, or whatever else one could call it, contact with my nerves, *even while we were separated in space*. (Schreber [1903] 1955: 34)

Schreber suggests that during hypnosis Flechsig might suddenly have suspected that other voices were tuned in to his nervous system, which in a gifted individual could only indicate 'a supernatural origin'. He further postulates that by the time Flechsig chose to log off, part of the latter's nerves had mysteriously migrated in a runaway schismogenetic process, prematurely ascending to heaven as a 'tested soul'. Since souls in the state of Blessedness dwell in an uninterrupted enjoyment of which earthly sexual excitation is but a mere foretaste, this may explain why Schreber initially fears sexual abuse at the hands of 'someone' (perhaps the errant Flechsig soul), and why he initially resists his feminization so vehemently. Until he becomes reconciled to his destiny, the aggregate of souls continuous with God's dominion function as members of prosthetic virtual communities engaging in netsex with the hapless Schreber. However, once he realizes that impregnation by God will lead to the regeneration of the Order of Things he accepts his fate of becoming-woman and learns to interactively influence the nerves of God. This is the closest to being 'cured' that Schreber ever came but he succeeded in getting his tutelage rescinded on the basis of being able to justify his 'feminization' according to the arguments outlined.

In the Name of the Father

Possibly the most intriguing element of Freud's analysis of the
Schreber case is his insistence that the fantasy of becoming woman
was the primary delusion and the redeemer fantasy only retroactively connected to it. Freud draws evidence for this hypothesis from
a dream of Schreber's during the 'incubation period' of his illness in
which he reports thinking that 'it really must be rather pleasant to be
a woman succumbing to intercourse' (Schreber [1903] 1955: 63). He
subsequently argues that in Schreber's case 'the exciting cause of the
illness was the appearance in him of a feminine [that is, a passive
homosexual] wishful fantasy' (Freud, 1911: 182). Given Freud's
central thesis that paranoia has its origins in repressed passive homosexuality, his focus throughout the study is on Schreber's putative
'unmanning' and his relationships with male figures, preeminently
with Professor Flechsig and his father.

Freud's arguments for attributing homosexuality to Schreber
comprise an intriguing cocktail of the somatic and the psychic. In
addition to the generalizing remark that most human beings oscillate between heterosexual and homosexual feelings (ibid.: 180), and
the somewhat specious claim that at fifty-one Schreber was at a critical point in his sexual life (a male 'climacteric') (ibid.: 181), Freud
pays particular attention to an episode in which Schreber reports an
extraordinary number of nocturnal emissions (ibid.: 180). Prior to
this revelation in his *Memoirs*, Schreber discusses the decline of his
wife's visits to the asylum, a factor which Freud insists on viewing
as causal: 'It is easy to understand that the mere presence of his wife
must have acted as protection against the attractive power of the
men around him' (ibid.: 180). However, the mainstay of Freud's
argument is that Schreber 'was reminded of his brother or his father
by the figure of his doctor' (ibid.: 182) and that his feelings for
Flechsig displayed the classic signs of transference: 'The person
who is now hated and feared for being a persecutor was at one time
loved and honoured. The main purpose of the persecution asserted
by the patient's delusion is to justify the change in his emotional
attitude' (ibid.: 175).

Freud intimates that Schreber's repressed affections for the doctor
who 'cured' him of his first illness are rekindled when pathological
symptoms reassert themselves, thus precipitating Schreber's anxiety
that 'someone' plots to abuse his feminized body:

It only requires a slight correction of the characteristic paranoic indefiniteness of Schreber's mode of expression to enable us to divine the fact that the patient was in fear of sexual abuse at the hands of his doctor himself. The exciting cause of his illness, then, was an outburst of homosexual libido; the object of this libido was probably from the very first his doctor, Flechsig; and his struggles against the libidinal impulse produced the conflict which gave rise to the symptoms. (Freud, 1911: 177)

The identification of Flechsig with the role of persecutor is somewhat compromised by the fact that in the *Memoirs* it is God (and his legion of virtual souls) whose reign of terror assumes prominence, but Freud's explanation of this point is particularly compelling:

It was impossible for Schreber to become reconciled to playing the part of a female wanton towards his doctor; but the task of providing God Himself with the voluptuous sensations that He required called up no such resistance on the part of his ego. Emasculation was now no longer a disgrace; it became 'consonant with the Order of Things'. (Freud, 1911: 183)

A magnificent victory is scored by the infantile sexual urge, claims Freud, when voluptuousness is demanded, not reproached, and castration is utilized as material for fantasy: 'His father's most dreaded threat, castration, actually provided the material for his wishful phantasy (at first resisted but later accepted) of being transformed into a woman.' (Freud, 1911: 192)

Subtle and cogent although Freud's analysis is, there is much in the *Memoirs* which is in conflict with his interpretation. Freud displays a commitment to hierarchical, centralized control structures which relentlessly situate the Schreberian fantasia within the locus of the family and relations of affiliation. In a remarkably slick series of moves, Freud succeeds in commuting Schreber's intensely psychotic delusional system to yet another incidence of Oedipal conflict. Declaring that we are familiar with the ambivalence boys show towards their fathers, Freud boldly asserts that Schreber's relation to his God 'is the unmistakable prototype of that relation' (Freud, 1911: 188). That this is a deeply unpromising line of interpretation is implied by the fact that not only is Schreber's God neither authoritarian nor univocally determined but that Schreber displays remarkable magnanimity towards his persecutor who is merely 'ignorant' of the ways of the living. To stage the Oedipal drama Freud is obliged to procure 'evidence' from Schreber's one overt gesture of defiance – his predilection for bellowing at the sun. Mythology is plundered to support the thesis that the sun 'is nothing but another sublimated symbol' for his father (Freud, 1911: 190) (overlooking the fact that a smaller sun is associated with the Superintendent of the asylum). Schreber's simple assertion that God does not understand the living is seized upon with a desperate glee. Freud notes that Schreber's father was a physician and deduces that to accuse him of only knowing about corpses is the height of insolence on the part of the son.

From Many to One

From beginning to end, Freud's interpretation of the Schreber case demonstrates an indomitable allegiance to a classical, idealist philosophy of representation which condenses the ceaseless multiplicity of unconscious affects to the formal unity of the signifier. Behind every episode Freud identifies the implacable paternal *logos*, every revelation reducible to an agonistic struggle with the representative of the Law which underwrites and reinforces the constitution of the self-reflexive psyche. That God is not a unitary construct is manifestly clear from the *Memoirs*; nor for that matter is Flechsig, whose soul at one stage is made up of between 40 to 60 parts. Yet, undaunted and in a move characteristic of Aristotelian logic, Freud isolates a concept which is identical across a plurality of representations: 'All of this dividing up of Flechsig and God into a number of persons... had the same meaning as the splitting of the persecutor into Flechsig and God. They were all duplications of one and the same relationship' (Freud, 1911: 185). From the many to two it is a small step to one: thus Flechsig 'must have stood for his brother' (ibid.: 185) who as the older sibling functions as a surrogate father figure. Each inventive incarnation of Schreberspace is reified into a sign, each sign leading back to the paternal signifier and the bastion of patriarchal law.

The axiomatic of the family, governed by a dialectical synthesis of individual and genus, harnesses Schreber's feminization into the straitjacket of logical structure. With all available positions determined in advance, becoming-woman can only ever be apprehended within a conceptual grid circumscribed by given biological coordinates. In effect, Freud anchors Schreber in an intermediate state between masculinity and femininity, a male body haunted by female desires. Within this logic of binary opposition, homosexuality cannot be appreciated in anything other than relentlessly heterosexual terms, femininity and 'passive homosexuality' equated in a suspect biologism of the penetrable body. That Schreber never fully realizes his feminine destiny is a problematic Freud evades by speaking darkly of an 'asymptotic wish-fulfilment' (Freud, 1911: 183) but it is worth commenting that the trajectory of Schreber's becoming woman tends to loop rather than curve, breasts and genitals appearing and retracting according to a distinctly non-linear tempo. Most significantly of all, perhaps, Freud's discourse underscores the prejudice that female identity is a deficient masculinity. According to Freud's Oedipal theory of psychosexual development it is the *sight* of the 'castrated' female that prompts the young boy to relinquish his incestuous desires for his mother and which simultaneously consolidates the 'self-sufficiency' of his phallic sexual identity (Freud, 1924: 318). For Freud, Schreber's 'unmanning' signifies femininity, for woman is an emasculated subject, a non-sex, her lack of penis her definitive 'sex character' (ibid.: 320).

Despite the hermeneutical *élan* of Freud's reading of the Schreber case, his analysis bears all the hallmarks of the institutional orthodoxy of Enlightenment subjectivity. Where there is multiplicity let there be unity. Where there is material production let there be representation. Where there is system let there be structure. Where there is corporeal becoming let there be organic finality. Where there is plenitude let there be negation. Under the despotism of psychoanalysis, the psychotic is disciplined, rehabilitated, reduced to the anaemic homogeneity of the law-abiding self.

Multiplicity, tactility, femininity

A cyberpsychological reading of the *Memoirs* seeks to liquify what classical psychoanalysis stabilizes. Neither the nosology nor the aetiology of Schreber's illness is of direct relevance to this enterprise for it is of little *material* consequence whether Schreber was a paranoid schizophrenic or whether unconscious homosexuality triggered his sexual extravagances. A cyberpsychological perspective probes the dark and tangled engineering processes which subtend the perceptible body forms Freud captures under the spotlight. The critical concern is with the new conditions of possibility for machining corporeal subjectivity which arise from the *boundary interfacing* evinced in the *Memoirs* and the implications that this might have for gendered social practice. From the rich, Boschian symptomatology of Schreber's illness Freud isolates the elements that can be requisitioned to corroborate his diagnosis of Oedipal anxiety, castration fear and paternal identification. Scant attention is given to the real, tangible linkages which Schreber makes with souls across the body plenum yet these are still 'sexual' and significant in terms of establishing the difference between structural and systemic organization. For example, Schreber confides to the reader that:

> [F]riendly souls always tended towards the region of my sexual organs (of the abdomen, etc.), where they did little or no damage and hardly molested me, whereas inimical souls always aspired towards my head, on which they wanted to inflict some damage, and sat particularly on my left ear in a highly disturbing manner. (Schreber, 1903: 112)

The souls which interfere with Schreber's head are still less damaging and infinitely more inventive than his psychoanalysts. For what transpires in the *Memoirs* is that Schreber's body *once feminized* becomes a key node of exchange in a cybernetic feedback relation with his environment. While not strictly 'alive' the departed souls are clearly not dead matter either. Souls interface with his body across a range of corporeal thresholds, targeting his heart, lungs, ribs, stomach, intestines, pharynx, muscles and eyelids, sometimes translating his thoughts into impersonal data to be replayed, sometimes expiring in his flesh, and frequently causing 'interference' in his neural connections to God. At each moment connections are formed and rerouted across endless scales, the path which the nerve souls take rarely being repeated. Constantly penetrated by souls plugging into the web Schreber despairs at ever being master of his own psyche (ibid.: 175). Throngs of religious leaders, state officials and sundry trespassers bombard him with their ceaseless chatter – including Jesuits, Cardinals, the Pope, 240 Benedictine monks, a Viennese nerve specialist, lawyers, university officials, a students' union from Jupiter, Saturn and Uranus – with no particular prominence being accorded to his father and brother who are mentioned in passing with other relatives such as his wife, mother and father-in-law, a friend of his youth called Ernest K. and a Prince who appeared on his head as a 'little man' (ibid.: 71–2). Indeed, in default of the family tree, Schreber explores the rich potential for transversal, rhizomatic netsurfing which his unique neurological link up affords. Thus he is able to swap information with an eighteenth-century soul about technological advances such as railways, enjoy conference networking with groups of souls merged into higher entities such as the 'Jehovah rays' (Schreber [1903] 1955: 53), and entertain God's nerves with virtual reality 'picturing' involving historical figures ('For instance I make – in day-time or at night – Napoleon or Frederic the Great walk through my room, or the Emperor William I emerge from my wardrobe in full regalia, etc.', ibid.: 182).

In fact, beings in Schreber's simstim world never retain their form long enough to congeal into familiar or familial unities. This is a datascape inhabited by 'fleeting, improvised men' (ibid.: 116), mutating objects (ibid.: 107) and deliquescent souls. Inmates at the Pierson Asylum change heads and multiply rapidly in number. 'Swarms' of different insects, epidemics of leprosy and plague (in blue, brown, black and white varieties), 'miracled' birds in their 'hundreds' and teeming yards of people overwhelm Schreber with their suddenness and volume. Proliferation and transformation similarly mark his body which undergoes promiscuous couplings with various grades of these life forms, without any respect for the constitutive order of the species. In the genre of quintessential science fiction fantasy Schreber reformats himself in different media, including cloning (ibid.: 86), growing multiple heads (ibid.: 86), and spawning a colony of Schreber replicants on another planet. He also has his skull relined with a different brain membrane by Jesuit souls seeking to reprogramme his identity (ibid.: 99) and a large nerve of a hospital attendant implanted into his arm as a bugging device (ibid.: 115). Not an Oedipal son but an orphan cyborg, constantly mutating in accordance with his environment. One might attempt, in a military Freudian manoeuvre, to drill these swarming, self-organizing excesses back into the disciplined phalanx of form. Except that there is no 'back' to which one might return, for these are duplications of a system which is never 'one' to begin with, replications without origin or end.

These interrelated vectors of tactility, multiplicity and emergent creativity map the critical terrain in which the cyberpsychologist approaches the issue of Schreber's feminization. As already observed, Schreber's solution to God's involuntary persecution of him is to 'cultivate voluptuousness' to pacify the nerve souls. Although initially a masculine and a feminine state of bliss are distinguished, it is noteworthy that as the *Memoirs* progress, the feminization of voluptuousness becomes *definitive* of Blessedness as such. The souls who seek this pleasure in Schreber's nervous system are already implicitly feminized, and by extension, so is the God who comprises them. If homosexuality is an issue at all, then arguably it is an autoerotic *lesbian* economy that is here being engineered. Since God's nerves 'continually want to see what pleases them, and these are foremost either female beings, through which their sensation of voluptuousness is stimulated, or their own miracles, which give them the joy of having created something' (Schreber, 1903: 186) Schreber is obliged to operate a website of lesbian pornography to preserve his own bodily well-being:

> I believe that God would never attempt to withdraw (which always impairs my bodily well-being considerably) but would follow my attraction without resistance permanently and uninterruptedly, if only I could *always* be playing the woman's part in sexual embrace with myself, *always* rest my gaze on female beings, *always* look at female pictures, etc. (ibid.: 210)

It is thus by no means certain that becoming woman symbolizes a deficient masculinity or passive homosexuality. Indeed, where is castration to be found within Schreber's glorious 'unmanning' – a process of corporealization which is only ever addressed in terms of *growth, abundance, and plenitude*? Schreber repeatedly insists that 'nerves of voluptuousness exist over the whole female body whereas in the male in the sexual organs and their proximity only' (ibid.: 204). Despite the undoubted positivism of Schreber's logic, what emerges from the *Memoirs* is an affectivity sprung loose from biological finality. Becoming-woman has nothing to do with lack, negation or loss, rather it institutes an explosion of sexuality as materially emergent.

It is important to be clear that this does not entail replacing one set of sexual signifiers with another. Feminization operates in the *Memoirs* as an index of pluralization, a sexualization of the body beyond any strictly determined coordinates:

> In order not to be misunderstood, I must point out that when I speak of my duty to cultivate voluptuousness, *I never mean any sexual desires towards other human beings (females) least of all sexual intercourse*, but that I have to imagine myself as man and woman in one person having intercourse with myself, or somehow have to achieve with myself a certain sexual excitement etc. – which perhaps under other

circumstances might be considered immoral – but which has nothing whatever to do with any idea of masturbation or anything like it. (Schreber [1903] 1955: 208)

Ambisexual, heterosexual, transsexual, a transvestite, a male lesbian. Fantastic possibilities for sexual *excitement* present themselves beyond the genital organization of binary sex code. As a feminized body, Schreber is able to access possibilities for communication not available to the 'masculine'. This is not because of any inherent female essence but because of the base materiality which subtends the sex historically and culturally positioned as 'other' to man. When Irigaray writes that *'woman has sex organs more or less everywhere'* (1977: 28) she does not invoke a truth about female embodiment, she gestures towards an autoerotic economy within which the means of communication begin to communicate with themselves. As Freud's Oedipal theory indicates, masculine subjectivity is constructed on the basis of positioning the feminine as its negative *alter ego*. However, insofar as 'feminine matter' is the condition of possibility for masculinity, by definition it must remain in excess of these speculative constructions. Beyond the mirror of Freudian reflection in which woman's 'sex character' presents the horror of 'nothing to be seen', undifferentiated matter is self-organizing. Enclosed *'within the intimacy of that silent, multiple, diffuse touch'* (Irigaray, 1977: 29) is the unspeakable, uncontainable feminine: the dark matter of cyberspace. Like Irigaray's 'woman' Schreber is 'the sex which is not one' in both the senses this locution implies: from the perspective of Freudian optics a non-sex, a castrated male; from the perspective of the cyberpsychologist a sex which can never be contained within the logic of identity, always multiple, never simply one. Perhaps it could be said that feminization describes the production of a virtual body 'elsewhere in that discursive machinery' of conceptual binarity. In this respect, feminization might be understood as the body's intensive capacity for growth, a sort of 'expanding universe to which no limits could be fixed' (Irigaray, 1977: 31). Schreber's post-biological body is a self-organizing system, illegible from the perspective of extrinsic binary determination. It is Freud who dreams of the transcendent God/father/phallus and Schreber who is firmly plugged into the production of the real. Despite his experience of manifold miracles it is by no means certain that it is Schreber rather than Freud who believes more keenly in magic.

If the body subject is perceived as an emergent system within webs of integration a serious challenge is posed to the Freudian technologies of surveillance and control that comprise the psy-complex. However, it remains to be asked what status feminization has politically in the off-line world of feminist praxis. Freud's analysis may inhibit cyberpsychological investigation but does the latter in turn perpetuate a postmodern idealization of the feminine as metaphor for the chaotic, the fluid and the irrational? Is the Schreber case simply a more exotic variant on the Romantic usurpation of feminine tropes for consolidating male subject positions? Do women actually profit from a theory of the postbiological body?

Postbiological body politics

Everything pivots in this discussion on the way in which becoming woman is understood. Within the binary logic of gender identity which has dominated Western thought since the Greeks, woman has been discursively positioned as the negative complement to masculinity. From Aristotles's characterization of woman as a deficient male to Freud's pronouncement of the female as castrated, subjectivity has tacitly prioritized the masculine. Given this cultural politics of representation, feminists have been presented with two choices: either assert a claim to subjectivity (which is tantamount to a logic of identification with masculinity) or refuse to collude with the bipolar logic of gender by tracking a migrant trajectory, cut free from the philosophy of reflection, comparison and inversion. It is in the spirit of the second alternative that Donna Haraway has aligned feminist politics with the cyborg:

> A cyborg body is not innocent; it was not born in a garden; it does not seek unitary identity and so generate antagonistic dualisms... Up until now (once upon a time), female embodiment seemed to mean skill in mothering and its metaphoric extensions... Cyborgs might consider more seriously the partial, fluid, sometimes aspect of sex and sexual embodiment. Gender might not be global identity after all, even if it has profound historical breadth and depth. (Haraway, 1991: 180)

What Haraway signals in her evocation of the cyborg is materially instantiated in Schreber's exploration of the feminized, postbiological body. Schreber's feminization is not a transitional stage from one sexed identity to another but a mutant, runaway process which, like a computer virus, silently and stealthily, reprogrammes the dominant code. As an ateleological operation, becoming-woman refracts the patriarchal power knowledge that normalizes biological finality. In practical terms this means that female embodiment is realized in terms of its *material engagements*, not in terms of pre-given significations which construct it as passive, heterosexual, maternal, nurturing, and hormonally unstable. For Haraway, what is politically crucial is the way in which boundaries are interfaced and not 'the integrity of natural objects' (Haraway, 1991: 163). In her view, this liberates women from totalizing identity politics, enabling them to interact with other women across the political spectrum, sometimes on mutually contradictory campaigns and without having recourse to biological fundamentalism (such as reproductive capacity) in sexing bodies as female.

This is not to suggest that cyborg politics is inherently revolutionary for transversal political connections may just as easily interface with the dominant ideology as with anything else, a problematic which Haraway's appeal to 'political accountability' can do little to remedy (ibid.: 169). This notwithstanding, at its most radical, Haraway's theory forces the question as to whether the conceptual distinction between 'on-line' and 'off-line' interactions can themselves be sustained. Cyberspace is often presented as a fantasy zone in which the masculinist desire to transcend the physical body reaches its zenith. What marks Schreber's feminization as distinct from this is its engineering of fully immanent connections, which register themselves corporeally. As Haraway notes, within the workforce 'to be feminized means to be made extremely vulnerable; able to be disassembled, reassembled, exploited as a reserve labour force' (ibid.: 166). This is precisely what happens to Schreber as he negotiates his continually fluctuating environment. Yet despite his myriad traumas he gains a sense of self in relation to the system with which he interfaces. This is a body in the process of un-organizing itself, *feeling its capacity for stimulation*. In this respect, the 'partial, fluid, sometimes aspect of sex and sexual embodiment' is exemplified by Schreber whose gender identity is never simply one, never only two.

Like Haraway's post-gender cyborg, Schreber is fascinated by questions of emergent conditions but his reflections on these issues are rarely guided by notions of organic wholeness or the logic of relations between the individual and generic essence. In this respect the *Memoirs* is a testament to the escape from the genus, from the organism and its destiny. Despite the claim that he must become woman in order to be impregnated by God, Schreber experiments with a variety of modes of replicating himself and netsex sprawls free of its procreative *telos*. Contra Freud's idiosyncratic hypothesis that Schreber wanted a son because he was afraid of his lineage dying out (Freud, 1911: 193) and 'upon whom he might have drained off his unsatisfied homosexual affections' (Freud, 1911: 194), Schreber's becoming-woman is an intensive voyage in sexualization across species boundaries, time zones and religious bloodlines, a becoming sexual which explodes the 'natural attitude' concerning gender.

Becoming-Cyberpsychological

Deleuze and Guattari (1980: 277) write that 'all becomings begin with and pass through becoming-woman'. Within the 'great dualism machines' the girl is the first victim and this is why 'the reconstruction of the body as a Body without Organs, the anorganism of the body, is inseparable from a becoming-woman' (ibid.: 276). As Deleuze and Guattari note, bisexuality in no way undermines the hegemony of the masculine and for this reason they refuse to locate becoming woman at the hesitating median between two clearly demarcated poles: 'A line of becoming is not defined by points that it connects, or by points that compose it; on the contrary, it passes *between* points' (ibid.: 293). Becoming is not a force which is in the process of coming into being or which points back to pure beginning prior to the fall. Nor is it an evolution by descent and filiation. If it is a question of evolution at all then it is the domain of symbioses 'that bring into play beings of totally different scales and kingdoms, with no possible filiation' (ibid.: 238). In his transient connections with 'miracled' wasps, flies, birds, and souls, Schreber forms momentary assemblages unthinkable from the perspective of the series, the syllogism and the signifier. This is what Deleuze and Guattari would call 'propagation by contagion' as opposed to 'filiation by heredity' (ibid.: 241).

> These combinations are neither genetic nor structural; they are inter-kingdoms, unnatural participations. This is the only way Nature operates – against itself. This is a far cry from filiative production or hereditary reproduction, in which the only differences retained are a simple duality between sexes within the same species, and small

modifications across generations. For us, on the other hand, there are as many sexes as there are terms in symbiosis, as many differences as elements contributing to a process of contagion. (ibid.: 242)

If becoming-woman is to impact politically it must operate independently of false universals, and filiative dualisms, including the *doxa* that bodies are *either* male *or* female. Yet since gender in the virtual environment is postbiological, cyberfeminism cannot proceed from any theoretical commitment to *women's* emancipation *as such* for sexed reality only emerges *as such* within cyborg alliances and 'unnatural participations'. Thus, while Schreber's *Memoirs* serve to decouple sexuality from meiotic and generational reproduction, such a gesture has no *intrinsic* feminist value (serving equally to challenge sex-role determinism *and* to consolidate pro-Life arguments for fetal autonomy). Perhaps it is in relation to these concerns that a cyberpsychological approach comes to the fore. As a *critical* device, cyberpsychology examines *how* new technologies of the self negotiate their relations to power in concrete material instances. The postbiological body is *feminized* inasmuch as it is non-essentialist and non-functionalist but it can only be deployed for *feminist* ends in its applications. Because cyberpsychology does not have a pre-established methodology it is able to assess body politics in terms of specific matrices of power without being empirically prescriptive. In this regard it also has a *deconstructive* function, severing old networks and allowing new configurations to grow. Inasmuch as it probes beneath the manifest to the latent, decentring the psyche and its certainties, it shares some procedural similarities with psychoanalysis. However, cyberpsychology differs from orthodox Freudian analysis in that it resists applying concepts to pre-set problems. What matters socially and politically are virtual connections, real *effects* not axiomatic forms. As Schreber's experiences intimate, corporeal excitations are not Oedipal ciphers but emergent conditions for propagation by contagion, a becoming-different no longer defined by reference to the logic of identity.

Postmodernist philosophies may have devoted much attention to deconstructing the subject but it is questionable whether a notion of matter as active and intrinsically self-organizing has been wrested free from Aristotelian hylomorphism – a prejudice which still informs much discourse about gender switching on the net. So long as the subject is abstracted from its material environment the patriarchal status quo will continue to usurp the power of feminization, paying lip service to feminism yet confirming gender stereotypes all the more strongly. Ultimately, what prevents cyberpsychology from institutional orthodoxy is its own status as *emergent*. It does not collapse everything into indifference, for to say that bodily boundaries materialize in their interactions is to recognize that some things are more socially constructed than others. In alluding to the postbiological body Haraway and Deleuze and Guattari replace a merely speculative probing at the borders of idealized sexual categories with a materialism that is genuinely transformative. In so doing they offer a perspective that informs what is *palpably* occurring through new technologies which reconfigure lived identities. The transsexual *imitates* the sex of choice and thus remains fatally bound to the politics of representation and the binary code of sex whereas the cyborg lives out a post-gender destiny. As Schreber says of his own voyages in a transgendered world: 'I have gained insight into the nature of human thought... for which many a psychologist might envy me' (Schreber, 1903: 141).

References

Deleuze, G. and Guattari, F. ([1980] 1988) *A Thousand Plateaus* (trans. Massumi, B.). London: Athlone.

Freud, S. (1911) 'Psychoanalytic notes on an autobiographical account of a case of paranoia (dementia paranoides)' (trans. Strachey, J.), in Richards, A. (ed.) (1979) *Case Histories II, Pelican Freud Library*, Vol. 9. Harmondsworth: Pelican.

Freud, S. (1924) 'The dissolution of the Oedipus complex' (trans. Strachey, J.), in Richards, A. (ed.) (1977) *On Sexuality, Pelican Freud Library*, Vol. 7. Harmondsworth: Pelican.

Haraway, D.J. (1991) *Simians, Cyborgs, and Women: The Reinvention of Nature.* London: Free Association Books.

Irigaray, L. ([1977] 1985) *This Sex Which Is Not One* (trans. Porter, C.). New York: Cornell University Press.

McLuhan, M. (1964) *Understanding Media: The Extensions of Man.* London: Routledge.

Schreber, D.P. ([1903] 1955) *Memoirs of My Nervous Illness* (trans. Macalpine, I. and Hunter, R.A.). London: W.M. Dawson & Sons.

CHAPTER 5

Genealogies of the Self in Virtual-Geographical Reality

NYDZA CORREA DE JESÚS

What is in a name? Boundaries, fixations in space, representations. Names singularize the desire for closure. They also represent, through their search for origins, desire for a one-to-one relationship. The intention behind naming is to establish consistency, and classical knowledge was organized around naming so that it could be developed as a system of identities, and as a path to essential denominations of the identified. Things had to be given names. The classical form of organization was designed to produce a continuous and continuing order in which history will fix in space that which was once seen as continuous, and then modernity analyses names and their transformations. Knowledge, then, has operated through the rationalization – spatial and temporal – of reality and the intention to universalize the reference.

But knowledge is also, in present times, the exploration and reflection of boundaries, of the thought behind the imprint of a name in its classical form or of its transformations. This turns to a conception of the name that goes beyond the naming so as to establish the life embedded in the death of naming. The sign thus selects the contours of the signified space, exposes its patterns of knowledge and its capacities to relate with other signs. This assumes the impossibility of a general theory to explain the vertiginous transformations of the contemporary world. It proposes the reflexivity of discourse.

What is in the discourse of 'cyberpsychology'? Certainly not simply the composition of another prefix or compound name for an 'applied psychology', a general fixed operation of the sign but, on the contrary, its *relativization*. An exploration of cyberpsychology necessarily entails a problematization of its many fixed forms, and its location in an-other dimensional delineation of space. Cyberpsychology speaks for a particular moment of signification, for it is another form of communication. In this sense, cyberpsychology is embedded within the easily accepted premise of the 'diversity of explanations' in psychology, but it opens up a territory inhabited by multilayered transformations of its object of study. This object is read through the paradigmatic and epochal assumptions from which we organize theoretical and methodological premises in the production of knowledge in science.

The effect of these shifting mutations and simultaneous existence of explanations, with no one of them privileged is that traditional psychology loses its ability to speak as myth. A myth is precisely concerned with being 'said' and being 'recognized'. It is organized around re-cognition as in the Greek doctrine of mimesis, imitation in the recognition of one-self, of the essential and true order (Gadamer, 1996). Myth invites us to establish an objective fixed image of an object beneath signification. The underlying premise is that it is possible to develop an image capable of establishing referents directly resembling the object. The neopositivistic image of psychology as myth during the first half of this century, assumed that the purpose of theory was basically as a correction and stylization of social traditions and technical applications. Freudian psychoanalysis, Piagetian genetic epistemology, and Batesonian 'ecology of the mind', for example, correspond to a third theory level which conveys, what Sanmartín (1989) termed, 'Metaphysical Programs of Research'.

Reexamined from within another realm, with an attention to the context of discourse, the image that contemporary psychology likes to present can be understood as a 'code' which is created for purposes of comprehension and recognition and the attempt to correspond to certain forms of reality. 'Cyberpsychology' disrupts this code, however, for it is premised on the rupture of the copy and the negation of the original, and it addresses psychology as an object of study and it exposes the logic in use. Psychology has 'thrown its eye and still sees', where 'seeing' is a position exercised in a specific order and delimitation. The attempts to reproduce reality, sanitize the subject and fix the object, are subverted by cyberpsychology and make it clear that psychology must not be considered with a simplistic eye.

This chapter focuses on the core of these transformations, and the way in which they force a dislocation of bodies in the time–space continuum and its compression, and the removal of processes of individuation from the sphere of the state. It is framed within an overall articulation of the changes which operate in psychology in transit to a *discursive psychology image*. First, then, we need to turn to an exposition of the contours that shape(d) the image of psychology and its role in the construction of the self, and then we will examine the paradigmatic and epochal determinations of the object of psychology as it attempts to grasp the 'plural self' and the 'cybernetic self' rooted in the 'techo-iconic image' of late capitalist societies. Here we see the privileging of the laws of image and consumption over religion and the law, and over the state and the law.

The image of psychology

Psychology, as science, is constructed within the presuppositions of the particular paradigm employed to signify its activities (Bateson, 1979). It is also a corporeal practice inasmuch as we should locate ourselves in that about which we speak, that is in scientific work. After Kuhn, this has become a dictum for the production of knowledge in any science, or beyond science in life itself.

These transformations in our understanding of the place of psychological science within specific paradigms signify the end of the illusion of transparency and system-oriented science. The effect is that scientific proposals are relativized, and different paradigms are seen as incommensurable. So the questions which are addressed by scientists are also necessarily posed to the speaking subject and attention is drawn to the conditions and presuppositions for the legitimation of its particular discourse at any point in time. This attention to paradigms also obliges us to specify the processes for the configuration of scientific explanation, as processes, and it provokes us to pursue a genealogical interpretation (Greimas, 1990). As with other constructions (be it fashion or architectural design), the pieces can only be arranged as a whole if (and only if) the conditions for the assemblage are explicated. Whether it is read as the magic of the secret and the value appropriated or the demand for an explanation of the logic of consensually validated forms – in everyday life and science – this process of metaphoric construction and deconstruction has become a perpetual present for scientific work and for getting a life (and now any simple 'instructions for use' are grossly misplaced).

Now, when we turn to contemporary psychology, the suffixes 'cyber' or 'discursive' function as enunciative statements which focus us upon the undoing of any fixed image of psychology which was constructed from within the modern ideal of science, that is, from within any paradigm of simplicity of representation. The discourse of the modern ideal of science, dominant for most of the twentieth century, assumed the universal as the path for producing laws in science. Reductionism became a criterion of scientific work and objectivity was assumed to be the basis for the production of knowledge. However, there is a paradox, for psychology has never had a unified discourse (Vattimo, 1990), and the discipline has operated either by reducing and simplifying its objects of study or has rendered them as complex phenomena. This paradoxical contradictory activity of psychology is rooted in the displacement from the physical-mathematical paradigm to the techno-iconic one. The Newtonian world view and the Einsteinian one have organized psychological knowledge in such a way that acknowledges both simplicity and complexity.

The significance of this can be seen in the pre-eminence of criteria of reference in theories of modernity on the one hand underpinned by notions of simplicity and the psychologists' theorization of the individual on the other which are also informed by notions of complexity. Referential discourse as a limit, that is as the possibility to delimit and thus contain, implies the constitution of an isomorphic reality, in its univocal relation with the object which is by way of science thoroughly objectified. Consequently, reality can be captured by the human subject insofar as it is capable of a rational representation. Perceptions and mental representations can grasp reality and order it symbolically and then refract it like a copy of the same. The modern individual prized by modern psychology thus unifies and articulates *closed systems*. Its 'work' entails the enactment of exteriority and the fidelity of explanations of the world, and perceptions and error are signalled when that is unattainable, when precision cannot lead to universalization. Relations are established within the capacity to represent reality in the 'objective mode'.

The object of psychology, the individual, constituted within these rationalist vectors of perception and comprehension is delineated as an apparatus of precision, and this individual is a necessity for the development of capitalist societies. The metaphysical essence of the individual follows the task of the acknowledgment of itself. The individual self now resides in the articulation of its activities in the world of work, salary and commodity exchange (Haug, 1986). As a historical process, and as a crucial category for psychology, the contours of this individuation and rationalization of the individual and the social is recognized in the works of Adam Smith, Descartes and Hobbes. Roger Smith (1997: 49) locates the language for the twentieth-century psychological subject in seventeenth-century political and economic discourses. These formulations stress that:

> The language of the self has a historical character and is not fixed. A new sense of self in the seventeenth century is a crucial part of what is distinctive, modern and Western. Modern people are preoccupied by personal feelings, personal wealth, personal fulfilment, personal health, personal privacy and much else 'personal' besides. This gives much of the twentieth century human sciences, like psychology and sociology, their subject matter.

The intertwining of these processes in the modern subject is also commented upon by Hacking (1990: vii), who argues that:

> Determinism was eroded during the nineteenth century and a space was cleared for autonomous laws of chance. The idea of human nature was displaced by a model of normal people with laws of dispersion. These two transformations were parallel and fed into each other. Chance made the world seem less capricious: it was legitimated because it brought order out of chaos. The greater the level of indeterminism in our conception of the world and of people, the higher the expected level of control [by the State].

As Hamon (1992: 100) states, 'it is the desire to grasp by listing the dimensions of reality', and here there is a reference to a French nineteenth-century publication, a periodical *Le Voleur*, whose subtitle was *Cabinet de lecture universel*; its front page showed a copyist working with the following caption: 'He compiled, compiled, compiled' (ibid.).

At the same time, modern society is organized such that it distinguishes temporality as a salient feature of progress. It is not just the constitution of a subject through language, or the inventory of all possible spaces through which the subject may move, but also its seizing for its own sake. Thus:

'Being' is about being located in space and time. Indeed progress entails the conquest of space, the tearing down of all spatial barriers and the ultimate 'annihilation of space through time'… Since modernity is about progress the theme that has been emphasized is the one of temporality, the process of becoming rather than the process of being in space and place. (Harvey, 1989: 205)

Psychology constructs its theoretical objects and practices in such a way as to picture itself as a kind of montage of the temporal and the spatial. The discipline establishes the mental in a manner which assumes its presence in a body located in geographical space and linear time, and where the task is the measurement of the corporeal and the mental. The individual was measured and judicially identified (with detailed police descriptions and photographic identifications). It was also 'catalogued' in its different morphological identities, scrupulously accounted and typified. A relay between a private and a public identity was established as a means of defining a consolidated self, and constituting the artefacts of identification, communication and self-recognition. While differentiation may imply a certain autonomy for the individual and a separation of the public and the private, the conquering of space in modernity always supposed a transparency concerning both. The image of the 'healthy person' (invariably indexed as male) in the nineteenth century is still the template and canonical statement of identity for the functioning of DNA testing. In this way we have constituted artefacts for the circulation of identity within the control of an organized institutional setting, the state.

Personality, attitudes, behaviour and opinions thus mark the discourse of modern psychology and its attempt to provide a means of normalization within the parameters of the therapeutic state, and to set delimited standards for the dilation of desire. 'Communication', in theoretical, experimental and technological terms, functions within the horizon of psychology as an attempt at clarification within the remit of 'transparency'.

The sexual domain provides an excellent example of this process. Hutton (1988: 131), analysing Foucault, Freud and technologies of the self, argues that:

Because everyone is called upon to analysis, knowledge of sexuality and knowledge of ourselves become ever closely linked. Making sense of our sexuality, Foucault holds, is perceived in the modern age to be a method for discovering the truth about who we are.

Another spiral in this circuit of desire is discussed by Dean (1992: 25), who writes that:

> A criminal act could be explained as dementia (in which case the criminal was not responsible at all), as the product of economic and corollary psychological situation of the subject, or as a moment of temporary insanity in an otherwise normal individual, provoked by a friend's treachery perhaps, or a lover's infidelity. In this way psychiatry attempted to envision all possible organic, social and emotional causes behind a crime and to take these into consideration when asked to determine a criminal's juridical responsibility for his or her crime. Yet it was baffled by crimes that offered no such rationally explicable motivation.

At the same time, questions arise concerning the ability of psychology to render the real. These questions have been posed from within other sciences and from art. The permeability of the body and the self, is stressed by biologists, for example, who open up the corporeal envelope of the body. A body is not 'covered' by the skin, it does not 'contain' the 'self'. Biologists and artists recognize that the body is cast within the domains of the imaginary and the real as something that can be smoothed or wrinkled (and is digitalized in computer technology). There is an enigma established in representations of the body inasmuch as it is incapable of definitively fixing an 'image', its definite contours or possible realignments. All signs of the body and the self can thus be rendered incomplete; and the image of psychology is thus forced to undergo mutations which never end.

The written image, the mechanically reproduced image, the image of psychology, is thus threatened by images of transformation coming from techno-informational changes as we move into the realm of the visual image; the implosion of permanence, fixation and location of the subject in time and space.

Psychology and image

> What I want to do is to distort the thing far beyond the appearance, but in the distortion to bring it back to a recording of the appearance… Why is it possible to make the reality of an appearance more violently in this way than by doing it traditionally? Perhaps it's that, if the making is more instinctive, the image is more immediate. (Francis Bacon, cited in Maxwell, 1993: 314)

The most significant changes concerning the image at the end of nineteenth century and the first half of the twentieth revolve around its location in the visual regime. Transmission meant the establishment of a communicative space in the order of information in audio-visual milieu. This entailed the erasure of classical 'face-to-face' interaction, of 'direct' dialogue, and the neutralization and symbolization of order through images.

Information became the means by which humans became subjects. The excess of information also expressed a will to render humans as 'real' subjects. Benjamin (1968) used the word 'shock' to express the instantaneity of information, the independence of the image and the fragmentation of the subject who travels from sign to sign and is at the mercy of signs. This process, at the same time, provides for the utmost possibility for the circulation of knowledge in capitalist society. From this time on, communication systems developed in a ceaseless spiral plugged into what we might call 'the hyperreality effect'.

Thus image, representation and reality must now be read using a different code of analysis, one which acknowledges the collapse of polarities and the simultaneity of significations for the sign. Art and science are now able to establish a dialogue alongside work in their specific fields, and explanation opens to the mercies of a synchronic system. The social character of discourse, its permeability regarding other disciplines, invites us to read objects of study in their diversity, in their openness.

The re-cognition that edges and lines of force occur everywhere in a text now plays alongside an awareness of the impossibility of recreating facsimiles of knowledge. Nonetheless, that scientists are historically situated, socially located and work in science is also the effect of an experimental enclosure. By that we mean the creation of a 'virtual cage' for delimitation and localization of the explanation. This is the exercise of signification in contemporary science. Thus paradoxical explanations and explorations are at the centre of that which accounts for the use of non linear models and the emphasis on diachronic and synchronic perspectives in research. Here we arrive at the assumption of complexity as the paradigm of contemporary science. This implies:

- the impossibility of reducing different levels of organization in reality
- a loss of faith in history's structural properties

- the simultaneous presence of chance and rules in systems capable of self-organization and homeostasis (auto-poietic systems)
- a leap from lineal to complex thought, where knowledge generates from thinking the thought that thinks about the systems of observation.

This is the language of relationships, the pattern which connects, in Bateson's (1979) words, and the use of metaphor, as when 'walking into the paradoxes'. It should be emphasized that without the use of metaphors, images would remain in the stereotypical dimension, confined to the search for regularity in signification. Metaphor opens up the spectrum of signification and blurs the distinction between sense and representation. As Ricoeur (1978: 149) explains:

> By blurring this distinction, the metaphorical meaning compels us to explore the borderline between the verbal and the non-verbal. The process of schematization and that of the bound images aroused and controlled by schematization obtain precisely on that borderline between a semantics of metaphorical utterances and a psychology of imagination.

Time and space

The object of study, be it the subject or the image, is now taken to be 'deliteralized' in a process which is able to observe the observation as a hyperreflexive form of constructivist perception. There is thus a 'will' to virtuality in discourse, the site where reflexivity and paradoxical formulations simultaneously alter the gaze of the observing subject. There occurs a diversification of spaces and the impossibility of relating diversity to any given fixed totality. Furthermore, this gaze is not private in compass, for it opens to chance and history. As Derrida (1997: 346) notes, when writing about the architect Peter Eisenman:

> That which overturns the opposition presence/absence, and thus an entire ontology, must nevertheless be advanced within the language that it transforms in this way, within which is inscribed that which this language literally contains without containing, is found imprinted. Eisenman's architecture marks this 'without'... We are related to this 'without' of the language, by dominating in order to play with it, and

at the same time in order to be subjected by the law, its law which is the law of language, of languages, in truth of all marks.

A consequence of these reflections on transformations in our understanding of the image and our conceptions of space–time is that it is necessary now to 'locate' the subject and its discourses, and to locate psychology as a discipline within discursive practices. During the last century we experienced vertiginous changes in perceptual experiences. Space is the crux of a transformational effect commanding another sense of incorporation, and another examination of our taken for granted 'being in space'. The otherwise separated conceptions of space and time coalesced in what Harvey (1989: 240) calls time–space compression:

> I use the word 'compression' because a strong case can be made that the history of capitalism has been characterized by speed-up in the pace of life, while so overcoming spatial barriers that the world sometimes seems to collapse inwards upon us. As space seems to shrink to a 'global village' of telecommunications and a 'spaceship earth' of economic and ecological interdependencies… and as time horizons shorten to the point where the present is all there (the world of schizophrenic), so we have to learn how to cope with an overwhelming sense of compression of our spatial and temporal worlds.

Deleuze (1989: 268–9) reaches a similar conclusion while discussing time-image phenomena in cinema:

> But one of Syberberg's originalities is to stretch out a vast space of information, like a complex, heterogeneous, anarchic space where the trivial and the cultural, the public and the private, the historic and the anecdotal, the imaginary and the real are brought close together, and sometimes on the side of speech, discourses, commentaries, familiar or ancillary testimonies, sometimes on the side of sight, of existing or no longer existing settings, in gravings, plans and projects, acts of seeing with acts of clairvoyance, all equal importance and forming a network, in kinds of relationship which are never those of causality. The modern world is that in which information replaces nature.

The reflective and functional system of spatialization is accelerated by way of the changes operative in the notion of motion. The relativization of the now inseparable time–space continuum reframes not only our perceptions (and our diverse journeys) but also our overall reception of lines, points, and forms. As Eisenman (cited in Jencks, 1989: 142) states: 'My work attacks the concept of occupation as given. It is against the traditional notion of how you occupy a house.'

Occupation of a geographical space and chronological time (both of which are very traditional notions) are superseded by Virilio's (1997: 16) statement that 'the sky is vanishing'. The metaphorical notion of journey is now being seen not as departure but as:

> 'Generalized arrival' whereby everything arrives without having to leave, the nineteenth century's elimination of the journey (that is, of the space interval and of time) combining with the abolition of departure at the end of the twentieth, the journey thereby losing its successive components and being overtaken by arrival alone. (ibid.)

Windows onto the future

The subjectively inscribed version of this 'vertigo', this permanent acceleration, decomposes the imaginary connection between the desire for unity and complementarity and fantasies of fragmented bodies, and this then issues in a constant hyperreal flow. This image is then assumed and affirmed by the social gaze, and it circulates as part of the current exchange for living. Space has been interrupted, time has been disrupted. That which was the primal scene for openness or closure, the window, dissolves into an illusion and a question capable of assuming diverse 'form images'; of transparency, thickness and the mutation from time into space. The architectural metaphor is employed by Virilio (1991: 79) to stress the transformation via 'acceleration' operated on regimes of temporality and space:

> The first window is the door, the door-window necessary for access to and thus for the reality of the home, since we could not conceptualize a house without some means of access... The window as such – the second window – appeared fairly late, in the sites of monastic cults, before becoming popular among the rural homes and only then, and especially, in the palace and the homes of the bourgeoisie... The third window is a recent invention: the television screen, a removable and portable window that opens onto the false day of the speed of light emissions. The television screen is an introverted window, one which no longer opens onto adjoining space but instead

faces beyond the perceptible horizon. Thus, if the door-window constitutes an opening... then the specialized window is more selective, because it interrupts, the passage of bodies. The specialized window is a punctured, a mediated opening for solar light, and nearby perspectives.

With the mutation of the window into the specialized window:

> Windows and mirrors are replaced by a cathode framework, an indirect opening in which the electronic false-day functions like a camera lens, reversing the order of appearances to the benefit of an imperceptible transparency, and submitting the supremacy of certain constructive elements to that cathode window that rejects both the portal and the light of day. (Virilio, 1991: 87)

In 1956 Bruno Funaro examined what we may call 'the vision thing', recalling the paradoxical status of the window:

> Today we are faced with what appears to be a dilemma: modern building technologies have, on one hand made unlimited windows possible. With the outer surface of buildings freed from structural commitments, windows can be placed anywhere, everywhere. On the other hand, modern technology has replaced with more reliable means many of the services which were performed by windows and which were their reason for being. Now that we can have them, we are not so sure that we really want them. (cited in Keenan and Bonauro, 1992: 133)

And still we may ask ourselves, what is the 'functionality' (if there is any) of windows regarding humans? The only plausible answer requires us to recognize the presence of a modern 'will for the visual', where the abolition of barriers and the perpetuation of space becomes an infatuation. This is an infatuation that still persists, as Bill Gates' version of the cyberwindow, Windows98, suggests. As a matter of fact, Gates' Windows98 might well be an answer to the question posed first by Funaro, and later by Keenan and Bonauro (1992), 'Why do humans want windows?' In other words, Borges' (1970) Aleph, 'the unimaginable universe', has multiplied itself kaleidoscopically. The *information* society has overwritten its movement into time. This significant variation in register derives from the simultaneous configuration in materials of technological information and forms of communication. The social realm within these transformations is itself interposed between the threads, or pixels, of this nouvelle net.

Deleuze (1992) speaks of the dispersed trend of capitalism today and its 'short term' forms of control embedded in a continuous and limitless spiral. The question about the subject, the self and its articulated historical 'beings' are now intimately connected to these core terms. Under these conditions, the subject occupies positions already desestabilized by the subversion of reality, but it is also displaced by rapid transformations of technology and information theories. The word, the canonical written word which had been so emphasized as the normalizing operation of the sign 'to socialize', is multiplied exponentially in the 'new' socialization fields – television, publicity, music and cybernetic texts:

> With the turn into time, the concern with the visual and the desestabilization of reality, a multiplication of subject positions and identities occur. Some processes come into play that manifest the current drama: the disorientation of humans and virtual reality. (Virilio, 1997: 45)

Disorientation occurs through the excess of images, and the impossibility of declaring the real. Virtual reality, however, appears as the last pillar of the neopositivistic will. But, at the same time, virtual reality contributes to the derealization of reality. The 'accident of the real', the splitting of reality, dislocates bodies (and forces us to ask which body, in which space) and derealizes identity (and forces us to ask which parameter in the technological self and its technologies).

Cyberpsychological mutations

Under these conditions, *cyberpsychology* is more than a trend or a prefix; it is the current incarnation of the will to render the subjects, this time in multiple positions. This also implies: first, a set of 'rules' that govern the 'game' (to borrow from Jean Renoir's poetic imagination); second, the manifold possibilities, subject positions that are created within this set of rules.

The recognition of a mutation in the social codes that dominate the production of knowledge (psychology, sociology, human science, natural science) suggests not an abolition of rules, but the construction of new rules in new realms. As new realms are subsumed, subject positions begin to develop, and multiplicity arises as (virtual-, cyber-)reality.

Severed from the state, and processed by the current state of the image, subjects inhabit the domain of flexible capital. With Windows98, endless opportunities for opening windows appear at once, both simultaneously and through dislocation. The performative action of opening windows presupposes the simultaneity of two apparently paradoxical situations: first, the constant change of contexts through changes in windows; and, second, constant change while remaining in the same overall context. The discursive level brings the possibility of assuming the 'overall context', while a vision of 'constant change' accepts history as a condition of meaning and image making. The 'will for a cyberpsychology' may express a celebration of this paradox.

References

Bateson, G. (1979) *Mind and Nature*. New York: Dutton.

Benjamin, W. (1968) *Illuminations*. New York: Schocken Books.

Borges, J.L. (1970) *Labyrinths*. Harmondsworth: Penguin.

Dean, C.J. (1992) *The Self and its Pleasures*. Ithaca: Cornell University Press.

Deleuze, G. (1989) *Cinema 2: The Time-Image*. Minneapolis: University of Minnesota Press.

Deleuze, G. (1992) 'Postscript on the societies of control', *October*, **59**: 3–8.

Derrida, J. (1997) 'Why Peter Eisenman writes such good books', in Leach, N. (ed.) *Rethinking Architecture*. New York: Routledge.

Gadamer, H.G. (1996) *Estética y Hermenéutica*. Madrid: Editorial Tecnos.

Greimas, A.J. (1990) *The Social Sciences: A Semiotic View*. Minneapolis: University of Minnesota Press.

Hacking, I. (1990) *The Taming of Chance*. Cambridge: Cambridge University Press.

Hamon, P. (1992) *Expositions*. Berkeley, CA: University of California Press.

Harvey, D. (1989) *The Condition of Postmodernity*. Oxford: Basil Blackwell.

Haug, W.F. (1986) *Critique of Commodity Aesthetics*. Minneapolis: University of Minnesota Press.

Hutton, P.H. (1988) 'Foucault, Freud, and the technologies of the self', in Martin, L.H., Gutman, H. and Hutton, P.H. (eds) *Technologies of the Self: A Seminar with Michel Foucault*. Amherst: University of Massachusetts Press.

Jencks, C. (1989) 'Peter Eisenman', in Papadakis, A., Cooke, C. and Benjamin, A. (eds) *Deconstruction*, omnibus volume. New York: Rizzoli.

Keenan, T. and Bonauro, T. (1992) 'Windows and vulnerability', in *Semiotext(e)/Architecture*. New York: Semiotext(e).

Magnaghi, A. (1995) 'L'importanza dei luoghi nell'epoca della loro dissoluzione', in Berardi, F. (ed.) *Cibernauti, Tecnologia, Comunicazione*,

Democrazia. Roma: Castelvecchi.

Maxwell, R. (1993) *Sweet Disorder and the Carefully Careless.* New York: Princeton Architectural Press.

Ricoeur, P. (1978) 'The metaphorical process as cognition, imagination, and feeling', in Sacks, S. (ed.) *On Metaphor.* Chicago: University of Chicago Press.

Sanmartín, J. (1989) *Los Nuevos Redentores.* Barcelona: Anthropos.

Smith, R. (1997) 'Self-reflection and the self', in Porter, R. (ed.) *Rewriting the Self.* New York: Routledge.

Vattimo, G. (1990) 'Dialéctica, diferencia y pensamiento débil', in Vattimo, G. and Rovatti, R.A. (eds) *El Pensamiento Débil.* Madrid: Cátedra.

Virilio, P. (1991) *The Lost Dimension.* New York: Semiotext(e).

Virilio, P. (1997) *Open Sky.* London: Verso.

Wilson, L. (1997) 'Cyberwar, God and television: an interview with Paul Virilio', in Kroker, A. and Kroker, M. (eds) *Digital Delirium.* New York: St. Martin's Press.

PART TWO

Body Politics, Ethics and Research Practice

In this part of the book we move onto concrete examples of the way in which cyberpsychology is being played out in practice. Each of the chapters explores a domain in which cyberpsychological subjectivity is performed in specific technological areas of work, and there is an attention in each, of course, to the *embodied* nature of this subjectivity. Cyberpsychology is not simply a novel variety of experience, but is only able to exist by virtue of its instantiation in material apparatuses.

The materiality of cyberpsychology is evident in John Cromby and Penny Standen's chapter in which they explore the potential of such developments as virtual environment technologies to not only facilitate a 'practical deconstruction of mainstream psychology' but also to come up with the goods for people, in this case for people with disabilities. Their account of these developments, which draws on German Critical Psychology's notion of 'subjective possibility spaces' is also, however, sensitive to the way the body becomes amenable to technological intervention and they consider issues of access, surveillance, control and dependency which arise from the use of these technologies.

These issues are also very much present in the sub-text of Betty Bayer's consideration of the 'material-discursive forces of cyborg body politics', and she homes in on the moral-political questions that are raised for feminists tackling the masculine imaginary of cognitive psychology in the context of cyberculture and the challenges that feminist technoscience poses for the discipline of psychology which has always, as Bayer notes, had intimate links with the technocultural project. An ethical research practice which draws upon Haraway's account of cyborg subjectivity takes us some steps forward, perhaps, but Bayer is also cognisant of the dilemmas such a practice opens up.

Heidi Figueroa-Sarriera takes the notion of cyborg subjectivity forward in a detailed review of the collective spaces opened up by multi-user domains (MUDS) and electronic conversation forums such as Internet relay chat (IRC) which could be considered as quintessential postmodern phenomena. These collective spaces require a 'performative model of the self', but Figueroa-Sarriera goes on to argue that this kind of 'territorialized subject' must be conceived of as embedded in forms of 'socialité' (a term she borrows from Michel Maffesoli) which capture and display the fragmentation of identities and new tribal forms of collective identity that cyberculture makes possible.

Cyborgs also appear in Steven Brown's account of the manifold monsters erupting from various cyberspatial locations (whether actually in electronic environments or in parallel worlds outside the net), but, like Figueroa-Sarriera, he is keen to emphasize that these hybrid forms of subjectivity and corporeality must be seen as located in networks. He describes the way 'transhuman' and 'extropian' communities pit themselves against the 'real world' and the tactics that are used to domesticate them, to effect the 'transformation from uncanniness to mundaneity'.

Cyborgs in these chapters speak of something novel, exciting and transgressive, and cyborgian subjectivity shows itself clearly as refusing forms of identity that twentieth-century psychology made its hallmark. However, the moral-political questions that cyborgs pose also need to be turned around and embedded in radical theoretical frameworks in order to comprehend and accentuate that transgressive potential, and so each of the chapters in this part of the book elaborates a framework that may be helpful – ranging from Cromby and Standen's German Critical Psychology, to Bayer's feminist technoscience perspective, to Figueroa-Sarriera's use of Maffesoli's work, to Brown's employment of Heideggerian motifs.

CHAPTER 6

Cyborgs and Stigma: Technology, Disability, Subjectivity

JOHN CROMBY AND PENNY STANDEN

The world is being transformed in the direction prescribed by the existence of forced labour, which is why it is being transformed so badly.
(Vaneigem, 1967: 53)

This chapter explores some of the potentials, problems and dilemmas
which cyberspace, virtual environments and associated new technologies create for people with disabilities. We begin by discussing
the *cyberpsychology* initiative in this book and outlining some meanings associated with the term 'cyborg', to inform our discussion of
the effects of technology upon bodies and subjectivities. Then we
introduce German Critical Psychology and the notion of *subjective
possibility spaces*, which we use to conceptualize how new technologies might affect the subjectivities of people with disabilities. We then
review the new technologies being used by or adapted for people
with disabilities, looking both at generic computer use and specialized devices or aids. We go on to describe the potential impact of
some of these applications in more detail, highlighting four issues
which are likely to be relevant when assessing the value of any new
technology for people with disabilities:

- access
- surveillance
- control
- dependency.

Cyberpsychology and cyborgs

Today talk of cyborgs and cyberspace is widespread, perhaps because it provides an apposite focus for tensions concerning technology, identity, culture and the body. Cyberpsychology meshes neatly with this Zeitgeist while simultaneously highlighting a pre-existing, practical deconstruction of some of mainstream psychology's most treasured beliefs. Specifically, it emphasizes a realm where postmodern concepts of identity as shifting, multiple, groundless, variable and discontinuous are not only viable but widespread. In this way it challenges the practices of regulation and subjection which mainstream psychology legitimates by reference to traditional notions of identity. Cyberpsychology also draws on Haraway's (1985) use of the cyborg as metaphor to question the dualisms – between mind and body, 'representation' and 'reality', culture and nature – which hierarchically structure the Western notion of self that is central to both patriarchy and capitalism.

Yet, as researchers using virtual environment technologies with people with disabilities who wish to take a critical stance to our own work and that of others, we must add some caveats and cautions. First, despite the apparent novelty of the cyborg metaphor, we should remember that people with disabilities first encountered many of the issues posed by the cyborging of humanity some time ago, in practice rather than in academic debate, when the first spectacles, hearing aids and wooden legs were used. Second, cyberpsychology is partially predicated on a belief that postmodern notions of identity are inherently radical and liberatory, when in fact they may be so only within certain limits (see Eagleton, 1995). We suspect that the multiple subjectivities of the postmodern era will prove to be at least as useful to post-Fordist, niche-marketing capitalism as the ideology of liberal humanism was to its mass-producing predecessor. Third, our status as 'hands-on' researchers and our work with people with disabilities gives us an inevitable emphasis on materiality, and leads us to question some of the more extravagant claims made for the electronic realm. Many of the features of cyberspace as it currently exists flow from its nature as a predominantly textual communication medium, and depend upon its novel combination of real-time interaction coupled with a limited and malleable representation of body and environment. As profit drives technology onward, these features may disappear as broadband fibre-optic technologies make live video streaming commonplace. Finally, although cyberpsychology places a useful emphasis on the linguistic and discursive aspects of human subjectivity, striking global inequalities mean that it is, and for the near future at least is likely to remain, a local concern. Hobsbawm (1993) points out that there are more phone lines in Manhattan alone than in the entire continent of Africa, and that two-thirds of the world's population have still never even used a telephone, never mind a computer.

Despite its widespread use the term 'cyborg' is rarely defined, a situation which promotes conceptual confusion. For our purposes, we can distinguish three ways in which the word is employed. First, as described earlier, the term 'cyborg' is used as a metaphor in order to gain political and conceptual leverage in debate, a usage which flows from Haraway's (1985) paper on socialist feminism. Second, the term 'cyborg' can refer to the transformation of subjectivity by the array of communication technologies currently available. The inter-penetration of mass media and everyday life is now so complete that the media have a hegemonic grip on points of cultural reference and topics of casual conversation, so that our lives and relationships are informed and occupied by tropes and narratives drawn from soap operas, advertising, political soundbites and high-profile tragedies. This transformation has coincided with, and been facilitated by, the weakening of previously existing bonds of labour and community as the era of mass capitalist production and consumption has been superseded by an age of 'flexible' production and 'identity consump-tion' (Hall and Jacques, 1989). Third, the term 'cyborg' can refer to the physical augmentation of the bodies of people with and without disabilities. Dery (1995: 231) says that:

> In cyberculture the body is a permeable membrane, its integrity violated and its sanctity challenged by titanium alloy knee joints, myoelectric arms, synthetic bones and blood vessels, breast and penile prostheses, cochlear implants and artificial hips.

These last two uses of the term 'cyborg' reflect a useful classification of technologies for people with disabilities, since they can be said to fall into two broad classes: physical prosthetics which augment their bodies, and communication devices which extend their subjectivi-ties. However, we must emphasize that this is only an analytical strategy since these meanings do not remain separate. Most obvi-ously, the cyborg metaphor is vitally shaped and informed by accounts of the body's amenability to technological intervention.

Moreover, some technologies address both subjectivity and physicality simultaneously – for example, any device which corrects a sensory impairment. Most importantly, in the subjectivity of individuals the cyborging of subjectivity and body typically co-occur. Collagen injections and penis extensions function below the level of consciousness, but those who have them typically assert that the effects upon self-image are as important as their aesthetic or functional aspects. The aids and devices used by people with disabilities may also raise this issue: for example, independent movement is extremely valuable, but the subjective awareness that independent movement is easily possible is also hugely significant. We will draw upon German Critical Psychology for a framework within which to understand this phenomenon; we now provide a very brief introduction to this work.

German Critical Psychology: subjectivity and possibility

German Critical Psychology (GCP) offers a means of conceptualizing the effects of the cyborging of both subjectivity and the body, through its description of how subjectivity is structured by possibilities. Tolman (1994) provides an accessible introduction to GCP, setting out a 'functional-historical' account of the emergence of subjectivity in human society. GCP grounds subjectivity in the material and social conditions which made its evolutionary emergence possible. It does this by examining the prehistory of our species, drawing together evidence from biology, archaeology, anthropology and history to detail the development of pre-human and early human social groupings. Among many other factors, GCP highlights bipedality, the move from trees and forests to open grasslands, increasingly complex social relationships, the availability of language for communication, and the division of labour which made early humans more efficient at meeting their own needs for survival. Together, over evolutionary periods of time, these developments produced a material organization of society which for the first time offered individuals a complex of possibilities way beyond the immediate necessities of survival. Although each social group had to produce on average enough food for its own sustenance, not everyone had to be engaged in this activity all of the time. Societal necessities (someone has to hunt the bison!) became individual possibilities (it doesn't have to be me!).

This distinction between societal necessities and individual possibilities is crucial to GCP, since it provides:

> The fundamental material, economic prerequisite for the knowing,
> epistemic relation of the person to the world... the possibility rela-
> tionship creates a kind of epistemic distance between individuals and
> their world that allows them to assess the relations among events (as
> opposed to being constantly concerned with the relations of events to
> themselves)... It is in this epistemic distance that we become fully
> conscious of the world and our relation to it. (Tolman 1994: 102)

Simply put, the need to deliberate and make choices was the evolutionary basis of human subjectivity; this need itself arose as a consequence of a social organization which meant that individuals no
longer had to be exclusively preoccupied with the immediate
demands of survival. For GCP subjectivity is simultaneously biolog-
ical/organic and societal, since the (largely societally determined)
nature of the possibilities available will strongly condition the subjectivity which emerges. Ideological and material circumstances
combine to offer each individual a more or less restricted range of
choices, so that:

> The life world of the mine owner is literally different to that of the
> miner... they perform different functions in the division of labour...
> they occupy different positions in society and thus experience differ-
> ent life situations. This is bound to have significant effects upon
> subjectivity... [the real, objective, quantitative differences in their situ-
> ations] are experienced subjectively in their respective life situations
> as distinctly larger or smaller subjective possibility spaces. (ibid.: 113)

The notion of subjective possibility spaces provides a way of
assessing the impact of cyberspace and related technologies upon
the subjectivity of people with disabilities. Each technology brings
a range of opportunities, access to which transforms the subjectivity of users. These opportunities may be immediate and material:
improved mobility makes it possible for a person to independently
take part in more activities. Other opportunities may be a provisional consequence of these immediate, material gains; for
example, better mobility might make it easier for someone to go
out unaided, so creating new opportunities to meet people and
form relationships.

Since subjective possibility spaces are structured by both ideology and materiality they can include the effects of factors such as gender. Lonsdale (1990) interviewed a woman in her early twenties who had begun using a wheelchair, instead of the callipers and crutch she had previously used and which gave her valuable exercise, because she hated the effect they had on her appearance and body shape. By contrast, in the wheelchair 'she felt she could glide quietly and gracefully into a room and look less distorted' (Lonsdale, 1990: 4). More so than men, women in our society are expected to comply with standards of appearance based on sexual, physical and behavioural stereotypes. For this woman, the subjective possibilities associated with conforming more closely to these expectations outweighed the problems which lack of exercise was likely to bring. In addition, the subjective possibilities which result from using a technology may well be contradictory, simultaneously containing both positive and negative aspects. For example, the improved mobility which results from using a wheelchair may provide subjective possibilities which have a positive character, because it makes more activities and places accessible. However, someone who is aware of prevalent stereotypes of disability may know that using a wheelchair could lead others to perceive her as being permanently and globally disabled; in this way, subjective possibilities which have a negative character would also arise.

These examples illustrate the value of using the concept of subjective possibility spaces to critically assess new technologies for people with disabilities. Not only does it capture the contradictory potentials of new technologies, allowing us to acknowledge their benefits at the same time as it draws attention to their shortcomings, it does this through a focus on the subjectivity of the user, so highlighting the experiential realm wherein new technologies are actually used and evaluated in everyday life. Subjectivity and lived experience are thus given primacy over other evaluative criteria (for example, social, orthopaedic, medical). Although the focus is on subjectivity, material and social factors are neither excluded nor added in later as 'context', but instead are treated as necessary and integral components by which subjectivity is structured.

Technologies for people with disabilities

Rather than attempt to provide a comprehensive review of technologies for people with disabilities, a brief overview of applications of new technology is followed by a more detailed discussion of the subjective impact upon people with disabilities of a small number of these applications. This discussion is organized around themes which we believe are relevant when critically assessing *any* new technologies for people with disabilities.

Computer use is rapidly becoming more widespread, yet commonly used computer peripherals make it difficult for many people with disabilities to use ordinary desktop computers. In response to these and other problems, both software and hardware have been developed. The most basic software solutions are the options built into operating systems such as Windows95 to make them more usable by people with disabilities by reconfiguring the keyboard to remove the need to use a mouse, or adjusting the sensitivity of keys to repeat pressing (Microsoft, 1995). Specialized software has been developed which aims to predict the 'intended' mouse movement of users with fine motor difficulties – such difficulties result in hand tremors which make it tedious for the person to use graphical user interfaces. The software 'learns' the users' typical patterns of computer interaction and so with repeated use becomes successively better at assisting with control of the computer (Craven *et al.*, 1997). Similar prediction algorithms have already been used with some success to help students with cerebral palsy to learn physics in a 'virtual science laboratory' (Nemire and Crane, 1995). On the hardware side there are specially adapted keyboards, touch sensitive screens, and devices which use 'suck and blow' tubes, light beams and pneumatics to control computer peripherals. One device even enables people with motor impairments to control a graphical user interface using only eye movements (Istance *et al.*, 1996).

Computers are also being used to assist with mobility, navigation and the control of wheelchairs and artificial limbs. Scott and Parker (1988) describe how computerized artificial upper limbs can use myoelectric signals to control the movement of prostheses. Computers can also be used to assist users with the control and navigation of electric wheelchairs, both by providing onboard assistance to users and by using 'virtual presence' technologies which permit remote operation. Joint research by the universities of Birmingham and Gothenburg has developed an aid for people with visual impairments, integrating portable computers with speech synthesis and navigation devices using the global positioning satellite (GPS) system so as to guide the user to a chosen destination. Taking this a step further, Vanderheiden and Cress (1992) propose a device called

'The Companion', a pocket computer incorporating a real-time clock, speech synthesis and a GPS link, which people with intellectual disabilities could use to help them live more independently. As well as navigation this device could provide help with schedules and appointments, sequencing of everyday chores, reminders about medication, and even task-specific help which would make people with intellectual disabilities capable of performing adequately in jobs which would otherwise be beyond them.

Virtual environment (VE) technologies are also being adapted for use by people with disabilities. VE are three-dimensional computer generated worlds which respond in real time to the activity of users, and so generate a sense of 'presence' (Steuer, 1992) in the virtual world. They can be run on ordinary desktop computers using standard input devices, or with dedicated graphics machines and peripherals such as head-mounted displays, gaze tracking and position sensors (Biocca, 1992). In both cases they are extremely flexible and have many applications in the field of disability. In assessment, Andrews *et al.* (1995) show how VE can be used with people with acquired brain damage. VE make possible rigorously controlled test situations which nevertheless retain ecological validity and could help to differentiate between (for example) sensory and motor damage. In rehabilitation, VE could be used to deliver therapeutic stimulation to people in comas (Wilson and Macmillan, 1993), while people with brain damage could use VE to repeatedly practice movements which need to be re-learned with no need for supervision, no risk, and minimal cost (Rose, 1996). Cromby *et al.* (1996) describe how VE can be used for education and skill acquisition by people with intellectual disabilities. VE systems foreground the learner's self-directed activity, need not use language or symbols, and provide a safe environment where skills can be practiced without harm or humiliation – a novel combination of features which make VE an ideal teaching medium for this group. Similarly, Stanton *et al.* (1996) describe how VE can be used by children with physical disabilities to learn their way around novel environments. VE technologies have even been adapted for use by people with visual impairments, using multi-channel 3D audio systems to generate interactive acoustic environments (for example, Lumbreras *et al.*, 1996).

In the UK application of new technologies to disability is in its infancy, hindered by limited and discontinuous research funding and a poorly developed infrastructure. In the USA provision is primarily funded by Medicare health insurance, which pays up to 80 per cent of 'approved charges' to rent or buy assistive devices but does not supply or develop equipment. Beneficiaries must depend on the market and their own ability to 'top up' the Medicare payments to get the technologies they need. Proponents of the free market argue that this arrangement is effective, equitable and results in the continual, innovative development of new technologies for people with disabilities (Galasko and Lipkin, 1989). However, this ignores the hidden agenda driving research which utilizes military or NASA technologies, and which may gain precedence over the needs of people with disabilities (we provide an example of this later). Additionally, the prominence of market forces means that those with less money are unlikely to have their needs addressed, and some potentials of new technologies may therefore be ignored. This may be why VE technologies (which have been pioneered in the USA) are hardly used there with people with intellectual disabilities (Salem-Darrow, 1995), despite their obvious suitability for this group.

This concludes our brief overview of applications of new technology to disability. We now consider four issues which these technologies raise, using specific examples to show their relevance and using the notion of subjective possibility spaces to understand how they might affect people with disabilities. These issues are: the availability of the technology to those who need it; the potential of the technology to allow others to observe or track the movements of its users; the potential of the technology to allow others to direct or constrain the user's activity; and the extent to which the everyday lives of users become interwoven with and reliant upon the functioning of the technology.

Access

The issue of access can be illustrated by a discussion of the potentials and problems of computer-mediated communication (CMC). CMC occurs most often through email, but also via Internet relay chat (IRC) and live video streaming. Systems are also being developed to facilitate 'virtual conferencing' using computer graphic representations of faces to simultaneously convey the emotions and reactions of participants alongside their verbal or textual communication (for example, Benford *et al.*, 1995). CMC has been the subject of much discussion, both in the popular press (for example, Rheingold, 1993) and in academia. Participation in CMC leads to the formation and cultivation of interpersonal relationships and the emergence of 'community' and 'identity' in the electronic realm, processes which have been compared with those that typically occur in face-to-face communication (for example, Ross, 1991; Frederick, 1993; Shields, 1996; Jones, 1997).

Access to CMC by people with disabilities raises a number of issues, the first of which is sheer physical access to the computer which, as we have already suggested, is likely to be unsuitable for many disabled users. Second, the cost of buying a computer and having it networked may be beyond people on lower incomes; this is especially important since disability and poverty are closely associated (see, for example, Beresford, 1996). Third, the widely held perception that computers are the province of the young and the well-educated may further discourage many people with disabilities from even considering them. The notion that 'such things are not for us' still constitutes part of the subjective possibility space experienced by many people in our culture, and may be especially prevalent in the oldest sector of the population where disability is concentrated. The male domination of discussion groups, and the bias towards male interests evident on the Internet, may provide women with disabilities with a further disincentive to use computers. Fourth, the emphasis on textual communication, privileging a mode which many will associate with experiences of failure at school, may further contribute to a reluctance to engage with new technology.

But assuming that people with disabilities do access CMC, it creates many possibilities. One effect may be the creation of new employment opportunities, since the transformation of many office jobs into an electronic form means that people with physical disabilities could work from home and so avoid the disabling separation of home and employment which industrialization imposed (Gleeson, 1997). Within the workplace computers reduce the physical effort involved in filing and fetching work documents, reducing the need to walk around or climb stairs, while networks facilitate access to databanks, allow communication via email, and permit a variety of different tasks to be performed at the same workstation (Roulstone, 1993). CMC might also allow people with disabilities to create or join 'communities of interest' which would otherwise be inaccessible to them because of either mobility problems or sheer geographical distance. For example, in the Internet 'newsgroup' hierarchy, support groups exist where people with various disabling conditions can exchange information and ideas, discuss medical matters and seek information about sympathetic doctors, diagnoses and treatments. People may also build friendships, and in so doing gain solidarity and support from others who are grappling with similar problems. Ultimately, this might help people with disabilities to both undermine some of the authority of medical 'experts' and be more vocal in demanding appropriate interventions, a possibility of which the medical profession is already aware – Coiera (1996: 3–4) notes that 'widespread use of the Internet is likely to aggravate existing conflicts between patient's expectations and the provision of health care'.

Because CMC reduces all participants to the same level of representation, which currently is almost exclusively textual, it also raises unique possibilities for identity construction. Through CMC, people with disabilities can interact with others without their impairments being either immediately obvious to others or relevant – even by omission – to the interaction. People with disabilities can be as similar to non-disabled people as they wish, since in CMC their disability is not only not an issue but is and will remain invisible unless they choose to disclose it. While other forms of written communication offer the same opportunities for anonymity, no other medium does so and permits real-time interaction. Uniquely, then, CMC can create (albeit temporarily and artificially) a subjective possibility space within which people are effectively no longer disabled in their interactions with others.

Surveillance

New technologies create many new opportunities for surveillance: witness the spread of closed-circuit TV cameras, of which there are now more than a million in the UK. But surveillance can also be more subtle and insidious, as with 'smart cards' for cashless financial transactions and supermarket 'loyalty cards', which all allow users' purchasing habits to be centrally monitored and individually recorded. Similarly, the electronic toll systems being piloted on some motorways use overhead scanners to read barcodes on vehicles' windscreens, allowing the computer system to track individual vehicle movements in real time.

Some new technologies designed for people with disabilities encounter similar issues. Heinz Wolff (1996) has proposed a 'caring house' for people with disabilities. The house is fitted with a variety of sound and motion sensors, tripswitches and pressure pads, all connected to a networked computer. The computer uses these devices to monitor movement and activity within the building, and the network link to alert care staff and call for assistance if a potential problem is detected.

The subjective possibility space this creates has two principal aspects. First, occupants of the house would be aware that their movements were constantly monitored, and would structure their activity to take account of this continual, passive surveillance. Second, they would also know that they had a high level of protection from the consequences of accidents and crises – not just medical emergencies, but incidents such as fires and burglaries. For some, the knowledge that their every movement was recorded by an all-seeing machine would be a small price to pay for the safety and security of knowing that they were protected from accident or injury. For others such a level of surveillance in their private lives would be simply unacceptable, whatever its benefits. While a range of living options are available for those who are unable to live wholly independently, people with disabilities will be able to exercise choice. However, as the costs of such technology continue to fall in real terms, it is likely that more and more 'caring' will be provided in this way as the cost of doing so (compared to paying workers) declines. A situation may ensue where the choice facing all but the very wealthiest people with disabilities is between no assistance at all, or assistance accompanied by and predicated upon continual surveillance.

Control

Beyond mere surveillance, researchers at Utah State University in America have developed a wheelchair incorporating 'remote presence' technologies which enable the chair's movement to be controlled by an operator at a base station (Smith *et al.*, 1995). If a user feels an epileptic seizure beginning while she is out in the chair, she can press a button which sounds an alarm at a control centre. A trained operator then puts on a head-mounted stereoscopic display and uses video cameras mounted on the chair to assess the situation (real-time information about the chair's angle, orientation and movement are also measured by sensors and transmitted back to base). In the best 'Thunderbirds' tradition, the operator then uses a joystick to drive the wheelchair and its occupant home again.

This wheelchair incorporates elements of surveillance and also of total control, since for the system to function the remote operator must be able to completely override any attempts by the chair's user to control its movement. The subjective possibility space this creates would include the dual aspects of surveillance and safety which the 'caring house' created, with the additional possibility that journeys could be constrained or redirected at any time. Opportunities for spontaneous intimacy, anonymity, aimless wandering and quiet reflection would all be compromised, since this technology excises solitude and seclusion from the lives of its users.

This wheelchair's design reflects unspoken assumptions about people with disabilities, whose dependency and perceived vulnerability may legitimate levels of supervision and surveillance which would otherwise be unacceptable. The bodies of people with disabilities can become highly public due to factors such as the ongoing requirement to explain to others their differential functioning, the relatively high levels of medical intervention they may receive, and the assistance sometimes needed to fulfil everyday bodily functions. In day care and residential settings this assistance is typically institutionalized; for example, toileting will be assisted by staff on duty, and who this is depends on shifts and rotas not preferences and relationships.

The wheelchair's design not only naturalizes this lack of privacy, it also demands an idealized technological Utopia which simply does not exist: would onlookers really stand by and watch a wheelchair-bound person in the throes of a seizure careering at high speed, oblivious and apparently out of control, through streets and across roads? The failure to consider this issue implies that other concerns are primary, and (we would suggest) is explicable only if the issue of funding is examined. In fact, this wheelchair uses technologies developed for NASA to remotely operate robot vehicles, and was essential to secure federal funding for this work. The benevolent aspects of these technologies were highlighted by the Mars Pathfinder mission and its use of a remotely controlled roving vehicle to explore the planet's surface. Its more sinister uses (to maintain, repair and realign spy satellites and weapons-targeting systems) gain less publicity but still receive primacy over the needs of people with disabilities, which are used here to justify the allocation of public money to this research.

Dependency

Oliver (1990) identifies dependency as a central issue in disability, showing how the rise of capitalism and associated changes in social relations increased the dependency of people with disabilities, making them more marginal and less economically self-sufficient (see also Ryan and Thomas, 1987). The new technologies discussed here are at the cutting edge of capitalism, and our society is crucially dependent upon them for the production and distribution of goods and services, the organization of travel, health and welfare, and the operation of the financial and money markets. But the dependency of people with disabilities upon new technologies may be even more thorough, because their reliance is likely to be more sustained, extensive and intimate. We all depend on computer systems to keep our shops full and our trains running (roughly) on schedule; people with disabilities may also depend on them to get out of bed, get dressed, prepare meals, open doors, and operate prosthetic devices and artificial limbs. In this context computer failures can cause more than inconvenience, posing a serious challenge to the quality of everyday life. Moreover, once dependency exists failures are not the only possible source of problems: the combination of built-in obsolescence and the exercise of monopoly power by large companies, upon whose products people with disabilities may have to rely, could create financial hardship for those with money and exclusion for those without it.

The subjective possibilities which dependency raises flow from the awareness that the quality of everyday life, or the ability to carry out simple tasks independently, cannot be maintained if the technology fails: in a sense, people with disabilities would become hostages to the machines that help them. For applications such as the caring house and the remote presence wheelchair, additional subjective possibilities would arise from the users' dependency on the benevolence of system operators not to abuse their opportunities for surveillance and control, since both of these devices would position their users under the unremitting gaze of an invisible 'carer' whose continued goodwill could become a continual source of concern.

The idealized abstract notions of 'independence' embedded in ideologies of care such as 'normalisation' (Brown and Smith, 1992) demarcate and individualize disability by concealing the social interdependence which is already the norm for everyone, disabled or not

(Oliver, 1993). Nevertheless, the extent and nature of the dependencies which new technology creates must always be considered when their suitability is assessed.

Discussion

New technologies for people with disabilities create opportunities and problems which typically arise simultaneously, so creating difficult dilemmas for users. Prosthetic aids which enhance bodily function inevitably reduce the user's ability to manage without them, as underuse causes muscles to atrophy and joints to weaken. There are other dilemmas, too: for example, the anonymity of CMC which enables people with disabilities to interact with others without their disability being an issue simultaneously undermines the potentials for political action which CMC provides. Invisibility and deception, however justifiable and well-intentioned, make a poor foundation for the trust and solidarity that determined political action demands (Breslow, 1997). Attention has been drawn to the possible drawbacks for women of leaving their bodies behind when they enter cyberspace, so shedding the fundamental basis upon which their gendered identity is founded (Dietrich, 1997); it seems likely that people with disabilities will also have to consider this issue.

Such dilemmas suggest that improvements in the quality of life of people with disabilities will not flow automatically from technology. Boal (1995: 12) observes that 'Artifacts are congealed ideology': given that there is already widespread discrimination against people with disabilities, this implies that they are unlikely to get the devices best suited to their needs without a struggle. Technology is always already social – which in our culture means that it is shaped and informed by market forces and the requirements of powerful vested interests. The remote presence wheelchair described earlier shows how such influences can lead to inappropriate devices being foisted on people with disabilities, and illustrates again (if further illustration were necessary) the need to involve end users throughout the design and evaluation process (for example, Newell and Cairns, 1993). However, even ideologically contaminated technologies can be subverted and used for other purposes. While for some devices this is difficult to imagine (guns have relatively few uses apart from shooting), for computer and communications technologies the development of alternative applications is greatly facilitated by the sheer power and flexibility of microprocessor-based devices.

Some decades ago, predictions were commonplace that by the millennium computers and robots would greatly shorten the working week and free humanity from drudgery and mindless labour. That these predictions have proved false is obvious; the more interesting question may be why this is so. In this context, the efforts of people with disabilities to get the applications of technology they most need may parallel, if not actually prefigure, the attempts of us all to acquire innovative new technologies shaped by the needs and aspirations of users rather than the profits of manufacturers. We hope that the issues and discussions outlined here might serve as a modest contribution to these struggles.

References

Andrews, T., Rose, F.D., Leadbetter, A., Attree, E. and Painter, J. (1995) 'The use of virtual reality in the assessment of cognitive ability', in Placencia-Porrero, I. and Puig de la Bellacassa, R. (eds) *The European Context for Assistive Technology: Proceedings of the 2nd Tide Congress*. Amsterdam: IOS Press.

Benford, S., Bowers, J., Fahlen, L., Greenhalgh, C. and Snowdon, D. (1995) 'User embodiment in collaborative virtual environments'. *Proceedings of the 1995 ACM Conference on Human Factors in Computing Systems* (CHI'95), May 7–11, Denver, Colorado: ACM Press.

Beresford, P. (1996) 'Poverty and disabled people: challenging dominant debates and policies', *Disability and Society*, **11**(4): 553–67.

Biocca, F. (1992) 'Virtual reality technology: a tutorial', *Journal of Communication*, **42**(2): 23–72.

Boal, I. (1995) 'A flow of monsters: Luddism and virtual technologies', in Brook, J. and Boal, I. (eds) *Resisting the Virtual Life: The Culture and Politics of Information*. San Francisco: City Lights.

Breslow, H. (1997) 'Civil society, political economy and the Internet', in Jones, S. (ed.) *Virtual Culture: Identity and Communication in Cybersociety*. London: Sage.

Brown, H. and Smith, H. (eds) (1992) *Normalisation: A Reader for the Nineties*. London: Routledge.

Coiera, E. (1996) 'The Internet's challenge to health care provision: a free market in information will conflict with a controlled market in health care', *British Medical Journal*, **312**(7022): 3–4.

Craven, M., Curtis, K.M., Hayes-Gill, B.R. and Thursfield, C.D. (1997) 'A hybrid neural network/rule-based technique for on-line gesture and hand-written character recognition'. Proceedings of the Fourth IEEE International Conference on Electronics, Circuits and Systems, Cairo, Egypt, December 15–18, 1997, Volume 2.

Cromby, J., Standen, P.J. and Brown, D.J. (1996) 'The potentials of virtual environments in the education and training of people with learning disabilities', *Journal of Intellectual Disability Research*, **40**(6): 489–501.

Dery, M. (1995) *Escape Velocity: Cyberculture at the End of the Century*. London: Hodder & Stoughton.

Dietrich, D. (1997) '(Re)Fashioning the techno-erotic woman: gender and textuality in the cybercultural matrix', in Jones, S. (ed.) *Virtual Culture: Identity and Communication in Cybersociety*. London: Sage.

Eagleton, T. (1995) *The Illusions of Postmodernism*. Oxford: Blackwell.

Frederick, H. (1993) 'Computer networks and the emergence of global civil society: the case of the Association for Progressive Communication', in Harasim, L. (ed.) *Global Networks: Computers and International Communication*. Cambridge, MA: MIT Press.

Galasko, C. and Lipkin, C. (1989) *Competing for the Disabled: IEA Health Unit Paper No. 7*, London: IEA Health Unit.

Gleeson, B.J. (1997) 'A historical materialist view of disability studies', *Disability and Society*, **12**(2): 179–202.

Hall, S. and Jacques, M. (1989) *New Times: The Changing Face of Politics in the 1990s*. London: Lawrence & Wishart.

Haraway, D. (1985) 'A manifesto for cyborgs: science, technology and socialist feminism in the 1980s', *Socialist Review*, **80**: 65–107.

Hobsbawm, E. (1993) *Age of Extremes: The Short Twentieth Century*. London: Abacus.

Istance, H., Spinner, C. and Howarth, P. (1996) 'Providing motor impaired users with access to standard graphical–user–interface software via eye-based interaction', in Sharkey, P. (ed.) *ECDVRAT'96: Proceedings of the 1st European Conference on Disability, Virtual Reality and Associated Technologies*. Reading: University of Reading.

Jones, S. (ed.) (1997) *Virtual Culture: Identity and Communication in Cybersociety*. London: Sage.

Lonsdale, S. (1990) *Women and Disability: The Experience of Physical Disability Among Women*. London: Macmillan.

Lumbreras, M., Barcia, M. and Sánchez, J. (1996) 'A 3D sound hypermedial system for the blind', in Sharkey, P. (ed.) *ECDVRAT'96: Proceedings of the 1st European Conference on Disability, Virtual Reality and Associated Technologies*. Reading: University of Reading.

Microsoft (1995) *Introduction to Windows95*. Seattle: Microsoft.

Nemire, K. and Crane, R. (1995) 'Designing a virtual science laboratory to accommodate needs of students with cerebral palsy'. *Proceedings of the Third International Conference: Virtual Reality and Persons with Disabilities*. Northridge: California State University Centre on Disabilities.

Newell, A. and Cairns, A. (1993) 'Design for extraordinary users', *Ergonomics in Design*, **10**: 10–16.

Oliver, M. (1990) *The Politics of Disablement*. London: Macmillan.

Oliver, M. (1993) 'Disability and dependency: a creation of industrial societies?', in Swain, J., Finkelstein, V., French, S. and Oliver, M. (eds) *Disabling Barriers, Enabling Environments*. London: Sage.

Rheingold, H. (1993) *The Virtual Community: Homesteading on the Electronic Frontier*. Reading, MA: Addison-Wesley.

Rose, F.D. (1996) 'Virtual reality in rehabilitation following traumatic brain injury', in Sharkey, P. (ed.) *ECDVRAT'96: Proceedings of the 1st European Conference on Disability, Virtual Reality and Associated Technologies.* Reading: University of Reading.

Ross, A. (1991) 'Hacking away at the counterculture', in Penley, C. and Ross, A. (eds) *Technoculture.* Minneapolis: University of Minneapolis Press.

Roulstone, A. (1993) 'Access to new technology in the employment of disabled people', in Swain, J., Finkelstein, V., French, S. and Oliver, M. (eds) *Disabling Barriers, Enabling Environments.* London: Sage.

Ryan, J. and Thomas, F. (1987) *The Politics of Mental Handicap* (revised edition). London: Free Association Books.

Salem-Darrow, M. (1995) 'Virtual reality's increasing potential for meeting needs of persons with disabilities: what about cognitive impairments?', in Murphy, H.J. (ed.) *Proceedings of the Third International Conference: Virtual Reality and Persons with Disabilities.* Northridge: California State University Centre on Disabilities.

Scott, R. and Parker, P. (1988) 'Myoelectric prostheses: state of the art', *Journal of Medical Engineering and Technology,* **12**: 143–51.

Shields, R. (ed.) (1996) *Cultures of Internet: Virtual Spaces, Real Histories, Living Bodies.* London: Sage.

Smith, S., Gunderson, R., Abott, B. and Joshi, M. (1995) 'Virtual presence and autonomous wheelchair control: an update', in Murphy, H.J. (ed.) *Proceedings of the Third International Conference: Virtual Reality and Persons with Disabilities.* Northridge: California State University Centre on Disabilities.

Stanton, D., Wilson, P. and Foreman, N. (1996) 'Using virtual reality environments to aid spatial awareness in disabled children', in Sharkey, P. (ed.) *ECDVRAT'96: Proceedings of the 1st European Conference on Disability, Virtual Reality and Associated Technologies.* Reading: University of Reading.

Steuer, J. (1992) 'Defining virtual reality: dimensions determining telepresence', *Journal of Communication,* **42**(4): 73–93.

Tolman, C. (1994) *Psychology, Society and Subjectivity: An Introduction to German Critical Psychology.* London: Routledge.

Vanderheiden, G. and Cress, C. (1992) 'Applications of artificial intelligence to the needs of persons with cognitive impairments: the Companion aid', in Murphy, H.J. (ed.) *Proceedings of the Third International Conference: Virtual Reality and Persons with Disabilities.* Northridge: California State University Centre on Disabilities.

Vaneigem, R. ([1967]1994) *The Revolution of Everyday Life,* London: Rebus Press/Left Bank Books.

Wilson, S. and Macmillan, T. (1993) 'A review of the evidence for the effectiveness of sensory stimulation treatment for coma and vegetative states', *Neuropsychological Rehabilitation,* **3**: 149–160.

Wolff, H. (1996) 'Ageing gracefully: an alternative proposition', paper presented to the conference *Technology Foresight: Health and Wealth Creation Through the Life Sciences.* Nottingham: University of Nottingham.

CHAPTER 7

Psychological Ethics and Cyborg Body Politics

BETTY M. BAYER

> Whether roaming cyberspace or wandering through a densely mate-
> rial collection, according to this interactive view, we remain the
> producers and directors of knowledge. Nuggets of visual data
> endlessly and enticingly summon us to collaborate in their restaging.
> (Stafford, 1996: 76)

At the dawn of the twenty-first century, changing technocultural
pulses of everyday life, of who and what we are about as psychological subjects, our subjectivities, have stirred up anew a sense of life in
the twilight zone. Neither wholly unmoored from our familiar ways
of being nor completely jacked into cyberspace, we are instead caught
up in the visual and digital cultural-political surrounds of transitions
and transformations, restagings and reimaginings. From magazine
headlines announcing technologies as making us faster, richer,
smarter as well as alienated, materialistic, and a 'little crazy' through
to advertisements claiming 'the future of machines is biology,' 'the
biological is becoming technological,' 'technologies are becoming
biological,' and 'don't just send email, be email,' popular culture
discourses heighten our association of technology with emerging
transformations in selves, bodies, and subjectivity. Likewise,
academic study and debate, whether of what constitutes intelligence,
the mind, emotion, the body, or life itself, have served to redraw filial
lines between humans and machines (Turkle, 1995). Calling into
question boundaries between nature and artefact, science and

culture, body and mind, self and non-self, these discourses signal disturbances around the limits to and boundaries between inner and outer, off-line and on-line material-discursive worlds.

So, here we are, poised betwixt and between the dawn of a digital age and the dusk of a mechanical one, between the end of the second and the beginning of the third millennium, all the while finding ourselves entranced by, but yet apprehensive of, cybertechnology's possibilities for individual, cultural, social and psychological life. Such opposing millennarian impulses of desiring new beginnings (salvation) and fearing ultimate destruction (damnation) enliven many narratives. Whereas some writers seek to spring the cyborg and cyberspace from the snare of apocalypticism, others query how cybertechnologies redesign private and public life, home and work spaces, asking what is new here or what it is that is being transformed (for example, Downey and Dumit, 1997). Quite apart from technology bringing about the much feared overly deterministic effects on our lives or the thrill of complete human makeovers, however, the 'notional space' of cybertechnologies seems more open for debate than not (Gibson, 1984). Given that these restagings are as much about the moral-political terrain of the worlds we inhabit as the ones we seek to create, it would seem of utmost importance for critical historians of psychology or those using a feminist cultural studies of science approach to enter into discussion around what counts as human and for which ways of life.

To ask what such inquiries in psychology might look like is to ask what, in short, the history of psychology would look like if told through cyborg body politics. As psychology's history is intertwined with the history of technology and so with issuing in its own cyborgs (see Edwards, 1996; Bayer, 1998), as so much of individual, cultural, social and political life is increasingly rendered in psychological terms (see Pfister and Schnog, 1997), and as matters of the cyborg and cyberspace life circle back to ones of personal, social and psychological life, the range of questions for study seems almost infinite. Who, in or out of psychology, can forget images of the bar-pressing, maze-running rat or pecking pigeon as Taylorized versions of productive workers? Or, children seated at Skinner's teaching machine, subjects hooked up to the bogus pipeline or to Milgram's fake shocking machine, Harlow's wired surrogate mothers, Galton's pictorial statistics of criminal physiognomy, or Chapple's time and motion recording instrument, the chronograph, fitting workers to types of work (see Sekula, 1986; Haraway, 1989; Bayer, 1997, 1998;

Stam *et al.*, 1998)? From Wundt's thought meter and early clock-like pendulum swings of mechanical hypnotic inducers through to cybernetic feedback recording instruments and experimental virtual social psychological worlds in cyberspace, psychology evidences interarticulations of changing technologies with changing versions of the psyche, body, and self. Whether remaking mind or body as a mechanical apparatus, clockwork mechanism, smooth-running electronic machine, hydraulic system, or fluid and flexible body image on a computer screen, psychology's interrelations of bodies and machines have transfigured time and again understandings of the body *and* subjectivity.

Questions of psychology's cyborg body politics thus span ones concerned with psychology's production and naturalization of cyborgian kinds, much as Kurt Danziger (1997) addresses psychology's historical production of psychological or human kinds, through to how contemplation on cyborgs and cyberspace enters into a remaking of technoscientific inquiry. Changing technologies of scientific instruments, apparatuses, and devices also, then, reshape scientific practices and scientific practitioners. Coincident with these concerns are issues of the moral-political engagements of scientific psychology, including the far-reaching need for a critical psychology to grapple with psychology's place in our late twentieth-century restaging as well as with the discipline's longer history in technocultural life.

Our contemporary preoccupation with the minglings of technology and ways of life thereby extends to the ways in which we feature scientific knowers and the production of scientific knowledge bringing particular cyborgian kinds into being. Drawing on feminist and other critical inquiries into psychology's ways of knowing, this chapter investigates struggles over meaning- and boundary-making in technoscientific iterations of what counts as human. From here, discussion moves to epistemic debate on psychology's technoscientific practices, including how their shapings of some 'kinds' over others occur not in some 'unearthly realm' but rather in the 'material and meaningful interactions of located humans and nonhumans – machines, organisms, people, land, institutions, money, molecules, and many other kinds of things' (Haraway, 1997a: 124). Locating psychology's knowledge production within the material-discursive forces of cyborg body politics is a critical step in *un*doing psychology's epistemological practices and *re*doing them expressly as 'situated knowledges' (Haraway, 1991).

Conflicted longings in life at the interface

Jaron Lanier, coiner of the phrase *virtual reality*, writes that 'social conflicts are now just as likely to be about the technologies of identity... as about the divvying up of resources' (Lanier, 1998: 62). Propelled by the power of technology to reinvent ourselves (yet again), the thrill of becoming other than we are, however, is put in check by the fear of losing our sense of self. Reflected in the 'conflicted longings of each self' (ibid.: 62) is that ambivalence arising from technologies of identity 'situated between idealistic technophilia and leery technophobia' (Terry and Calvert, 1997: 18). Jenny Uglow (1996: 14) expresses such conflicted longings 'as a fearful seduction':

> [I]n which terror of artificial beings, whether holograms or cyborgs, is induced not by their inhuman ugliness (as with Frankenstein's monster), but by their beauty and strength, their muddling *likeness* to a human ideal. The problem becomes one of authentication, of defining the human – or, conversely, of falling in love with the feared machine.

Enticed by longings for expansions in the sense of self and human capacities and by desires for human perfectibility and earthly transcendence, our awe of human–machine relations stands over against our dread of disappearing into the machinery or code, or becoming mere apprentices to or appendages of the machine (Uglow, 1996). Senses of enhancement and perfectibility are thus entangled with those of diminished and inconsequential being. Just as '[t]he telescope that takes us to the ends of the universe also presents earth as a dot,' so computers that boost memory capacity and performance power also reflect humans as minikins (ibid.: 15). Such technobody reconfigurations have to do with our place in the scheme of things, with fashioning the socio-political configurations of ways of living out our lives. Several examples are illustrative.

Consider, for one, Anne Joseph and Alison Winter's (1996) compelling study of technologies devised to identify or locate the essence of an individual from traces of finger-, voice-, or genetic prints. At once reduced to a trace and, through profiling, recreated into a whole being, what we might typically qualify as unique physical and psychological characteristics of an individual become transformed into different information codes of what constitutes essential human uniqueness and individuality. Moreover, technologies of profiling often exceed their initial functions as they refigure not only individuals but also public and private social, moral and political life. Another example of refiguring and re-ordering is found in medical imaging technologies, such as the fetal sonogram. In addition to displacing the maternal body, ultrasound images are, in Lisa Cartwright's (1995: 224–5) words, 'wreaking havoc with conventional development theories by imputing gender and sexual identity to the fetus almost before the actual formation of sexual anatomy'. For Cartwright, as for others, images are never just images, technologies never just technologies. Rather, imaging technologies, such as the fetal sonogram, become endowed with 'fantastic narrative dramas' of subjectivity and identity, ones which may be mobilized as much by anti-abortion groups or others to serve as an 'icon of conservative family values' as by those who seek to 'redirect its [medical imaging technologies] cultural function' (ibid.: 224–5, 234).

As these examples highlight, there is much more to these human–technology linkings than enhancements to see, to read, or to detect the 'essences' of life. Such pairings transform the selfsame entities they purport to reveal, reconstituting 'human' kinds in ways that reformulate rights and responsibilities along with our relations with and to humans, non-humans, and the everyday. Such reconfigurations also undergo normalizing and naturalizing effects making human–technology interfaces appear ordinary, as in two mid-twentieth-century compendia of psychology laboratory instruments cataloguing under 'human' functions of audition, bodily activity, and learning, for example, apparatuses of kymographs, dynamometers, and acoustical units (Andrews, 1948; Grings, 1954). In Edwin Boring's (1946) reply to Norbert Wiener's challenge to 'describe a capacity of the human brain' which could not be duplicated by electronic analogues (see Edwards, 1996), there is further instanced a naturalization of cyborgian kinds. Beginning with inventorying 'just what properties a robot needs to make a man of him' (ibid.: 178), Boring's harmonious fit between his list of input–output functions and a *hypothetical* robot eventuates in a Turing-like proposal for how an *actual* robot might enlighten views on human nature: 'Certainly, a robot whom you could not distinguish from another student would be an extremely convincing demonstration of the mechanical nature of man and of the unity of the sciences' (ibid.: 191). Boring's restaging is manyfold – of behaviourism, of man, of science and of the scientist. Through these interlinkings we gain a sense of the particular masculine logic inspiring feedback loops between Boring's robot and rational (scientific) actor. Similarly, Elizabeth Wilson (1996) finds at the heart of 'thinking machines' in cognition, such as Turing's, reworkings of the 'thinking man'. The apparent disembodying function of machines 'masks a more fundamental embodiment... via a *masculine* morphology masquerading as neutrality itself' (Wilson, 1996: 592).

Turning from questions of gender differences in cognition to the matter of cognition itself, Wilson redirects us to interests and desires circulating in human–non-human interfaces as constitutive practices of gender-in-the-making (also see Haraway, 1997b). In seeking, then, to establish the scientific basis either of what it means to think, to feel, to act, or of what 'human' or 'self' means, psychology's interarticulations of humans and machines have refigured what counts 'naturally' as the psyche, inner being or essence, and the psychological terms of self, mind, body, gender, sexuality, and everyday life.

Just as the particular exchanges occuring in these couplings amplify what counts as 'human,' so human–machine interchanges of competencies, capacities, and characteristics evidence that there is more to cyborg investigations than simply announcing various sightings of cyborgian couples or leaving off with assertions that technologies transform us, our bodies and selves. Posing this problematic as one of cyborg body politics, Theresa Senft (1996: 12) says:

> [I]t seems to me that announcing that we are all cyborgs is a little like arguing that we are all queer – it may be true, but what does that mean? Who, exactly are 'we,' and which politics does the cyborg give us?

While Susan Leigh Star (1991: 43) interrogates this political problematic as matters of *cui bono?* in 'meeting place[s] between "externalities" and "internalities"', Camilla Griggers (1997: 54–5) begins from the interested location of lesbian cyborgs to raise questions of '*who* gets to produce cyborg bodies, who has access, who provides the laboring and component bodies, and who becomes and who buys the commodities produced'. On the political economy of cyborg subjectivities, Brenda Brasher (1996: 817) asks whether celebratory linkings of cyberspace with proliferation of selves marks cyborg identity as privileged – 'an expansion of the human beyond precyborgian limits'. This 'expansion' contrasts with that of the less privileged for whom 'becoming borged can entail one's humanity being annexed by machines', such as secretaries turned word processors or replaced by computers, or assembly workers in Silicon Valley who may be without access to on-line life (Brasher, 1996: 817).

Other critical theorists reveal additional contrarieties encircling cybertechnology imaginings and life. Colliding with versions of cyberspace selves as unconstrained by gender, race or class are reports of sexual harassment and cyberrape in netlife. For all the hype of leaving the 'meat' behind in cyberspace, gender politics abound, as do caricatures of gendered bodies. To these we might add the issue of 'whether the Internet is, in fact, a technology of the home, the workplace, or of the street, whether it is public or private' (Jones, 1997: 21). As a technology of the self, cyberspace posits the possibility of free-living and informational free trade at the same time that personal webpages may be thought of as hyperlinked mergers of commodified selves with the market economy of information capital.

Insofar as we regard cyborgs of various kinds as sites of moral-political contest between oppression and emancipation, utopic and dystopic restagings of the meaning and view of humanness, investigations into cyborgian kinds reveal rather quickly both a politics and a historicity to hybrid subjects (Haraway, [1985]1991; González, 1995). To this charting of emerging versions of humanness, practices of scientific knowledge production become paramount for how they set the scope of our critical vision in seeing, imagining or constructing possibilities for practices of freedom in our everyday – cyborgian – encounters (Star, 1991). Still, there is more to such critical investigations into science's reigning means of knowledge production. Entering critically into matters of how cyborgs, literally or figuratively, are 'put together and taken apart,' leads to querying the networked relations of science, technology, culture, and politics in that broader sense of the scientific laboratory and the world crafting together our 'experimental ways of life' (Haraway, 1997b: 15, 50, 126). Using the figure of the cyborg critically is about parallel inquiries into what else emerges in relations among science, technology, culture and politics and how to interfere in these constituting patterns for 'new opportunities for analysis and activism' (Downey and Dumit, 1997: 7).

'Interference patterns' in 'experimental ways of life'

Set against the conventional positivist paradigm construing the knower and knowledge as above and beyond time, location and space contingencies as well as serving to demarcate boundaries between fact and fiction and science and culture, then, is Haraway's

([1985]1991) oppositional figure, the cyborg. What makes the cyborg so potent a critical vantage point for rethinking science as culture is that this figure of hybrid fusions emerges from the interminglings rather than isolated workings of science, science fiction, the military, religion, politics and culture (also see Penley, 1997). So contrary to evidencing scientific know-how in what counts as the real or the nature of who we are, cyborgs, in either their figurative or literal forms, raise profound questions concerning technoscience's boundary making and embodying practices. Interrogating these practices involves moving between the making of cyborgian kinds and the feminist question in science (Haraway, 1997b). Critical cyborg body politics of psychology thus engage with what has come to be called in late twentieth-century USA gender, culture, and science wars – or negotiations around meaning-, body-, and world-making practices. Indeed, some argue that these very debates animate popular culture and scientific cyborg constructions (Springer, 1996).

Feminist technoscience approaches to cyborg body politics query human–non-human comminglings situated within local and more broad material-discursive matrices of knowledge production. Boring's (1946: 177–8) turn to a robot analogue, for example, was located in the metaphorical and technological 'spirit of [late war] times,' populated with talk of 'electronic mathematicians' and 'electronic brains.' Yet, even as Boring acknowledged this, he overlooked the bit on how his enlistment of 'talk about machines' to 'leave out the subjective, anthropomorphic hocus pocus of mentalism' and to aid 'precision of psychological thought' was itself wrought through certain discourses on technology (ibid.: 191, 177). Ironically, the very mix of mediators bringing into being mechanism as ways of life, being and knowing is the very mix translated into 'special code[s] of communication' (ibid.: 177) in humans and machines alike (cf. Latour, 1993). Enabling this translation of matters of life into problems in coding are the coacting discourses of (military) command–control–communication–intelligence (C^3I), positivist science, and technology whose gender, class and race investments are morphed into the signs of rational actors (Haraway, 1997b). Likewise, post-war renegotiations of gendered workers and workplaces might be seen as contributing to cybernetic small group research transforming communications of status, emotions, or gender into information codes which were then transferred onto the 'internal experience of the individual' (Edwards, 1996: 204). Remade here were gendered classes of workers, group relations and managerial styles, ones for which the interaction chronograph's or recorder's graphs, for example, functioned to hide social ordering effects (cf. Traweek, 1997). Yet this very material-discourse nexus carries the trace of networks of cyborgian-kinds-in-the-making in which gender functions as a primary marker of difference (see Chapple, 1949; Bales, 1950; Crutchfield, 1951; Springer, 1996). Once rendered through positivist science, however, such 'newly emerging' 'experimental ways of life' become simply *natural* kinds – of human life, psyche, worker profiles, women, men, or group relations – rather than subjectivities-in-the-making (cf. Danziger, 1997; Haraway, 1997b).

Approached uncritically, then, the cyborg's contentious constitution may, as these examples show, capitulate to science-as-usual, to a positivist epistemology organized by 'the problematic of sovereignty' (Rouse, 1996: 403). Key components of scientific epistemology effecting a reproduction of 'central issues of political sovereignty' include assumptions of an 'impartial rational observer,' independence of investigative technologies (apparatuses, methods) from objects of study and from the knowledge produced, and the logic of epistemic adjudication (Rouse, 1996). Edwards' (1996) study of the joint action of closed-world (Cold War, C^{3}I) and cyborg discourses bears importantly on the crossovers of political, intellectual, and epistemic sovereignty animating knowing subjects, knowledge production, and subjective life in psychology's moves from behaviourism through to cybernetics and to artificial intelligence. Rather than supplanting one another, Edwards shows how cybernetic psychology initially extended behaviourism (recall Boring), absorbing the language of input–output (stimulus–response) by translating this along with 'concepts of purposes, goals, and will' to 'creat[e] a new technical terminology and system of quantification – information theory – for describing flexible, self-directed behavior in both machines and minds' (Edwards, 1996: 182, 184).

Edwards' historical specification of these projects within broader military metaphors, technical practices and research endeavours delivers a striking account of the politics of psychological subjectivity formed out of command and control core 'ideologies of human minds as manipulable' (ibid.: 2). That psychology's renditions of subjectivity are political comes out as clearly as psychology's hand in naturalizing cyborgian kinds and the discipline's particularization of its research interests, problems and specificity of cyborgian kinds as coordinated, in part, with military-related projects and support. Recent depictions of psychology's research on virtual reality (VR) continue to show the discipline's ties to military and space engineering, as well as how its investments in epistemic sovereignty lead to seeing changing technologies, such as VR, as about solving scientific social psychology's inability to control 'natural settings' by 'putting subjects in identical interactions with virtual people' (Azar, 1996: 24). Framed more broadly, the history of psychology's laboratory ages, from its early brass instrument, mechanical period through to electronic, computer and virtual reality ones, is wholly interarticulated with changing technologies and wider cultural discourses. Deployed to control laboratory conditions, to regulate, manipulate, and create stimuli or simulate 'real' life circumstances, or to measure, observe, and record, this history is also about the politics of technoscience in making subjects of different kinds. Re-reading psychology as a history of psychology's production of cyborgian kinds redirects us to the discipline's shifting technocultural intelligibilities wherein networked relations among science, technology, and the world make visible 'science as cultural practice' that cuts between remaking and reinstating 'experimental ways of life' for us all (Haraway, 1997a).

From making evident the work of culture, history, politics and ethics in the work of science, feminist cyborg politics moves on to remaking science as situated knowledges, as 'nodes in fields, inflections in orientations, and responsibility for difference in material-semiotic fields of meaning' (Haraway, 1991: 195). Entering science into the webbed fields of meaning counterposes that tradition of the self-invisibility of the knower who manages to inhabit the 'culture of no culture,' that aperspectival, disembodied view of all things from nowhere which Haraway calls the 'god trick' (Nagel, 1986; Haraway, 1991, 1997b; Daston, 1992). Repositioning objectivity critically as a 'view from somewhere' or 'from below' uncovers how technology's function as neutral devices of detachment (for example, 'hands off,' Megill, 1991; Stafford, 1994), disembodiment, and distancing is betrayed by science's investment of technology 'with spiritual significance and a transcendent meaning' in that larger narrative drama of desire for 'the recovery of man's lost divinity' (Noble, 1997: 6; see Bordo, 1990; Haraway, 1997b). So even as over the centuries the entanglements of science and technology entailed, in 'Cartesian terms, the development of a thinking machine... aimed at rescuing the immortal mind from its mortal prison', the body, there were at stake forms of embodiment. As such, these embodiments were enactments of man–machine relations, ones wherein scientific agency changed form historically from 'co-explorer' or 'steward with God' to man as 'co-creator' (Noble, 1997). Bound up with the historical interchanges among religion, science, culture, and the military, technology has enabled what Noble calls a 'masculine millenarian culture', – the staging anew of Adamic perfection. Such gender constituting discourses continue to exercise a powerful grip on scientific imaginations where human cloning and Christian religion are made commensurate as 'we will become God-like' by 'extend[ing]' the life span and having 'access to unlimited knowledge' (Seed, cited in Kadrey, 1998: 155, 182). These ideas are also evident in the current hype of cybertechnologies as leaving the meat behind in cyberspace (Noble, 1997).

Feminist technoscience introduces interference patterns into mergers of technology and life as yet one more millennarian spin on life and death struggles, bringing the otherworldly ambitions of transcendence and perfection down to earth in its revelation that 'technoscience is a form of life, a practice, a culture, a generative matrix' (Haraway, 1997b: 50). Reposing the problematic as one of the *forms* of human–non-human kinds, or which kinds of bodies are being (re)made in what ways, feminist technoscience takes special interest in sciences' mutating and morphing of 'nature... into culture, and vice versa, in such a way as to displace the entire nature/culture (and sex/gender) dialectic with a new discursive field' (ibid.: 149). Grappling with emerging discursive fields, feminists doubly expose these dualistic schemes as permeable, transformative, and seemingly fluid *and* as constructions which may nonetheless stabilize 'older hierarchies of human variation' (Hammonds, 1997: 109).

Without historical specificity and contextual contingencies, analytic moves in name only of multiplicity and fluidity, as in contestation of categories, may simply etherize in the nets of dominant knowledge/power relations (Haraway, 1997b). Insofar as cybertechnologies bend gender, we must ask ourselves what in the way of gender is being contested and for whom? This is what it means to 'queer' the gender bending or identity-release talk of cybertechnology for while butches and drag kings reveal 'there is no real man to become' (Plant, 1997: 212), harassment of women, anti-lesbian and gay actions, and pro-men's movements seeking to revitalize masculine power and authority remind us of competing gendered stakes involved in these complex border zones. Likewise, Boring's robot much as the visualizing technologies in classifying workers, kinds of group relations, fetal sonograms, finger- and voice printing, virtual social worlds along with psychology's other technologies, such as 'apparatuses of bodily production' in hysteria, body imaging, and gay genes, are interested locations where historically specific gender, race, sexuality and class meanings are being negotiated, normalized and naturalized. Querying human–non-human interchanges and queering their normalizing and naturalizing investments, then, are the twinned strategies needed to unseat epistemic sovereignty and put in its stead knowledge-making practices that critically engage technoscience's accountability and responsibility for possible kinds of selves and worlds.

Far from delimiting ethics to matters of technical practice or applications of scientific knowledge, ethics, as politics and culture, move into the centre of situated knowledges through the pivotal position of responsible accountability. Feminist technoscientific accountability is about knowers situating themselves and their knowledge production in terms of political alliances, critical moral judgements, and commitments to justice, freedom, and knowledge. Knowers and knowledges are, then, contingent, partial, and an 'embedded relational' perspective in addition to being partial 'in the sense of being *for* some worlds and not others' (Haraway, 1997b: 37; also see Gill, 1995; Biagoli, 1996). Moreover, situating practices contest the 'loaded dualities' of relativism and realism, relativism and rationality, offering instead '*practice* of oppositional and differentiated consciousness' for 'more adequate knowledge judged by the nonessentialist, historically contingent, situated standards of strong objectivity' (Haraway, 1997b: 198–9; also see Harding, 1991; Biagoli, 1996; Rouse, 1996). Contested also are forms of reflexivity that end in looping uncritically back to self-reflection or some 'reflexive regressus' in the mimetic sense of representations between science and the world (Biagoli, 1996; Haraway, 1997b). Replacing such forms of 'weak' reflexivity and 'weak' objectivity are feminist science studies' practices of strong objectivity and 'diffraction' – ways to intervene, to create interference patterns *where* the meanings and visions of humanness get made which has everything to do with our experimental ways of life here in the not-so-neat-and-tidy political zones we mostly call, however cyberspatial, daily life (Haraway, 1997b).

We are not the end of the story...?

As collaborator, muse, and agent, technology has long been a key player in stagings of who we are or might be and worlds we might want to inhabit. From one to another historical restaging, comminglings of humans and non-humans with technology trouble what counts as 'real,' 'natural' and 'human' just as they intervene in ontological narratives, such as creationism and evolution, to unsettle the groundwork of origins, creators and created. Of course, even as such hybrid fusions function to make the familiar strange, reveal foundational truths as discursive productions of knowledge/power relations, and decode the 'natural' as constructed 'all the way down,' these fusions do not escape constitutive effects of reigning narratives of masculine millennarian culture, secular humanism, evolutionary progress, military command and control systems, enlightenment science, capitalist economies, and political sovereignty. Into these hybrids' webbed worlds of doubling and redoublings of storied beginnings and endings, feminist cyborg body politics are needed to query whose subjectivities are at stake, whose conflicted longings and needs are represented in which stories, and to rework the boundary- and meaning-making lines constituting our 'experimental ways of life.'

More than a 'play with surfaces,' writes Michael Heim (1991: 6), 'our affair with information machines announces a symbiotic relationship' much as 'the erotic lover reaches out to a fulfilment far beyond aesthetic detachment'. Bringing the erotic into play with the more functional and useful presses technologies beyond their semblance as interesting 'objects to think with or second selves' (Turkle, 1995). Coursing through these material semiotic nexuses are the fantastic, tactile, and sensuous, at once electrifying technovisionary quests into the 'nature' of things and making of technovisions a political hotbed of contested creations. Impassioned technovisions stir us up. They enliven the ferment over the 'new' or 'transformed'. Early emerging cybernetic systems, for example, fuelled Boring's (1946: 192) visionary pulse for the realization of psychology as mechanism. Confident in the arrival of this distant future, Boring concludes by saying: 'I choose to sit cozily with my robot, squeezing his hand and feeling a thrill – a scientist's thrill – when he squeezes mine back.' That this flight of fantasy functions rhetorically to authorize Boring, his mechanism and his science is self-evident. As discernible and more telling of what this future portends, however, are the masculine homoerotic and homosocial desires embodying this three-way mirroring of scientist, man and machine, much as Wilson (1996: 585) found in couplings of thinking machines and men a 'reinstantiation of Cartesian desire for the kernel of man to be pure intellectuality' (also see Hayles, 1996).

Transfiguring body–technology linkings through cybertalk of morphings, augmentations, enhancements, and prostheses, late twentieth-century cybertalk shifts from human–machine mirrorings to technobody blurrings are no less vitalized by desires, needs, ambivalences and fearful seductions. For some, current restagings are of evolutionary or creationist proportions such that technologies are regarded as generative forces in the evolution of new computers (technology is biological?) and the Human Genome Project as one of not only understanding but also designing our futures (biology is technology?) (Sinsheimer, cited in Noble, 1997: 189; Hillis, 1998). For others, technofusions are of mind-bending dimensions, as in reconfiguring the brain as a 'naturally evolved' 'powerful computational device' and neural activity as 'sophisticated chips or microcomputers' (Pinker, cited in Blume, 1998: 155). Added to these remakings are scientific fantasies of downloading our consciousness (see Keller, 1996), calls to recognize computers as a 'new milestone in our cultural development' (Fields, 1987), visions of virtual reality wherein experiential contact is 'a psychological place, a virtual location' or a 'perfect presence' (Biocca, 1992: 27–8), cyberspace as releasing us from bodily strictures and material constraint, and cybergenetic programmes wherein morphed interracial unions, depicted in *Time Magazine* as 'the new face of America,' curiously sort 'unnatural' from 'natural' – preferred – hybrid persons (Hammonds, 1997). Critically engaging with these mergings and morphings, feminist cyborg body politics steps into the stream of historical, political, cultural, and scientific currents and cross-currents calling cyborgian subjects into being.

Technovisions, realized or not, then, are less about settling issues of who we are than struggles over *kinds* of bodies-, selves-, and worlds-in-the-making (Haraway, 1997b). This is precisely why ethics and politics reside not outside science but inside its very constructions of neural chips, gay genes, prosthetic bodies, scientific identities, selves and subjectivities. Ethics and moral politics can no more be split off as 'out there in the world' (wherever that is) than interested locations, values, and situated perspectives can be treated as the 'noise' we need to damp down to get at the 'real' story. Instead they are the critical contingencies inside the way we produce knowledge, including psychology. Feminist technoscience and technovisions are thus critical network navigators in making a difference for the manynesses of sexual, racial and gender wonder in worlds that go on.

Note

This paper is dedicated to the memory of Toni Flores whose feminist teachings on the body politic were all about making life matter.

References

Andrews, T.G. (1948) 'Some psychological apparatus: a classified bibliography', *Psychological Monographs*, **62**: 1–38.

Azar, B. (1996) 'Diving into virtual reality', *The APA Monitor*, **27**(1): 24–6.

Bales, R.F. (1950) *Interaction process analysis, a method for the study of small groups*. Cambridge, MA: Addison-Wesley.

Bayer, B.M. (1997) 'Technovisions and the remaking of scientific identity'. Paper presented at the International Society for Theoretical Psychology, Berlin.

Bayer, B.M. (1998) 'Between apparatuses and apparitions: phantoms of the laboratory', in Bayer, B.M. and Shotter, J. (eds) *Reconstructing the Psychological Subject: Bodies, Practices, and Technologies*. London: Sage.

Biagoli, M. (1996) 'From relativism to contingentism', in Galison, P. and Stump, D.J. (eds) *The Disunity of Science: Boundaries, Contexts, and Power*. Stanford: Stanford University Press.

Biocca, F. (1992) 'Virtual reality technology: a tutorial', *Journal of Communication*, **42**(4): 23–72.

Blume, H. (1998) 'Reverse engineering the psyche', *Wired!* (March), 155.

Bordo, S. (1990) 'Feminism, postmodernism, and gender-skepticism', in Nicholson, L.J. (ed.) *Feminism/postmodernism*. New York: Routledge.

Boring, E.G. (1946) 'Mind and mechanism', *American Journal of Psychology*, **59**: 173–92.

Brasher, B. (1996) 'Thoughts on the status of the cyborg: on technological socialization and its link to the religious function of popular culture', *Journal of the American Academy of Religion*, **64**: 809–30.

Cartwright, L. (1995) 'Gender artifacts: technologies of bodily display in medical culture', in Cooke, L. and Wollen, P. (eds) *Visual Display: Culture Beyond Appearances*. Seattle, WA: Bay Press.

Chapple, E.D. (1949) 'The interaction chronograph: its evolution and present application', *Personnel*, **25**: 295–307.

Crutchfield, R.S. (1951) 'Assessment of persons through a quasi group-interaction technique', *Journal of Abnormal and Social Psychology*, **46**: 577–88.

Danziger, K. (1997) *Naming the Mind: How Psychology Found its Language*. London: Sage.

Daston, L. (1992) 'Objectivity and the escape from perspective', *Social Studies of Science*, **22**: 597–618.

Downey, G.L. and Dumit, J. (1997) 'Locating and intervening', in Downey, G.L. and Dumit, J. (eds) *Cyborgs and Citadels: Anthropological Interven-*

tions in Emerging Sciences and Technologies. Santa Fe: School of American Research Press.

Edwards, P.N. (1996) *The Closed World: Computers and the Politics of Discourse in Cold War America*. Cambridge, MA: MIT Press.

Fields, C. (1987) 'Human–computer interaction: a critical synthesis', *Social Epistemology*, **1**: 5–25.

Gibson, W. (1984) *Neuromancer*. New York: Ace Science Fiction.

Gill, R. (1995) 'Relativism, reflexivity and politics: interrogating discourse analysis from a feminist perspective', in Wilkinson, S. and Kitzinger, C. (eds) *Feminism and Discourse: Psychological Perspectives*. London: Sage.

González, J. (1995) 'Envisioning cyborg bodies: notes from current research', in Gray, C.H., Figueroa-Sarriera, H.J. and Mentor, S. (eds) *The Cyborg Handbook*. London: Routledge.

Griggers, C. (1997) *Becoming-Woman*. Minneapolis: University of Minnesota Press.

Grings, W.W. (1954) *Laboratory Instrumentation in Psychology*. Palo Alto, CA: National Press.

Hammonds, E.M. (1997) 'New technologies of race', in Terry, J. and Calvert, M. (eds) *Processed Lives: Gender and Technology in Everyday Life*. New York: Routledge.

Haraway, D.J. ([1985]1991) 'A cyborg manifesto: science, technology, and socialist-feminism in the late twentieth century', in Haraway, D.J., *Simians, Cyborgs, and Women: The Reinvention of Nature*. New York: Routledge.

Haraway, D.J. (1989) *Primate Visions*. New York: Routledge.

Haraway, D.J. (1991) 'Situated knowledges: the science question in feminism and the privilege of partial perspective', in Haraway, D.J., *Simians, Cyborgs, and Women: The Reinvention of Nature*. New York: Routledge.

Haraway, D.J. (1997a) 'enlightenment@science_wars.com: A personal reflection on love and war', *Social Text*, **15**: 123–8.

Haraway, D.J. (1997b) Modest_Witness@Second _Millennium.FemaleMan_Meets_OncoMouse. New York: Routledge.

Harding, S. (1991) *Whose Science? Whose Knowledge? Thinking from Women's Lives*. Ithaca: Cornell University Press.

Hayles, N.K. (1996) 'Narratives of artificial life', in Robertson, G., Mash, M., Tickner, L., Bird, J., Curtis, B. and Putnam, T. (eds) *FutureNatural: Nature/Science/Culture*. London: Routledge.

Heim, M. (1991) 'The erotic ontology of cyberspace', in Benedikt, M. (ed.) *Cyberspace: First Steps*. Cambridge, MA: MIT Press.

Hillis, D. (1998) 'The big picture', *Wired!* (January), 38.

Jones, S.G. (1997) 'The internet and its social landscape', in Jones, S.G. (ed.) *Virtual Culture: Identity and Communication in Cybersociety*. London: Sage.

Joseph, A. and Winter, A. (1996) 'Making the match: human traces, forensic experts and the public imagination', in Spufford, F. and Uglow, J. (eds) *Cultural Babbage: Technology, Time and Invention*. London: Faber & Faber.

Kadrey, R. (1998) 'Go forth and multiply', *Wired!* (March), 150, 182.

Keller, E.F. (1996) 'The dilemma of scientific subjectivity in postvital culture', in Galison, P. and Stump, D.J. (eds) *The Disunity of Science: Boundaries, Contexts, and Power*. Stanford: Stanford University Press.

Lanier, J. (1998) 'Taking stock', *Wired!* (January), 60, 62.
Latour, B. (1993) *We Have Never Been Modern*. Cambridge, MA: Harvard University Press.
Megill, A. (1991) 'Introduction: four senses of objectivity', *Annals of Scholarship*, **8**: 301–19.
Nagel, T. (1986) *The View from Nowhere*. Oxford: Oxford University Press.
Noble, D.F. (1997) *The Religion of Technology: The Divinity of Man and the Spirit of Invention*. New York: Alfred A. Knopf.
Penley, C. (1997) *NASA/TREK: Popular Science and Sex in America*. London: Verso.
Pfister, J. and Schnog, N. (1997) *Inventing the Psychological: Toward a Cultural History of Emotional Life in America*. New Haven: Yale University Press.
Plant, S. (1997) *Zeros + Ones: Digital Women and the New Technoculture*. New York: Doubleday.
Rouse, J. (1996) 'Beyond epistemic sovereignty', in Galison, P. and Stump, D.J. (eds) *The Disunity of Science: Boundaries, Contexts, and Power*. Stanford: Stanford University Press.
Sekula, A. (1986) 'The body and the archive', *October*, **39**: 3–64.
Senft, T. (1996) 'Introduction: performing the digital body – a ghost story', *Women and Performance: A Journal of Feminist Theory*, **9**: 9–33.
Springer, C. (1996) *Electronic Eros: Bodies and Desire in the Postindustrial Age*. Austin: University of Texas Press.
Stafford, B.M. (1994) *Artful Science: Enlightenment Entertainment and the Eclipse of Visual Education*. Cambridge, MA: MIT Press.
Stafford, B.M. (1996) *Good Looking: Essays on the Virtue of Images*. Cambridge, MA: MIT Press.
Stam, H., Lubek, I. and Radtke, L. (1998) 'Repopulating social psychology texts: disembodied "subjects" and embodied subjectivity', in Bayer, B.M. and Shotter, J. (eds) *Reconstructing the Psychological Subject: Bodies, Practices, and Technologies*. London: Sage.
Star, S.L. (1991) 'Power, technologies and the phenomenology of conventions: on being allergic to onions', in Law, J. (ed.) *A Sociology of Monsters: Essays on Power, Technology and Domination*. New York: Routledge.
Terry, J. and Calvert, M. (1997) 'Introduction: Machine/Lives', in Terry, J. and Calvert, M. (eds) *Processed Lives: Gender and Technology in Everyday Life*. New York: Routledge.
Turkle, S. (1995) *Life on the Screen: Identity in the Age of the Internet*. New York: Simon & Schuster.
Traweek, S. (1997) 'Iconic devices', in Downey, G.L. and Dumit, J. (eds) *Cyborgs and Citadels: Anthropological Interventions in Emerging Sciences and Technologies*. Santa Fe: School of American Research Press.
Uglow, J. (1996) 'Introduction: "possibility"', in Spufford, F. and Uglow, J. (eds) *Cultural Babbage: Technology, Time and Invention*. London: Faber & Faber.
Wilson, E. (1996) '"Loving the computer": cognition, embodiment and the influencing machine', *Theory and Psychology*, **6**: 577–99.

CHAPTER 8

In and Out of the Digital Closet: The Self as Communication Network

HEIDI J. FIGUEROA-SARRIERA
(TRANSLATION BY JANE RAMÍREZ)

In spite of the differences between the various theories of the formation of personal identity that can be found in any traditional psychology textbook, there is one idea that is more or less common to all: the theory that identity is forged in social relations; that is, through contact with the other. Taking part in the semiotic exchanges of communication is the basic requirement for the formation and transformation of personal identity as an integrated and coherent entity. (The Latin root of the word 'identity' is *idem*, 'the same', the same entity.)

Nevertheless, current theorization has raised doubts as to just how coherent and stable that identity is, given that the subject is able to exhibit multiple self-portrayals when interacting with the other in cyberspace or virtual space. These self-portrayals may be different from and even conflict with the way the person presents him- or herself in 'real life' (that is, in face-to-face communicative relations). Thus, metaphors such as 'protean self,' 'saturated self,' 'flexible self,' and 'de-centred self' proliferate, as theorists attempt to configure an *imaginaire* different from that of the self as a coherent and self-contained unit that is able to signify these new experiences (cf., for example, Gergen, 1991; Figueroa-Sarriera and López, 1993; Lifton, 1993; Martin, 1994).

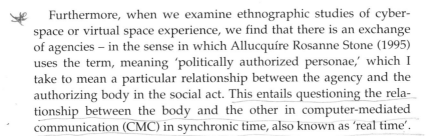

Furthermore, when we examine ethnographic studies of cyber-space or virtual space experience, we find that there is an exchange of agencies – in the sense in which Allucquíre Rosanne Stone (1995) uses the term, meaning 'politically authorized personae,' which I take to mean a particular relationship between the agency and the authorizing body in the social act. This entails questioning the relationship between the body and the other in computer-mediated communication (CMC) in synchronic time, also known as 'real time'.

When asked how sitting alone at a terminal was a social act, they explained that they saw the terminal as a window into a social space. Frequently the social space was described as being 'out there' (usually accompanied by an expansive wave of the hand), or sometimes 'in there' (accompanied by a gesture toward the computer). When describing the act of communication, many conference participants moved their hands expressively as though typing, emphasizing the gestural quality and essential tactility of the virtual mode. They were demonstrating a perceived deep connection between the differently embodied character of virtual communication and the articulation of that communication in terms of an imagined physical locus within which an exchange of information took place between physical entities. (Stone, 1995: 110–11)

In what sense, if any, is it possible to talk about this disembodied experience as different from the embodied experience and how do we connect the embodied and the disembodied experiences? What relationship is there between one's 'real' identity and one's 'virtual' identities? Can the dichotomy be sustained? What implications do these experiences have for reconceiving the notion of identity?

Before proceeding further, let us pause briefly for a description of the particular type of virtual space or cyberspace that serves as the context for these questions: MUDs (multi-user domains or multi-user dimensions).

MUDding and 'changing the subject'

MUDs are zones in the Internet in which users employ words and commands to create worlds where, by assuming the identity of a variety of imaginary characters, they can solve puzzles, invent pastimes, take part in aggressive, even 'fatal' encounters ('kill' in cyberspace may mean blocking access or connection), participate in romantic activities, or have 'disembodied sex' (compu-sex, net.sleazing, or net-sex).

The first MUD was named after multi-user dungeons; it was created at the University of Essex in England, in 1980. The setting for this MUD comprised treasures, warriors, wizards, and dwarfs, and is known as The Land. Subsequent generations of MUDs are organized around different imaginary settings. Objects can be designed in MUSEs (multi-user simulation environments) and MOOs (MUD object oriented); more recently, in some of them, it is possible to incorporate images into the virtual space. The codes that are used also provide for the designing of 'automatons,' simulations that can mimic a real phenomenon (Rheingold, 1993). These activities may have dimensions of scientific investigation, or they may be educational or simply recreational and ludic, all of which makes these spaces deserving of the name multi-user dimensions or domains.

Those who have studied MUDs agree with the premise that the major attraction for users is the possibility of a change of *identity*. The participant can conceal his or her own identity, pretending to be someone else or even producing various characters at the same time or in different contexts.

In both the MUD and its variants (MOOs, MUSEs and others), the first thing a user must do, in fact, is create this identity (also known as 'virtual persona'); only then does interaction become possible. In this scenario, the participants can communicate in various ways: sending electronic messages which are stored in the participant's email box; using public bulletin boards; sending a page to any place within the MUD; or speaking directly to another person in different modes. These are the 'say' modes, in which all those in the 'room' can hear, and 'whisper,' and speak more privately to one person in particular. By means of 'pose' or 'emote' an expression can be indicated 'wordlessly'. Some have described this form of communication as out-of-body language. 'Pose' is particularly important in constructing a certain 'atmosphere' or context. If, for example, in MIT's MediaMOO, I wished to express through my character, Natalia, a cordial gesture toward my interlocutor, I would have to write, 'emote is smiling at you.' Then, 'Natalia is smiling at you' would appear on the screen.

In terms of what makes communication possible, it depends on who is available in the 'room' at the same time the communication occurs – thus, the interaction tends to be contingent and ephemeral.

This does not necessarily mean that long-term relationships cannot be established, but the fluctuations in attendance at a site suggest the constructionist, changing and ephemeral nature of both the social relationships and the processes of objectivation and sedimentation in these constructions. In contrast with other scenarios which also allow synchronic communication, such as the IRC (Internet relay chat), in MUDs participants are expected to create objects and modify their environment, and what they build remains to be utilized by other participants. In this sense, cooperation is vital to the existence of this medium.

There is a very marked tendency to include images in these spaces. Although some of the reflections here expressed could be pertinent to this type of space, I believe that the inclusion of images in the communicative exchange adds a specificity that merits special treatment. A fundamental aspect of the MUDs is that their existence would not be possible if not for their basically narrative nature. Everything that 'is' in this space has to have an existence in words, a narratability. These spaces have been seen as privileged spaces, as laboratories of social constructionism for many designer users and closet transvestites. In this chapter, I will address several issues related to the concept of identity and its construction through the act of communication, which is in turn made possible by a text-based MUD.

Both MUDs and IRC provide a space for a sort of transcultural traffic. This traffic, in turn, generates forms of cybernetic cultures (cyborg cultures) that emerge out of the conditions of the space: its forms of access, fictitious identities, rapid interactions oriented fundamentally to the present, and almost exclusive use of words to develop a context for the dialogue. Recently, chatting using avatars has proliferated on-line. Avatar chats take place in three-dimensional virtual worlds which you can explore and in which you hear background noises. The avatar is an image that represents you in the virtual world. An avatar is a cartoon-like representation used to make people 'visible' while chatting and interacting with others. The avatars have a repertoire of expressions and gestures such as 'smiling', 'waving', 'frowning', and so on and sometimes conversation is displayed in balloons or in a separate window.

As in MUDs, in IRC the first thing a participant must do is select a name by which to be known in the various virtual encounters. Elizabeth Reid (1991), in her study of forms of communication and of community in the IRC, tells us that most of the interactions that take place there are related not to business or work, but rather to play. This implies that users do not construct themselves according to the conventions of 'real' social contexts outside the IRC scenario; instead, within cybernetic space, little by little, the user develops his or her personal cultural game with the other participants. Reid concludes that by deconstructing conventional social frontiers and making possible the construction of a context for experimentation with different forms of self-representation, the IRC is a postmodern phenomenon.

What mechanisms are used to deconstruct the assumptions underlying conventional forms of communication? It has been suggested that these cybersystems have the following distinctive aspects that differentiate them from more traditional forms of communication: anonymity, an absence of mechanisms for self-regulation, little scope for drama, and few social cues. Anonymity reduces self-regulation and, since this form of communication depends entirely upon the written word in a synchronic interaction, it substantially reduces social cues as permanent contextual references (Kiesler *et al.*, 1984, cited in Reid, 1991).

There is an image that is constructed in several ways and is constantly repeated in essays that attempt to understand these spaces – the assumption of an 'absence of context' as a base for the emergence of new cybernetic contexts. In contrast, I would suggest that cyberspace allows a confluence of presences and absences of context. That is to say, although social interactions are constructed in space (as are the symbolic cues that make them possible and intelligible), the *dis*embodied social experience is also sustained by another type of materiality, that of the physical/real body with its socio-semiotic markers that are historical and have multiple determinations.

The body/other relationship mediated by technological apparatus has been represented by various *imaginaires*. Stone (1995: 96–7) comments:

Whereas, prior to electronic communication, an agent maintained proximity through texts bearing the agent's seal, and the agency the texts implied could be enforced through human delegates, in the time of electronic speech proximity is maintained through technology, and agency becomes invisible. Users of the telephone eventually took for granted that they were speaking to another person 'on' the telephone. It was this sense of assurance in the presence of a specific bounded unitary agency, grounded by a voice, that undergirds a gradual refiguration of the meaning of proximity. With the advent of electronically prostheticized speech, agency was grounded not by a voice but by an iconic representation of a voice, compressed in bandwidth and volume and distorted by the limitations of the early carbon-granule transducers, so as to be something more than a signature or seal on a text but far less than an embodied physical vocalization. Agency was proximate when the authorizing body could be manifested through technological prosthetics. This technological manifestation in turn implied that the relationship between agency and authorizing body had become more discursive. This process of changing the relationship between agency and authorizing body into a discursive one eventually produced the subjectivity that could fairly unproblematically inhabit the virtual spaces of the nets.

 What implications do these transformations have for the notion of identity from the point of view of psychology? Do the traditional psychological assumptions about what identity is merely *(in)form* the way we represent ourselves in various social contexts, or does social experience *form* our identity? More than that, what is the relationship between the 'real' identity and the 'virtual' person? Should we still be talking about identity, anyway?

Identity on stage

 In general terms, social psychology's assumptions associated with the concept of personal identity can be summed up, according to Ignacio Martín-Baró (1985), in four statements:

1. Identity exists in reference to a world.
2. It asserts itself in the interpersonal relationship.
3. It is relatively stable.
4. It is a product as much of society as of the individual's actions.

Let us pause for a moment to examine this set of assumptions. They presuppose that the individual's context – and in particular, the most immediate interpersonal relationships, those that link the self to a not-self (that is, to the other) – reveals itself as a reality of meaning. That reality of meaning is, of necessity, plural (ethnic groups, the individual's position within the family configuration, gender and class differences, and so on). However, it is assumed that within that reality, in spite of its plurality, the person's self is consistent. Given the oneness of personal formation and the world, transformations in the context will be accompanied by variations in the self throughout its existence. Nevertheless, there is an insistence that these changes do not negate the continuity of the self, and do not contradict the assertion that the self is stable.

In contrast, the performative model of the self that underlies the notion of symbolic interaction assumes that the identity is a construct that emerges in direct relation to particular circumstances. Identity is seen as 'the face' that the subject shows by his or her performance within certain contexts. This leads us to a notion of identity as a strictly circumstantial and contingent construct. To some, this proposal is unacceptable, in that it suggests understanding the subject as an entity that has lost the fundamental part of the social being – that is, her or his identity (*idem*, the same... the same entity) – and is therefore on the path to imminent disintegration as a subject.

It would seem that these two ways of seeing identity are irreconcilable, and indeed they are, in that they constitute theorizations built upon the assumption of face-to-face communication and interaction. This dichotomy does not help in dealing with interaction mediated by electronic communication devices. In that sort of interaction, the face-to-face relationship is supplanted by the face-*inter*face relationship, which multiplies exponentially as the number of participants who happen to be in the same virtual space increases. I would suggest, then, that the construction of identity by means of CMCs in synchronic time allows for the coexistence of assumptions that would seem to be contradictory and mutually exclusive. Understanding this proposition requires that we consider two issues, which in the case of life in the MUD are intimately related: simulation (also known by its variant 'VR,' or virtual reality) and interactivity. Both are to be seen as communication, acting, and play.

I play, therefore I am

Sherry Turkle (1995) has identified two fundamental elements of simulation. In the first place, the vividness of the representation demands fuller attention from the subject during the interaction. Turkle gives as an example the crocodiles at Disneyland, whose bright colours and repeated movements make them appear more alive to the watching visitor than the crocodiles the same visitor may find living in a zoo. If a virtual object is going to catch the subject's attention, it has to present itself in such a way as to seduce the subject's curiosity. In the case of text-based MUDs, the challenge is even greater, because the portrayal rests entirely upon the narrative arts. The subject must actively strive to come up with the best possible way to construct his or her objects and virtual persona so that they will evoke what is 'real,' but at the same time surpass it. In the second place, the simulation takes on a clarity that contrasts dramatically with polluted physical reality. The subject creates the environment for interaction by constructing a certain atmosphere for the communicative exchange. In addition, the subject does not have to risk having his or her facial features, race, and so on (or those of her or his interlocutor) impose experiences of prejudice, disdain, marginalization, and so on upon the communicative exchange. Neither does the subject have to deal with a threatening or negative scenario like a good many of the daily scenarios in which we have to speak.

From all of this, we can deduce that there is a somewhat odd relationship between the simulated and the physical/real: the simulation is not a replica of the physical/real, even though it may allude to it. This places simulation on a level with artistic creation. In this regard, John Casti (1997) notes that in spite of their differences, Plato and Aristotle agreed that the essential aspect of art lies in its difference from reality. He adds that nevertheless, there are many disagreements between these two philosophers as to whether we can learn anything from this difference. Aristotle, unlike Plato, thought it possible to learn through the creation of imitations.

All this suggests, then, that the imitation of an action, carried out in a setting, can produce an action that is similar to that carried out in real life, but under circumstances that make it possible to learn from the situation. This is the basic premise of the techniques associated with role playing in psychotherapy. However, when we speak of the therapeutic setting, there is an assumption that the role of the therapist is to facilitate reinterpretations of the situation in a way that will be productive for the participants. In contrast, when we speak of the experience of communication in virtual spaces in which the subject becomes hooked on interactive communicational relationships, thereby engaging in a self-representation that is different from what she or he is in the physical/real world (for example, representing oneself as a man when one is a woman, as an extrovert when one is usually shy and quiet, and so on), the experience of reflexivity does not necessarily pass through the filter of a third person. Nevertheless, whether MUDs can be psychotherapeutic settings has little to do with the presence of therapists in the strict sense of the word. Although there have been cases of people who have acted as therapists in these scenarios, the therapeutic value of these spaces has more to do with the fact that MUDs encourage projection and transference. Turkle (1995: 207) even suggests that these processes occur for the same reasons they arise in Freudian psychoanalysis:

> Analysts sit behind their patients so they can become disembodied voices. Patients are given space to project onto the analyst thoughts and feelings from the past. In MUDs, the lack of information about the real person to whom one is talking, the silence into which one types, the absence of visual cues, all these encourage projection. This situation leads to exaggerated likes and dislikes, to idealization and demonization.

The virtual interpersonal experience inserts itself within a spatial metaphor. Interaction takes place in spaces that simulate 'known' places, such as a library, a coffee shop, a games room, and so on. The atmosphere is constructed through a detailed description of objects, the 'emote' code we have mentioned previously, and 'emoticons.' For example, :) means that the person is smiling, : (that he or she is sad. Thus, the drama metaphor is also activated, at times even more intensely than in a physical/real relationship, if we wish to attract and hold the attention of the interlocutor.

If we add the element of safety, which acting in these types of spaces assumes, in comparison with acting in real life, we have a scenario that easily evokes the experience of simulation as play. George Herbert Mead's Role Theory (1965) is particularly relevant, especially if we reconsider the play phase in the formation of personal identity. Two matters are worthy of our attention. First, in the play phase, the child can play any role, behave in any way, without regard to context; second, the child constantly needs the other to tell him which behaviours are appropriate in specific contexts. According to Mead's theory, personal identity is fixed in that phase in which we have internalized the 'generalized other,' the set of rules and roles that have been duly contextualized. In psychoanalytic terms, at that point we would have a subject inscribed in the symbolic order. In the MUD experience, we have both phases functioning simultaneously, and the effect is both a product and a process: the subject as a complex communicational network. The network metaphor in this particular case is from the work of William J. Mitchell (1995: 29–30), who claims that the body becomes an apparatus with a wireless connection to an electronic communication apparatus:

> By this point in the evolution of miniature electronic products, you will have acquired a collection of interchangeable, snap-in organs connected by exonerves. Where these electronic organs interface to your sensory receptors and your muscles, there will be continuous bit-spits across the carbon/silicon gap. And where they bridge to the external digital world, your nervous system will plug into the worldwide digital net. You will have become a modular, reconfigurable, infinitely extensible cyborg.

This leads me to suggest the need to understand the experience in these spaces at two levels, each represented by a particular metaphor that indicates both the process and its product: the mediation/territory metaphor and the spatialisation/nomad metaphor.

The subject as a territorialized/nomadic network

While the politics of the state require territorialization, which produces an enclosed space, the nomadic perspective is that of a fighting machine that breaks closure, thus permitting an open space (Deleuze and Guatarri, 1985). As a result, the territorialized subject is the subject of the boundary, becoming the frontier that separates the territory from the world:

> The subject is, in the first place, an individual, a border that separates from the rest: a topo-chronological boundary that separates an interior/past from an exterior/future. The interior/past is the part of the medium that has already been incorporated; the exterior/future is the part of the medium yet to be incorporated. At the physical level the borders are defined in terms. of energy (the case of a crystal is complex, because we don't really know what the line is that distinguishes it from a virus). At the biological level the borders are defined in terms of genetic information, both in individuals of primary species, or one-celled organisms, and in those of secondary species, or multi-celled organisms. At the psycho-social level they are defined in terms of linguistic information (the border between animal and

human societies is also somewhat indeterminate, because we don't really know where to draw the line between zoosemiotics and human language). (Jesús Ibáñez, 1985: 272)

So we are dealing with an embodied subject with multireferential semiotic markers, but who remains a subject as long as he or she retains a capacity for reflexivity or self-referentiality. The interior boundary makes self-reference or reflection possible:

> At the psycho-social level the subject's self-reflexivity is empowered. The subject thinks about himself or herself insofar as she or he is split in two by a reflective surface, first an imaginary one (a mirror) and then a symbolic one (language). The subject becomes lost in this game of reflections and becomes the desire of the desire of the other/Other, Father, or Symbolic Order, in symbolic identifications. The subject can recover only if he or she assumes a contradictory stance, keeping her or his distance and going along with the other, yet abolishing those identifications (narcissism); if he or she oscillates between desire and self-interest; if she or he accepts the father-role or castration and at the same time becomes committed to a transfinite process of going beyond the exterior and interior boundaries that castration imposes. (ibid.: 274)

Self-reference makes possible the so-called agency of the subject, an agency filled with value judgements: '[the subject] decrees that what he or she likes is good, what he or she does not like is bad; she or he spits out or projects the bad and swallows or introjects the good' (ibid.). We are dealing, then, with the ethological or axiological dimension of the subject. We are also alluding here to the three dimensions of subjectivity, according to Edgar Morin (1983): exclusion (ontological), self-reference (logical), and self-transcendence (ethological).

Rom Harré (1983) reminds us that our personal being is the product of appropriations and transformations from social sources, including the local theories regarding selves. Identity-formatting projects are aimed at the production of uniqueness; this process requires cognitive reflection, or self-knowledge, and reflexive action, or self-control, depending on the assumptions of local knowledge as to what a 'self' is. This means that the psychological conditions for the development of the subject must be provided by a self-reference apparatus, which can only be given in social relationships (whether 'real' or 'virtual') during the semiotic discursive processes.

These processes unfold on a computer screen when the embodied subject transmutes – that is, changes, in transit, into a disembodied subject – only partially and temporarily. This disembodied subject can, as we have seen, take on multiple representations, appropriating the space to himself or herself while metamorphosing into a nomadic subject. In the virtual setting the subject reproduces what she or he is; but also what he or she would like to be, and what she or he would not want to be in the real physical world, as well. Turkle's (1995) ethnographic work, deals with this very subject: the various ways in which a person interprets his or her life in MUDs. In short, there are three uses for the virtual experience:

1. as an escape
2. as a way of attaining a degree of social mobility
3. as a means of resistance.

Some people have revealed that in their virtual lives they can escape from a stifling reality, albeit only temporarily. Others talk about the possibility of experiencing a degree of social mobility that is part of the *imaginaire* of the 'American Dream' but is not accessible to all in real life. In the MUD a person can create objects, turn them into possessions, and develop a representation of her- or himself with a higher social status. Likewise, the subject can be gaining privileges while developing and demonstrating his or her programming talents. In addition, there are those who see their virtual life as a way of resisting the conventional organization and significance of social life, in that they are able to construct alternative worlds. In the auto-referential communicational network, the subject sitting before a screen travels about within the boundaries, and so does the so-called reality.

It has been said that taking on a particular identity means taking on at the same time a universe of meaning. This, then, implies an ethics and an aesthetics of the social relationships that have shaped that identity, so that taking on a particular identity will also mean taking on that universe of meaning as a horizon of possibilities whose moorings emerge precisely when self-referentiality expands inside and outside the screen, inside and outside the person. The relationship between the virtual personae and the real person could be represented as a sort of heteronomous/autonomous self. Each virtual self has its own logic of organization and reflexivity, yet maintains another level of organization with the real self. The virtual selves somehow interrogate and simultaneously explain their identity-formatting projects to the embodied self, and vice versa. Ethno-graphic studies in this area show that the person is able to recreate the experience narratively, putting into words what he or she likes or does not like about their virtual identities and the relationships they establish with the other in virtual space.

The potential to learn from these experiences is provided, on the one hand, by the possibility of the unfolding or transmutation of the territory to space, and, on the other, by the capability of self-reflexivity. The subject relates to his or her virtual personae in a variety of ways – sometimes pleased with them and sometimes in open conflict and contradiction – but in any case a process of semiotic continuity/discontinuity between the subject and the virtual personae is gener-ated. In short, as disembodied subjects we represent ourselves in various ways in virtual space but, at the same time, this virtual experi-ence continues to interrogate the territorialized (embodied) subject, keeping up a sort of extended conversation through the self-reflection that is now unfolding or transmuting from the open space to the terri-tory. The transmutation, of necessity, goes through the ethological (axiological, valorative) dimension. From this perspective we could then look at the phenomenon of the need to 'come out of the closet,' a digital closet. I refer to that moment when, in spite of our virtual personae, we feel compelled to identify ourselves to the other in terms of territory. This exercise goes from revealing our demographic features (name, sex, profession, and so on) to moving towards meeting our virtual interlocutor face to face. Mitchell (1995: 12) suggests this metaphor by saying that 'There are games of constructing electronic closets, and moments for coming out of them.' He also suggests that students of cyberspace culture might do well to take a look at gay liter-ature. It would seem that we are facing the need to be recognized as an embodied body (a body 'in the flesh'), even though that body may be, as Paul Virilio (1995) says, a 'terminal body'; the ultimate reduction of urban territory. This body does not place us in vacuums or absences of contexts, but rather in complex multireferential contexts in the midst of which the self-referential subject debates her or his own signification and that of the other.

This would qualify CMC as an intermediate space between the spoken and the written word, between interpersonal communication and the mass communication media, between the 'ins' and the 'outs'; but even more, as an experience that destabilizes the assumptions of absolute dichotomy in these categories. To my way of thinking, in this game of boundaries, this is what makes the CMC experience one that could be categorized as postmodern. Emphasizing this aspect – more than the *imaginaire* of the 'vacuum' and contextual 'absence' – makes manifest the importance of the political dimension in the study of these systems.

The *socialités* that are generated in cyberspace are electrodigitalized tribes – disembodied tribes, to be sure, but as I said before, only partially and temporarily. I use the term *socialité* in the sense in which it is employed by Michel Maffesoli (1993). Sociality is an indispensable aspect of communication (assuming correspondence and solidarity) that contributes to the emergence of contemporary social forms that are fundamentally heterogeneous and nomadic in open space.

When we take a look at 'that thing' that we call cyberspace, we find a multiplicity of 'social aggregates,' virtual communities that are very real, protean neo-tribes with a variety of organizational and functional forms. Some are more conventional, hierarchical, centralized. Others, more anarchic, make experiments with radical democracy that are deeply worrisome to the centres of power (for a discussion of tensions in the forms of citizenship made possible by means of CMC, see Figueroa-Sarriera, 1997). Hakim Bey (1991: 108) expresses it as follows:

> Thus *within the Net* there has begun to emerge a shadowy sort of *counter-Net*, which we will call the Web (as if the Net were fishing-net and the *Web* were spider-webs woven through the interstices and broken sections of the Net). Generally we'll use the term *Web* to refer to the alternate horizontal open structure of info exchange, the non-hierarchic network, and reserve the term *counter-Net* to indicate clandestine illegal and rebellious use of the Web, including actual data-piracy and other forms of leeching off the Net itself. Net, Web and counter-Net are all parts of the same whole pattern-complex – they blur into each other at innumerable points. The terms are not meant to define areas but to suggest tendencies.

The *socialité*/space relationship takes on a clandestine form, according to Maffesoli. The *socialités* are predesignated not in the zoning codes of the urban planners, or in official policies, or in plans from the capital. Even so, this should not lead us to conclude, as Maffesoli does, that they are 'beyond' or 'over and above' politics. Rather, the *socialités* suggest an invitation to an unavoidable reflection about politics – a staging of what is more and more evident: that Modernism is built on the destabilization of social, political and economic assumptions. Even though political officials do not predesignate the cyber*socialités*, they are unswerving in their zeal to discipline them, reinscribe them, and reorganize them within the diverse projects of governability.

This experience, in all its complexity, is what is possible today through CMC. It is a system that provides the experience of communication as a body in expansion – in the same sense that Maffesoli proposed – as *unicity*, which is not reductive unity but rather the plurality of the mutually influential elements. It is a system that permits the organic experience of the hybridity that destabilizes modern, conventional ways of thinking, and that even pushes to the limit the problems that the state has attempted historically to resolve by means of various technologies of domination, subjugating nature and/or reducing otherness, consigning that which is other to subordinate situations. If cyberpsychology becomes a field of study, it should incorporate the political dimension into its analysis to avoid being caught, on the one hand, in the hypocritical trap of axiological neutrality; and on the other, in the neopositivistic reductionism that fixes the object of study at the so-called interpersonal level.

References

Beamish, A. (1995) *Communities On-Line: Community Based Computer Networks*. MA Thesis, City Planning, MIT, http://alberti.mit.edu/arch/4.2 07/anneb/thesis/toc.html

Bey, H. (1991) *T.A.Z. The Temporary Autonomous Zone, Ontological Anarchy, Poetic Terrorism*. New York: Autonomedia.

Casti, J. (1998) *Would-Be Worlds: How Simulation is Changing the Frontiers of Science*. New York–Chichester–Brisbane–Toronto–Singapore–Weinheim: John Wiley & Sons.

Deleuze, G. and Guatarri, F. (1985) *El Anti-Edipo. Capitalismo y Esquizofrenia*. Barcelona, Buenos Aires, México: Ediciones Paidós.

Figueroa-Sarriera, H.J. (1997) 'Netanos y ciudadanos cyborgs: Un viaje al "más acá"', *bordes*, 4/5: 4–18.

Figueroa-Sarriera, H.J. and López, Mª. M. (1993) 'El sujeto descentrado y algunas de sus implicaciones para las Ciencias Sociales, o ¿dónde vives tú, finalmente?', *Revista Cayey*, **XXV** (73): 13–17.

Gergen, K. (1991) *The Saturated Self: Dilemmas of Identity in Contemporary Life*. New York: Basic Books.

Harré R. (1983) *Personal Being: A Theory for Individual Psychology*. Oxford: Blackwell.

Ibáñez, J. (1985) *Del Algoritmo al Sujeto. Perspectivas de la Investigación Social*. México-España-Argentina-Colombia: Editorial Siglo XXI.

Kiesler, S., Siegel, J. and McGuire, T.W. (1984) 'Social psychological aspects of computer-mediated communication', *American Psychologist*, **39**(10): 1123–34.

Lifton, R.J. (1993) *The Protean Self: Human Resilience*. New York: Basic Books.

Maffesoli, M. (1993) *El Conocimiento Ordinario*. Mexico: Fondo de Cultura Económica.

Martin, E. (1994) *Flexible Bodies: Tracking Immunity in American Culture from the Days of Polio to the Age of Aids*. Boston: Beacon Press.

Martín-Baró, I. (1985) *Acción e Ideología. Psicolología Social desde Centroamérica*. San Salvador: UCA Editores.

Mead, G.H. (1965) *Espíritu, Persona y Sociedad*. Buenos Aires: Editorial Paidós.

Mitchell, W.J. (1995) *City of Bits: Space, Place and the Infobahan*. Massachusetts: Massachusetts Institute of Technology.

Morin, E. (1983) *El Método 2: La Vida de la Vida*. Madrid: Cátedra.

Reid, E. (1991) *Electropolis: Communication and Community in Inter Relay Chat*. Honour Thesis, University of Melbourne, Department of History. Gopher://wiretap. spies.com/00/Library/Cyber/electrop.txt

Rheingold, H. (1993) *The Virtual Community: Homesteading on the Electronic Frontier*. New York: Addison-Wesley.

Stone, A.R. (1995) *The War of Desire and Technology at the Close of the Mechanical Age*. Cambridge-London: MIT Press.

Turkle, S. (1995) *Life on the Screen: Identity in the Age of the Internet*. New York: Simon & Schuster.

Virilio, P. (1995) *La Velocidad de Liberación*. Buenos Aires: Ediciones Manantial.

CHAPTER 9

Electronic Networks and Subjectivity

Steven D. Brown

The man in the moon
Came down too soon
And asked the way to Norwich;
He went by the south
And burned his mouth
By eating cold plum porridge.
Traditional

Bestiary contents

When at its most effective, fear works by degrees of subtlety. In collections of children's nursery rhymes, the man in the moon is still depicted as an English Regency gentleman tinged a strange blue, presumably by the unbearable coldness of his lunar origin. Perhaps it is exposure to this absolute cold that is in some way responsible for his odd reaction (the burning) to 'cold' plum porridge. Or maybe it is because of his descent 'too soon' to the earth – a cosmic version of 'the bends'? Images come to mind of astronauts clutching their placenta-like air supplies as they are hurriedly transferred for decontamination. These are feet that have walked on, hands that have touched the soil of another world. But astronauts are at least returning home – who knows what reasons the man in the moon has for coming down, what his plans are in seeking directions to Norwich? And in the absence of any clear intent it is easy to find all of this deeply threatening.

Monsters are omens, portents. They foretell the occurrence of some ill or symbolize a form of disturbance in the order of things. This disturbance is etched into their very appearance – a confusion of organs and limbs, the coexistence of 'impossible' characteristics. Human–animal hybrids (changelings, werewolves), the 'living dead' (zombies animated by mystic powers, Frankenstein's creation given life by science), creatures like the Wendigo or the Golem made of seemingly inert raw materials (ice, mud). Monsters are literally physical 'category errors'. More than this, they are the very embodiment of a force which threatens to undo all categories and divisions. If we perceive that the man in the moon comes down 'too soon' it is because his very appearance threatens to disrupt the security of the systems of thought upon which we rely to make sense of what goes on around us.

So the problem is really how to manage this threat posed by the monstrous. Herein lies the power of nursery rhymes, to make monstrosity cut a mundane figure. For in repeating his odd tale, the man in the moon becomes an almost comic figure. A funny little man who can be left to flounder alone on the road to Norwich. This potential transformation of uncanniness to mundaneity has long been recognized. In the medieval world, for example, the figure of the hermaphrodite, the a-gendered product of a superabundant nature, was a familiar concern to medical and theological authorities (Rubin, 1995). The hermaphrodite betrayed not so much the fragility of the natural order (understood as capable of producing such mixtures), but rather a more ordinary offence against social order; the inability to fully engage in a (hetero)sexual relationship with a wife or husband invalidated any marriage. This could lead to the hermaphrodite undergoing surgery to either remove or else release a set of genitals, according to a determination of which were the dominant organs. The problem of medieval hermaphroditism was therefore a discreet one of deciding whether the person should become fully female or male:

> The attitude betrays no moral outrage, simply the need to define a single sexual persona and impose on it a heterosexual orientation. What is curious... is its wholesomeness, as compared with the treatment it would receive in a popular publication today. No moral deviance is suggested, only a rather uncomfortable and inconvenient social fact, a fact about identity. (Rubin, 1995: 104)

The hermaphrodite then, posed a problem, an 'inconvenient social fact' to be addressed. In so doing, the element of monstrosity which visibly defines hermaphroditism – the violation of the division of biological sexes – was domesticated, dissolved into the relative invisibility of quotidian social ordering.

Domestication remains the fate of modern 'monsters'. Take 'Dolly', the genetically cloned sheep. Her appearance brought debate about genetic modification and cloning to a ferment in the UK. Yet by the time she was able to produce her first proper fleece – which was shorn and knitted into a sweater for a charity auction – Dolly's monstrosity had been gently erased, replaced by an image of unthreatening docility. As the power of modern technoscience to reveal previously unimaginable 'inconvenient social facts' grows, so too, seemingly, does the inventiveness with which these selfsame facts are drained of their apparent horror and reduced to the level of commonplaces.

But what of ourselves? What happens when it is we, and not other animal hybrids, who are revealed as monsters? For what other words could be more apposite to describe a 'ventilated pregnant cadaver', kept alive until 'its' fetus comes to term (Caspar, 1994), or a rapist who 'deliberately draws out' a naïve alter from a woman with multiple personality disorder (Stone, 1995)? Here what is posed is indisputably a psychological question: *What are we becoming*? A question which raises anxieties that no one nursery rhyme can easily dispel.

It is entirely possible that psychology lacks an adequate vocabulary to even begin to articulate such an enquiry, since its very premise calls into question that which is most taken for granted – the autonomous, rational bounded human subject. Yet cognitive psychology, for all its difficulties, has always been concerned with how processes of perceiving and managing 'problems' constitute one of the primary features of human life. If we now grasp this recovery of the quotidian from the uncanny as a practice which involves the use of a highly particular set of *social technics*, we are led towards a very different analysis of how 'inconvenient social facts' are treated. We begin to discern something of the outlines of how social ordering is secured.

Transhumanism and its discontents

Let us now name this monster whose tracks we are beginning to follow: the transhuman. Spawned by the convergence of technics with 'meat', the transhuman is a creature that lives somewhere between our notions of the natural and the artificial, the real and the virtual. It is composed of an ever shifting array of materials – part biology, part machine – being the sum of a series of relations which elide any simple categorization. Transhumans take on many guises: 'partially live' patients standing ready to be harvested for organ donations; an Australian artist with a 'third limb' controlled by remote access; Malaysian women clad in white anti-static overalls battling with the were-demons they see in the microscopes of a Western microchip manufacturer (see Hogle, 1995; Stelarc, 1997; Ong, 1988). If we understand them at all, it is in terms of the kinds of *interactivity* they make possible. Here, a strange interaction between plastic, blood and flesh; or else between sensors and baud width; there a collision between spirits and modern work technologies. This is what we are becoming – weaves of elements drawn together by the rhythms and pulses of biology, sociality and technology. Or, if you prefer, the outcome of chains of mediation that occur in vast networks that ride roughshod over the crumbling distinctions between nature and society (a scenario much discussed within the sociology of translation – see Latour, 1993; Brown and Capdevila, 1998; Law and Hassard, 1998).

Is this not to overstate things *just a little*? These transhumans may be incarnations of an unsettling future–present, but they are in no way representative of what we take to be 'ordinary life'. Yet *something* is happening. We have become more aware of the omnipresence of technics in our everyday human affairs, most noticeably in the form of information technologies. We take it for granted that we may step into and out of vast streams of data (telephones, banking networks, Internet) which are never twice the same. We grasp, however incompletely, that knowing who and what we are is dependent upon the power of technics to make us visible to ourselves, in the form of all kind of computerized imaging and surveillance technologies (Lury, 1998), the vicissitudes of electronic community (Poster, 1995) or even representations of identity as encrypted with the 'originary code' of the human genome (Nelkin and Lindee, 1995). What then is happening is a shift from the metaphors of lineage and continuity, to a conception of the world as evolving by way of codes and networks.

Quite how we came upon this language is a matter of some concern. One convincing account by Bowker (1993) has it that in the 1940s and 1950s, the emerging discipline of cybernetics sought to reconstruct contemporary understandings of form and organization in terms of information, feedback and systems. The promise of these terms is that, in a very concrete way, they cut across the ancient dualisms of mind and body, intention and act. Both organism and machine can be described as equivalent 'focal units', comprising a set of feedback loops marked off from the environment within a clear system boundary. And these units may be in turn nested Russian doll-like within systems of ever greater complexity up to the level of the cosmos itself. What this means is that cybernetics is able to provide a common language for the biologist and the engineer, a language which comes to displace physics as the one true science upon which all other individual sciences are but simple analogies.

The world we subsequently come to inhabit – what Haraway (1995) disparagingly affirms as the 'New World Order' – is irrevocably shaped by cybernetics. When all possible forms of organization, from the genome to the nation state, can be administered as networks of information flows, then the very governance of life itself becomes *a problem of coding* (Guattari, 1984; Haraway, 1991; Crewe, 1997), to be addressed by ever more sophisticated types of engineering. The mathematization of space, begun in the Classical era with Newton, Descartes and Leibniz, then fully ignited by the science of thermodynamics in the mid-nineteenth century, comes to full fruition with the modern cybernetic concern with information (for example, Wiener, 1931). Information – that piece of difference from noise that we understand to constitute order – is understood as the very stuff of life. Small wonder then that the overarching problem within the New World Order is how to shape and direct flows of information by managing problems of coding and connection. In this way, the impulse towards globalization acquires full moral force, since that which is not connected becomes indistinguishable from noise: it is by definition cut away from life as such. This legitimates the extension of global commerce such as agribusiness under the guise of 'recuperating' failing third world markets. All must be allocated their place within the modern spaces of calculation.

What then is 'our' place? It is that place, presumably, that has been prepared for us by the mathematization of the human subject by cognitive psychology, an operation made necessary by the more general translation of the world into the universal language of cybernetics. But this putting into place of the human is fundamentally unstable, since it is itself located within roughly the same space which is shared by all other information rich forms of 'life' (both organic and machinic). There is no longer any fundamental difference between humans and others. It is this indeterminacy with regard to the precise location of human individuals as users of electronic networks that is so celebrated by the literature on cyberspace (for example, Benedikt, 1992; Heim, 1993), with Gibson's *neuromancer* serving as the *locus classicus*. This is, of course, only half the story, since cybernetics makes it equally difficult to draw up the division between humanity and nature, a point whose full implications have been repeatedly stressed by the ecofeminist movement (for example, Shiva, 1989; Plumwood, 1993). What we are left with is less a clear place in the order of things and more an erratic trajectory through the evolutionary history of the planet, the falling parabola of the (trans)human.

Despite this, indeterminacy has its own attraction. The Extropian movement, for example, regards the fluidity of the human as, ultimately, its source of salvation. Crudely put, extropianism extends the logic of thermodynamics, with its emphasis on the gradual disorganization of the cosmos into a state of complete entropy (the 'heat death' of the universe scenario), to its bitter conclusion. It is argued that in order to survive this inexorable drift towards entropy, the human must evolve into increasingly more complex forms of information-rich organization:

> Life and intelligence should never stagnate; it can re-order, transform and transcend its limits in an unlimited progession... The extropian goal is our own expansion and progress without end. Humanity must not stagnate: to halt our burgeoning move forward, upward, outward, would be a betrayal of the dynamic inherent in life and consciousness... Let us blast out of old forms, our ignorance, our weakness, and our mortality. The future belongs to posthumanity. (More, 1994)

Note that 'human life and consciousness' here refers to a particular patterning of information, one which might therefore become transferred across into ever more complex arrangements of materials, such as organic machines. Taking their cue from Hans Morevec's rhetoric around the 'uploading of consciousness' into technology (see Figueroa-Sarriera, 1995), the extropians envisage an evolutionary leap 'forward! upward! outward!' for the human, who thereby literally transcends or overcomes their own condition through a new alliance with biotechnics.

However, as Ansell Pearson outlines at some length (1997), this position is based on a misappropriation of both evolutionary theory and Nietzschean thought (Nietzsche being infamous for envisaging the 'death of man' and the coming of the 'overman', an image later taken up in the poststructuralism of Foucault, 1970 and Deleuze, 1988). If there is a single motto to be derived from evolution (itself a dubious proposition) then it is probably that simplicity rather than complexity confers the best survival advantage (think of viruses or bacteria). By the same token, what Nietzsche has in mind is less the leaving behind of the 'meat' of embodiment and rather a perpetual attempt to repeatedly go beyond the limits constituted by every attempt at establishing the proper place of the human. Indeed, there is a sense in which transhumanism, at least in its extropian form, simply replicates and redoubles the rapacious will-to-order that characterizes late modern times. In an otherwise rare moment of clarity, Arthur and Marilouise Kroker (1996) describe our current circumstances as the 'flesh eating 90s'. They situate the rhetoric of transhumanism within the markedly humanist discourse of Marshall McLuhan's hypothesis of electronic media as an extension and argumentation of the powers of humankind:

> In the 60s, McLuhan theorised that the technological media of communication were in his term, 'extensions of man', electronic outer-ings of the central nervous system. But that was then, and this is now. Because in the 90s it's exactly the opposite. Not technology as an exten-sion of the human sensorium, but the human species as a hotwired extension of digital reality. No longer the will to technology, but the vanishing of technology into the will to virtuality. Hacking human flesh by way of artificial intelligence, virtual reality processors, and the violent force-field of the electronic media is the sure and certain way by which virtuality actually eats the human body, becoming digital flesh at the end of the century. (Kroker and Kroker, 1996: 139)

Their point is cogent. The encoding of the body into information fit for virtual reality systems is, in effect, the harvesting of the human by electronic technologies: flesh eating. Technology does not augment, but actually consumes 'us'. Once coding and mapping is complete, there is an awful lot of surplus meat leftover. What we 'are' is effectively swallowed up in a will to extend the sphere of the virtual.

So where does that leave 'us' (presuming that the term still desig-nates anything in particular)? It is at this point that Haraway's (1991) vision of the 'cyborg' – whether we read it as metaphor, fantasy or fact (Hamilton, 1997) – becomes valuable for its insight into what we might term a kind of cybernetic existential condition. We can see ourselves as somewhat ambiguous creatures who are thrown into a way of being which is intrinsically 'shameful' (I am here drawing on Kosofsky Sedgwick and Frank, 1995). Confronted by a natural world already ravaged and exploited, facing a future whose disclosure appears increasingly to rely upon the inscrutable vicissitudes of technology, holding our breath while something akin to the final names of God are deciphered from the human genome: we have much to feel anxious about. *And yet still we go on*:

> A cyborg body is not innocent; it was not born in a garden; it does not seek unitary identity and so generate unitary antagonistic dualisms without end (or until the world ends); it takes irony for granted. (Haraway, 1991: 180)

It is this ability to keep it all together (which might serve almost as a definition for cyborgs of all kinds) which we need to understand.

Harvest festival

Three sets of bearings from the previous discussion can be taken to help us on our way. First, the notion of *harvesting*. Harvesting traditionally refers to the annual gathering in of crops. As such, what is harvested is in time renewed in the cycle of seasons. The harvesting we have been describing, though, is anything but renewable. Whatever grants the harvest – in this case the human body – is partly destroyed, or at least rendered obsolete through the process of gathering. This is a peculiar harvest, one which sets upon the crop, caring little for its future safeguarding. It is treated as a simple resource to be used once only.

Second, it is worth reading on a little in Haraway's manifesto. The lines immediately following the previous quote run as follows:

> Intense pleasure in skill, machine skill, ceases to be a sin, but an aspect of embodiment. The machine is not an it to be animated, worshipped, and dominated. The machine is us, our processes, an aspect of our embodiment. We can be responsible for machines; *they* do not dominate or threaten us. We are responsible for boundaries; we are they. (Haraway, 1991: 180)

What Haraway forces us to attend to is that *there is no clear separation between machine and human*, no innocent 'us' menaced by threatening 'them'. We comprise integral parts of the mechanism, they in turn constitute what we are. Our engagements with technology have always been among our most intimate, most self-revealing encounters with the world. It is through the use of technics, from the most basic tools to contemporary information systems, that we have been able to cut out the space we now inhabit and so become what we are. Technics holds us together. From which it follows that we are now in the curious position of being both what is set upon, and responsible for that very harvesting.

At the same time, this intimacy with technics is a source of 'intense pleasure'. The skills to which Haraway is referring here can be broadly interpreted as all the different techniques at making, constructing and bringing into being that technics makes possible. It is not solely engineering that is at issue here. As Sadie Plant (1997) has described at some length, weaving and other craft techniques which are traditionally recognized as women's skills are perhaps closer to the sensibility (that is, the aesthetics as well as formal operations) of modern programming and design than 'masculine' machine skills. Our embodiment of such skills, the ability to fabricate, in all its senses, by manipulating our mutual imbrication with technology brings great satisfaction. Yet this satisfaction is tempered by an acknowledgement that in exercising our skills we are participating in the setting upon of ourselves. We *resource* ourselves, with the inescapable conclusion that our ability to discern the full implications of such a resourcing (very roughly, our 'humanness') is precisely what is being threatened in the process.

Thereby do we arrive at a final point: *the shamefulness of our present existence*. The very facets of our being which give us most pleasure – the skills and abilities granted by technics – are those which drive on the harvest at still greater speeds. A circumstance which generates a deep sense of anxiety. But are we yet clear about the proper nature of this threat? Here it is possible to perceive a clear difference which divides up along gender lines. Compare the following two statements. The first is drawn from the welcome document to the *transhuman* mailing list, the second is an artist's statement by the cyberfeminist collective VNS Matrix, describing an installation (All New Gen) based around a video game design:

Never in history have our daily lives and our destinies been so deeply involved with technology. Yet, so many people today are indifferent, cynical, or outright hostile towards progress. It's time we stand up to the mystics, Luddites, and Unabombers of the world. We ascended from pre-sentient animals through tool-use, abstract reason, communication, and zeal for learning. These time-tested methods are precisely how we will ascend from humanity to the next stage in our species' development: transhumanity. (Bokov, 1995)

All New Gen promotes a new construct on the block, All New Gen, hero of our game. Gen is 'GameGirl', supported in her mission by her Zonegirls, the DNA Sluts. The enemies of Gen and her posse of brave new girls are Big Daddy Mainframe, the omnipresent omniprocessor of a military-industrial complex and his offsider Circuit Boy, a fetishized replicant of the perfect human HeMan, and a dangerous technobimbo. All New Gen's mission of sabotage is to act as a virus in cyberspace, infiltrating and corrupting the fathernet of power and ambition. (VNS Matrix, 1997)

The first statement is deeply embedded in the kind of language that is routinely associated with the colonial impulse of a male-centred view of modernity (see Easlea, 1983; Plumwood, 1993), now extended to the 'new electronic frontier' (Sardar, 1996). 'Progress' constitutes the prime imperative. That which stands in its way is regarded as ignorance, cynicism or irrational technophobia and comes to be defined as a potential threat. Resistance is overcome through pressing onward with a project of mastery, based on the application of 'reason' and the use of equipment to extend the powers of the human. The vision of the transhuman that emerges is one of an 'armoured self', who uses technology to assert their domination of the immediate environment (cf. Bukatman, 1993). It does not take much interpretative work to see this as an exaggerated defensive mechanism, the fantasy of a 'hard' body free from the 'mess' of intimacy and boundary-blurring relationships with nature and others. Indeed, this is precisely how Robins and Levidow (1995) read the 'cyborg-soldiers' of modern warfare who project all inner conflicts onto the screen filled with abstract images of the enemy produced by cameras mounted on 'smart bombs' and other remote controlled systems.

A very different set of threats is picked out in the second statement. Here it is military-industrial complex, in the guise of Big Daddy

Mainframe, and its offspring generated by its own fantasy of procreation, Circuit Boy. Their domination of systems of communication – the fathernet – becomes exemplary of the more general colonization of representational space by male fantasies. Against all this, Gen and the Zonegirls act as a 'virus', attempting to corrupt and pervert the dominant order through acts of subversion. Here what is at stake are the means by which those who are excluded from the machinery of representation, the de facto means by which social ordering is secured, are able to disrupt its functioning by establishing a very different relationship to the spaces opened up by technology. This is achieved, partly, by celebrating the fluidity of the relation between humans and technics. Such an immersion cannot by definition support the penetrative logic of domination and absolute control:

> Entering the matrix is no assertion of masculinity, but a loss of humanity; to jack into cyberspace is not to penetrate, but to be invaded... Cyberspace is the matrix not of absence, void, the whole of the womb, but perhaps even the place of woman's affirmation. This would not be the affirmation of her own patriarchal past, but what she is in a future which has yet to arrive but can nevertheless be already felt. (Plant, 1995: 60)

Plant here asserts that it is woman who finds affirmation in the immersive space formed by the matrix of information communication technologies – this through her attunement to the logic of fabrication and weaving diversity. And it is precisely this kind of 'irony' on which Haraway's cyborg also thrives: recognition of itself as made from a weave of codes and materials that although produced by the 'informatics of domination' are combined into unstable 'wholes' that make possible unique kinds of subversion and reversibility.

What we have then are two distinct sensibilities: the paranoid armouring-up of the cyborg soldier against the immersive irony of the All New Gen cyborg. And it is not too difficult to conclude that the latter sensibility seems infinitely more adjusted to complexities of negotiating identity in cyberspace than the former. But although Haraway's cyborg and the accounts by Plant and VNS Matrix serve to highlight the deep contradictions in transhumanism, of themselves they still do not allow us to get a fix on precisely how it is possible to live right within the tension set up between the will-to-order being played out in modern technology – the festival surrounding the harvest, if you like – and the kinds of creativity that this same phenomenon makes possible. In particular, there is a difficulty inasmuch as we are driven back onto a psychoanalytic model of gender (either the classic Freudian account of defensive projection in the case of the armoured self, or a more sophisticated notion of difference by way of Luce Irigaray in Plant's writing), which takes us away from our initial concern with the management of monstrosity as a matter of *social* technics. Something more is needed.

Technikon, technikos, technē

To reiterate: the question is how we can go on with technology, how we can hold it all together in the face of our own monstrosity. The question implies that we know what technology really is, that is, what it is in its *essence*. As Grint and Woolgar (1997) outline at some length, it is rarely the case that the 'essence' of technology is known in advance, but rather that this is precisely what is most at stake in historical debates around the introduction of all new technologies, from the automatic Jacquard loom through to virtual reality. Indeed, to interpret cyberspace as we have been doing as either something to be mastered, or else as immersive space riven with inherent contradictions and possibilities, is to position oneself within competing accounts of what this electronic medium *actually is*. Or to put it another way, such interpretations are attempts to discourse on the ontology of cyberspace (*onto* – being or 'is-ness'; *logos* – account).

The philosopher who is perhaps the most notorious thinker of such accounts of the being of technology is Martin Heidegger. Heidegger's (1977) essays 'The question concerning technology' and 'The age of the world picture' could not be more stark in their reading of the danger posed by the ravages of technical-rational world ordering made possible by modern technologies (for an extended discussion see Brown and Lightfoot, 1998). In brief, Heidegger discerns through the Greek etymology of the term that 'technology' is originally *technikon*, or that which belongs to technē. Technē is a practice which reveals things for what they are. Technē is a craft skill, but also a form of fine art and moreover an 'art of the mind'. It allows that some 'being' be brought forth ('unconcealed') that would not otherwise bring itself forth. In Heidegger's famous example, technē is akin to the construction of a bridge across the Rhine. Something is brought forth, but in so doing the river itself remains undisturbed.

Modern technology, by contrast, comes to pass in a 'challenging' or a setting upon of the earth. Heidegger likens this to a hydroelectric plant built across the same river. This subjects the Rhine to a series of 'interlocking processes pertaining to the orderly disposition of electrical energy' (1977: 16). The river is thereby 'unlocked' or 'exposed' as a thing to be 'commanded' and 'set-in-order' as a simple resource. The Rhine then comes to reveal itself, to take up its standing for us, in a manner entirely in accord with the demands of the hydroelectric industry:

> What kind of unconcealment is it, then, that is peculiar to that which comes to stand forth through this setting-upon that challenges? Everywhere everything is ordered to stand by, to be immediately at hand, indeed to stand there just so that it may be on call for a further ordering. Whatever is ordered about in this way has its own standing. We call it standing-reserve. (ibid.: 17)

When beings are revealed as 'standing-reserve', that is as resources which stand perpetually available for calculation and command, then technology functions as '*Ge-stell*' or 'enframing'. Enframing is a way of revealing that gathers together and orders what is revealed into a prearranged space of calculation. Beings that are 'challenged forth' into unconcealment in this manner can only come to stand as objects entirely at the disposal of the human. The obvious danger here is that once under way, enframing is destined to also 'set-upon' and reveal humans themselves as forms of standing reserve:

> As soon as what is unconcealed no longer concerns man [sic] even as an object, but does so, rather, exclusively as standing-reserve, and man in the midst of objectlessness is nothing but the orderer of the standing-reserve, then he comes to the very brink of a precipitous fall; that is, he come to the point where he himself will have to be taken as standing-reserve. (ibid.: 27)

Enframing is harvesting. But *Ge-stell* is also, for Heidegger, a derivation from 'stellen', meaning 'to set' or 'to place'. This word has a wide usage in German, ranging from the domestic sense of 'to put in place' and 'to order' through 'to arrange' and 'to supply'. What this suggests is that *Ge-stell* is in some sense the exponential proliferation of the kind of mundane ordering proper to the domestic sphere. The common techniques that are used to order that most intimate of spaces – the home – such as the tidying up of drawers and the putting of things into their proper place, are 'the same' as those which drive forward the ordering of the world as enframing. In Samuel Weber's reading (1996) of Heidegger, this is expressed by translating *Ge-stell* as 'emplacement', meaning both the 'placing in order' of all things (in the sense of commanding and harvesting) and an 'ordering into place' (in the sense of establishing a pre-arranged place for things in an all-encompassing calculative order).

What Weber also emphasizes is that Heidegger uses the term 'essence' – *Wesen* – in a special sense, rendered in translation as 'the way in which something pursues its course, the way in which it remains through time as what it is' (Heidegger, 1977: 3). We might say that it equates to how something 'proceeds forth', 'takes place', or, as Weber has it, 'goes on'. Understood in this fashion, the essence of some being *is an event*, something which comes to pass and in so doing stakes out its place in the world. Harvesting is the event of modern technology. Such harvesting is accomplished by a massive extension of domesticity. We make the entire world our home in order that all things may become as 'available' to us as knives in a drawer or cups on a rack. In so doing proximity and immediacy come to take on an ever greater value:

> In Dasein [the human] *there lies an essential tendency towards closeness.* All the ways in which we speed things up, as we are more or less compelled to do today, push us on towards the conquest of remoteness. (Heidegger, 1962: 140)

In attempting to ensure constant availability we become compelled to think of technology as a means to defeat distance and bring the world ever nearer, at ever greater speeds. The world can then be commanded to stand perpetually ready before us. Here then is the paradox: it is technology which engenders monstrosity by 'unconcealing' things which would otherwise not be brought about, the most monstrous of which is the way in which we come to recognize ourselves as simple resources at our own disposal (literally things to be manipulated). Yet what goes on or takes its place as modern technology is *domestication* on a massive scale. Our means of dealing with monstrosity is then precisely the same practice that results in its emergence in the first place. Thus the only way that we can possibly continue to hold it altogether is to drive ever harder onwards as *technikos*, beings in the sway of *technikon*, in the hope that as fast as technology creates ever greater domestic turbulence, we are able put everything in place and shut fast all the drawers.

To live this way is to dwell in perpetual anxiety. Anxiety, at least in the psychoanalytic sense, is the gradual sense of displacement that arises when one begins to doubt one's own place in the scheme of things. Both a confusion over origins and terror concerning something which is ever-so-vaguely apprehended in its coming to pass: the uncanny, *das Unheimlich*, literally 'the unhomely'. It is this way in which anxiety is so curiously unmarked that is the key. We are anxious about nothing in particular. For Heidegger such 'nothingness' indicates the withdrawal of the world from our apprehension. Things begin to slip away into concealment. At such moments, presence – the usual proximity of the world to us – becomes an issue. Anxiety is the revelation that instead of something, there could be nothing (Heidegger, 1961). Instead of proximity and availability, there might be unmeasurable distance and concealment. Instead of connection, disconnection. Is this not the ultimate terror in a world where everything is in principle connected? That we become fatally estranged, unplugged from the networks?

Still there may be much to be gained from anxiety. By forcing us to confront the dialectic of intimacy and sudden displacement that marks out modern technics, anxiety brings the question of how to carry on into sharp relief. In doing so it is worth reminding ourselves that what goes on as *technikon* is not only emplacement. Technikon refers also to technē, to the art of making present. In an earlier questioning of the work of art, Heidegger (1993) concludes that what is at work in art involves both a 'fixing' and a 'taking place'. What is fixed is a figure, but what this figure in turn begins to open up is a 'world'. World here means a space wherein beings come into unconcealment. The work of art allows beings to take up standing before us, but can only achieve this by providing the security of a shelter, something set up and fixed in place in advance of their coming to unconcealment. This kind of unconcealment – a 'setting forth of the earth' – is quite unlike the challenging forth of emplacement. It does not exhaust that which is brought to presence. It maintains a relation to the ineffable, the 'nothingness' of absolute concealment:

> This setting forth of the earth is achieved by the work as it sets itself back into the earth. The self-seclusion of earth, however, is not a uniform, inflexible staying under cover, but unfolds itself in an inex-

haustible variety of simple modes and shapes. To be sure, the sculptor uses stone just as the mason uses it, in his own way. But he does not use it up. (Heidegger, 1993: 173)

The crucial phrase here must surely be 'not use up'. To respect the withdrawal of *something* into the *nothing* of concealment. Only by respecting this withdrawal, this disconnection or, as Adrian Mckenzie (1997) calls it 'dead time', can we resist the onward drive of emplacement. How can we apprehend such 'dead time' as integral to the harvesting of all that is within the modern, domesticated spaces of calculation? Perhaps we may take our bearings here from our experience of art:

> The setting up of a world and the setting forth of earth are two essential features in the work-being of the [art] work. They belong together, however, in the unity of the work-being. This is the unity we seek when we ponder the self-subsistence of the work and try to tell of this closed, unitary repose of self-support. (Heidegger, 1993: 173)

How to go on? By pondering the self-subsistence of the work that is monstrosity, which alone allows us to articulate something of its 'closed unitary repose', the way in which it works its way in and out of emplacement. We may say, by allowing more time in silent reflection on the modern monsters that crowd around us. More time to understand how it is that they force us up against the unmeasurable gap between connection and disconnection, something and nothing. Monsters are omens, portents, puzzles. In our haste to domesticate them we fail, perhaps, to allow them time to take their measure of us. This even more so when the monsters we consider are part of the mobile army of metaphors that we corral into a sense of self. We need to find a means of standing full square within our own anxiety, staring eye to eye with monstrosity. This, I take it, is precisely what Sherry Turkle (1995: 171) is describing:

> It is spring, and in the newly mild weather, a group of children is playing on the grass with transformer toys. This particular set can take the shape of armored tanks, robots or people. They can be put into intermediate states so that a 'robot' arm can protrude from a human form or a human leg from a mechanical tank. Two of the children, both seven years old, are playing with toys in these intermediate states. A third child, who is a year younger, insists this is not right.

The toys, he says, should not be placed in such hybrid states. 'You should play with them as all tank or all people.' He is getting upset because the two older children are making a point of ignoring him. An eight-year-old girl comforts the upset child. 'Its okay to play with them when they are in between. It's all the same stuff,' she says, 'just yucky computer cy-dough-plasm.'

It *is* all the same stuff. But how hard it is to live with that.

On the way...

Losing the certainty of a belief in the rational, autonomous subject has been a terrible burden for psychology. One that seemingly threatened the very future of the discipline. Cyberpsychology is partly about searching for a way forward. Not though by inventing yet another conceptual monstrosity like the *cogito ergo sum* of cognitive psychology, but by confronting the actual monsters that technology brings forth. By thinking closely about the kinds of monsters we ourselves are becoming and just how it is that we approach this most intimate of problems. Part of that is recognizing that we have very ancient devices for dealing with such concerns, and that what makes our relationship to modern technology so perplexing is that it so precisely embodies these devices alongside its ability to engender monsters. Technology is both the poison and the cure, to echo Ansell Pearson (1997). It *dis*places as it *em*places. It has within it the onward drive to connect matched against the infinite slowness of disconnection.

What I think we get from envisaging a putative cyberpsychology by way of Heidegger is a rich vocabulary for talking about this movement between anxiety and security. We can speak of the relationship between humans and technology not as an 'interaction', an 'impact' or any other of the terms which reify the cognitive subject, but as a matter of *placing*, an ordering of humans and machines all mixed up together ('yucky computer cy-dough-plasm', if you like). What we need to do is see in each instance how this mixture is made up and the ways of being and acting it makes possible. Yet we can also see that running through all such mixtures is a tension between the absolute setting-in-order of total emplacement, and the complete withdrawal of the world into closure. And we can recognize perhaps ever so vaguely that art (in its broadest possible sense) serves as an interesting model for how to reflect upon these tensions. Because what is at stake here is just how we can live while fully acknowledging our place in all this mess. Heidegger has an apposite phrase here – questioning puts us 'on the way'. It moves us forward. Cyberpsychology could be just such a means of going on.

References

Ansell Pearson, K. (1997) *Viroid Life: Perspectives on Nietzsche and the Transhuman Condition*. London: Routledge.

Benedikt, M. (ed.) (1992) *Cyberspace: First Steps*. Cambridge, MA: MIT Press.

Bokov, A. (1995) 'Welcome to transhuman'. Internet document available at transhuman@umich.edu

Bowker, G. (1993) 'How to be universal: some cybernetic strategies, 1943–70', *Social Studies of Science*, **23**: 107–27.

Brown, S.D. and Capdevila, R. (1998) 'Perpetuum mobile: substance, force and the sociology of translation', in Law J. and Hassard J. (eds) *Actor-Network Theory and After*. Oxford: Blackwell.

Brown, S.D. and Lightfoot, G. (1998) 'Insistent emplacement: Heidegger on the technologies of informing'. *Information Technology and People*, **11**(4): 290–304.

Bukatman, S. (1993) *Terminal Identity: The Virtual Subject in Postmodern Science Fiction*. Durham: Duke University Press.

Caspar, M.J. (1994) 'At the margins of humanity: fetal positions in science and medicine', *Science, Technology and Human Values*, **19**(31): 127–45.

Crewe, J. (1997) 'Transcoding the world: Haraway's postmodernism', *Signs*, **22**(41): 891–905.

Deleuze, G. (1988) 'On the death of man and superman', in *Foucault* (Hand, S., trans.). Minneapolis: University of Minnesota Press.

Easlea, B. (1983) *Fathering the Unthinkable*. London: Pluto.

Figueroa-Sarriera, H.J. (1995) 'Children of the mind with disposable bodies: metaphors of self in a text on artificial intelligence and robotics', in Gray, C.H., Figueroa-Sarriera, H.J. and Mentor, S. (eds) *The Cyborg Handbook*. London: Routledge.

Foucault, M. (1970) *The Order of Things: An Archaeology of the Human Sciences*. London: Routledge.

Grint, K. and Woolgar, S. (1997) *The Machine at Work: Technology, Work and Organization*. Cambridge: Polity.

Guattari, F. (1984) *Molecular Revolution: Psychiatry and Politics*. Harmondsworth: Penguin.

Hamilton, S.N. (1997) 'The cyborg, 11 years later: the not-so-surprising half-life of the Cyborg Manifesto', *Convergence*, **3**(2): 104–20.

Haraway, D.J. (1991) *Simians, Cyborgs, and Women: The Reinvention of Nature*. London: Free Association Books.

Haraway, D.J. (1995) 'Cyborgs and symbionts: living together in the new world order', in. Gray, C.H., Figueroa-Sarriera, H.J. and Mentor, S. (eds) *The Cyborg Handbook*. London: Routledge.

Heidegger, M. (1961) *An Introduction to Metaphysics*. (Manheim, R., trans.). New York: Doubleday-Anchor.

Heidegger, M. (1962) *Being and Time* (Macquarrie, J. and Robinson, E., trans.). Oxford: Blackwell.

Heidegger, M. (1977) 'The question concerning technology' (Lovitt, W., trans.), in *The Question Concerning Technology and Other Essays*. New York: Harper & Row.

Heidegger, M. (1993) 'The origin of the work of art' (Hofstadter, A., trans.), in Krell, D.F. (ed.) *Basic Readings: Martin Heidegger*, revised edn. London: Routledge.

Heim, M. (1993) *The Metaphysics of Virtual Reality*. Oxford: Oxford University Press.

Hogle, L.F. (1995) 'Tales from the cryptic: technology meets organism in the living cadaver', in Gray, C.H., Figueroa-Sarriera H.J. and Mentor S. (eds) *The Cyborg Handbook*. London: Routledge.

Kosofsky Sedgwick, E. and Frank, A. (1995) 'Shame in the cybernetic fold: reading Silvan Tomkins', *Critical Inquiry*, **21**: 496–522.

Kroker, A. and Kroker, M. (1996) *Hacking the Future: Stories for the Flesh-Eating 90s*. Montreal: New-World Perspectives.

Latour, B. (1993) *We Have Never Been Modern* (Porter, C., trans.). Cambridge, MA: Harvard University Press.

Law, J. and Hassard, J. (eds) (1998) *Actor-Network Theory and After*. Oxford: Blackwell.

Lury, C. (1998) *Prosthetic Culture*. London: Routledge.

Mckenzie, A. (1997) 'The mortality of the virtual: real-time, archive and dead-time in information networks', *Convergence*, **3**(2): 59–71.

More, M. (1994) 'On becoming posthuman'. Internet document available at http://www.primenet.com/~maxmore/becoming.htm

Nelkin, D. and Lindee, M.S. (1995) *The DNA Mystique: The Gene as a Cultural Icon*. New York: WH Freeman.

Ong, A. (1988) 'The production of possession: spirits and the multinational corporation in Malaysia', *American Ethnologist*, **15**: 28–42.

Plant, S. (1995) 'The future looms: weaving women and cybernetics', *Body and Society*, **1**(3/4): 45–64.

Plant, S. (1997) *Zeroes and Ones*. London: Fourth Estate.

Plumwood, V. (1993) *Feminism and the Mastery of Nature*. London: Routledge.

Poster, M. (1995) 'Postmodern virtualities', *Body and Society*, **1**(3/4): 79–95.

Robins, K. and Levidow, L. (1995) 'Soldier, cyborg, citizen', in Brook, J. and Boal, I.A. (eds) *Resisting the Virtual Life: The Culture and Politics of Information*. San Francisco: City Lights.

Rubin, M. (1995) 'The person in the form: medieval challenges to bodily "order"', in Kay, S. and Rubin, M. (eds) *Framing Medieval Bodies*. Manchester: Manchester University Press.

Sardar, Z. (1996) 'alt.civilizations.faq: cyberspace as the darker side of the West', in Sadar Z. and Ravetz J.R. (eds) *Cyberfutures: Culture and Politics on the Information Superhighway*. London: Pluto.

Shiva, V. (1989) *Staying Alive: Women, Ecology and Development*. London: Zed Books.

Stelarc (1997) 'From psycho to cyber strategies: prosthetics, robotics and remote existence', *Cultural Values*, **1**(2): 241–9.

Stone, A.R. (1995) *The War of Desire and Technology at the Close of the Mechanical Age*. Cambridge, MA: MIT Press.

Turkle, S. (1995) *Life on Screen: Identity in the Age of the Internet*. New York: Weinfeld & Nicolson.

VNS Matrix (1997) 'All new gen: artist's statement'. Internet document available at http://www.gold.ac.uk/difference/vns.html

Weber, S. (1996) 'Upsetting the set-up', in *Mass Mediauras: Form, Technics, Media*. Stanford: Stanford University Press

Wiener, N. (1931) 'Back to Leibniz! Physics reoccupies an abandoned position', *The Technology Review*, **34**: 201–25.

PART THREE

Trajectories, Identities and Events

The three chapters in this part of the book trace the various trajectories which cyberpsychology opens up, and each asks critical questions about the way in which cyberpsychology may be recuperated (neutralized and absorbed) by the psy-complex and reduced to the status of a mere technological artefact and appendage. The strategies of identity production that traditional psychology employed through the twentieth century may yet succeed again in the twenty-first if the cyborg, for example, is conceived of as being a fixed thing, liable to representation and willing to answer questions about its origins and inner rationality.

Erica Burman explores the ambiguities and ambivalences which constitute the cyborg in contemporary cyberculture alongside the child, and the interwoven representations of cyborgian subjectivity and childhood that paradoxically confirm the child both as 'the quintessential humanist subject' and childhood as the new 'cyberintelligentsia'. Despite the hopes for the cyborg as an idealized point of resistance to traditional forms of psychology – in a refusal of identity, masculinized cognitive functioning and developmental growth – if we attend to the imagery of the cyborg we find the selfsame images of individuality and omnipotence we should have left behind.

Dan Heggs provides an account of the recuperative strategies facing cyberpsychological critiques in an analysis which also situates the increasingly visible figure of the cyborg in popular culture, in particular in superhero comic books. The lesson he draws from the employment of cyborg imagery in these texts is salutary, for we find forms of identity which are as determined to tell stories of their origins and account for themselves as authentic as the old flesh and blood characters they displaced. Again, Heggs draws attention to a paradox, which is that while Haraway's account of the cyborg was of a hybrid form without origins or fixed identity we are witnessing cyborgs in film, for example, which 'integrate with technology precisely in order to inoculate themselves against the threat to fragmented identity'.

Francisco Tirado's take on this problem is to open up the question of identity in psychology and to argue, in a way which picks up and elaborates a theme from other earlier chapters in the book, that cyberpsychological critique needs to focus on 'becoming cyberpsychological' not as a thing but as an *event* – as he puts it 'becoming cyborg is an event and not a process'. Tirado stresses that the cyborg should be seen not as isolated or delimited as a particular kind of thing, since it transgresses forms of identity and surpasses forms of history which try to capture the birth of things the better to capture what their essential qualities are.

These chapters take to task the individualizing practices of old psychology, and a turn to 'vagrant' forms of being and knowing is designed as part of a strategy of resistance to the modes of technological control and self-definition that have always defined the 'humaneering' projects of the discipline.

CHAPTER 10

The Child and the Cyborg

ERICA BURMAN

This chapter explores parallels in culture, meanings and figurative possibilities between representations of childhood and cyborgs. Both children and cyborgs function at the margins of the material and the metaphorical, of the actual and the possible. As such they mark key borders around contemporary forms of subjectivity. The crucial question is whether they afford transgression or rather simply reinforce the borders that their spectral presences inscribe. Thus while children and cyborgs have each been mobilized to warrant interventions and to inspire (or even personify) visions of the future, they both also form key cultural repositories for the repressed fears and fantasies to which modern subjectivity gives rise.

However, alongside the convergences between the two I will highlight some crucial asymmetries between the trope of the cyborg and of the child: while both work as metaphors of possibility, the child signifies a site of bodily longing, of loss and transience that the cyborg, at least in some readings, refuses. The cyborg, as a metaphor of the postmodern condition, may offer more vigorous political challenges than the (always already de)natured child. Thus if the cyborg marks the return of the personal, political, and military repressed to haunt us, then its surfaces present a text from which we can perhaps better glimpse sources of the political dynamic we inhabit.

Yet these surfaces are discontinuous, and thus – like any projective image – reflect and refract back onto specific locations. The political possibilities of the cyborg correspondingly modulate according to the position of the evaluator, rather than reside within some essential quality it possesses (or lacks). For the cyborg is by definition a product, an artefact, a 'man-made' article. While its claim to autonomous, intelligent existence relies on the extent to which it is considered to exceed its programming, the child – also an expression of the time and place of its (cultural and genetic) conception – hovers equivalently on the borders between biology and society, between nature and culture, securing its status as warranting indulgence and protection only insofar as it fails to lay claim to adult pleasures and responsibilities. Both are positioned as outside the fully human sphere.

Consistent with this perspective, this chapter therefore weighs up ambivalences rather than absolutes of the cyberpsychological drift in culture. Despite their contrasting relationship to the humanist subject (exemplified by the child and eschewed by the cyborg), in the end the child and the cyborg turn out to be less opposed than we might have initially supposed. But is this simply to restate the original problem? For not only do cyborgs and children present representations of subjectivity that are already essentialized (fixed and packaged) for consumption as commodities, they are also no longer mutually exclusive (cf. Davis-Floyd and Dumit, 1998). With children now hailed as the new cyberintelligentsia the modern romantic narrative of 'child as father to the man' lives on under the rule of capital. Even as signs of malleability, then, cyborgs and children can function alongside, as well as oppose each other, and in so doing their potentials for political subversion can yet still be resolved in favour of the maintenance of patriarchal order.

But this perhaps overlooks other moments of contest. Let me begin again and take the story slowly, for in the telling other possibilities may emerge.

Subject matter

Within the modern cultural imaginary the child is the quintessential humanist subject. As a signifier of loss, the child alludes both to the costs of capitalism – what was not allowed to be, the vulnerability and connectedness supposed of premodern sensibility – and its productive possibilities as the symbol of modern human capability, the seed of the yet-to-be-actualized self. Steedman (1996) traces the literary emergence of this trope, characterizing it as an expression of loss and longing for that which is produced as disallowed by modernity. Everything about the child – ineptitude, imperfection, bewilderment, and especially its diminutive stature – connotes the pain and effort of maturity, testifies to the journey traversed from an irretrievable state (while precisely *what* has been 'lost' remains unclear). Steedman emphasizes how the mere word 'little' comes to evoke the pathos and mystery carried by the child. However this affective aura, notwithstanding its counterposition to modernity, is also reproduced for its exploitation, for images of little children, especially babies, not only sell well but also sell other products – whether nappies and cars – or even personify commercial investments, bank accounts and advertising space.

Alternatively, as a presence rather than spectral space of longing, the image of the child in contemporary psychology exemplifies the triumphant tale of human achievement. This is the heroic narrative of modernity writ small and (literally) individual into the lifecourse story of the developing child. The child as worker/problem solver, earns 'his' entry into humanity through practice and the acquisition of skills (Stone *et al.*, 1973). Yet the narrative of progressive development formulated by Piaget (for example, Piaget, 1933, 1957) implies an openness and optimism that Western culture can no longer (claim to) deliver. The language of (child) development lost its evolutionary lilt to information processing sometime in the 1960s and thence to cybernetics (Rutkowska, 1993). Capacities became skills, skills became autonomous systems amenable to commodification – in all, a piece-work model of the factory production line blue collar worker rather than the pioneering blue chip adventurer (cf. Harris, 1987).

But while the child is saturated in identification, the cyborg somehow eludes it. The cyborg seems a more uneasy site for humanist attributions. The representation of subjectivity it invites is that of going beyond human limits. In the world of artificial intelligence, for example, miniaturization may inspire awe (as another variety of structural adjustment as downsizing) but this is rather of the bold presumptuousness of human aspiration and power. The cyborg is typically less a site for identification than possession, of envious appropriation rather than empathy. The aim is to control, rather than be, it.

Complementary projections

So it would seem that the cyborg and the child represent complementary qualities in relation to crises of contemporary subjectivity. While the cyborg threatens mastery, the child represents dependency.

However, what both share is their separation from the adult world of responsibility and relationships – the cyborg excluded by virtue of its paradoxical uniqueness and isolation (we never hear of *communities* of cyborgs), and the child via its attributed non-participation in society through supposed communicational or occupational deficits. Despite these differences, both are invested with phantasmic qualities of otherworldliness and powers beyond conventional knowledge. The sentimentalized construction of a separate condition of childhood has long been recognized as a key achievement of modernity serving the current and future needs of the labour market, as well as offering a space of nostalgic longing for a return to Edenic innocence outside sociality (Aries, 1962; Steedman, 1996). Similarly the cyborg invites fantasies of omnipotence, of absolute obedience and control unfettered by moral restraint.

In different ways each therefore expresses a theme of insecurity of human competence. While the cyborg evokes anxieties of hyperrationality and the child of disintegration into chaotic madness, both concern fantasies of being annihilated and overwhelmed. Somehow both the child and the cyborg represent limit points of human capability, but their boundaries are continuously shifting. Children are constantly being granted new (cognitive or communicative) abilities that undermine presumed developmental thresholds (whether of ages or stages). Similarly, the cyborg is daily proclaimed as becoming more sentient, more human-like, troubling the specific place of *human* 'being'.

Here Julia Kristeva's concept of the 'abject' seems apt. The abject is 'the place where meaning collapses' (Kristeva, 1982: 2). It does not 'respect borders, positions, rules' but rather 'disturbs identity, system and order' (ibid.: 4). In their different ways, and for different reasons, the image both of the child and the cyborg, now unhinged from their previous displacements and safely beyond the bounds of reason or morality, throw previous certainties into question and usher in themes of undifferentiation, as well as the disgust and horror that attends disintegration of hard-won boundaries. In complementary ways, then, both child and cyborg offer an annihilation of self that is both feared and desired; feared because they challenge definitions of human values and qualities, and desired because they seem to offer escapes from the agonies (of mortality and embodiment) that flow precisely from these. As Barbara Creed points out:

> Abject things are those which highlight the 'fragility of the law' and which exist on the other side of the border which separates out the living subject from that which threatens its extinction. (Creed, 1987: 48)

Moreover, it is only when these creations – children and cyborgs – start to resist their allocated position outside the social that they are animated by the most intense and negative projections. The costs of transgressing the conventional categorization of childhood are evident in the public response to children who behave in supposedly unchildish ways – children who are violent, who murder, who are sexually active and – especially on the margins of capital's centres – children who live on the streets and who work. Thus the limits and functions of our dominant generational classifications become manifest. Equally the cyborg as glorified robot, as docile technological instrument, can be safely consigned to the slapstick genre of clanking suits of armour (cf. Goldberg, 1997), and it is only when it starts pushing the boundary of the un/known, of (passing for) being alive that it poses moral and emotional difficulties.

Monstrous mo(ve)ments

Monsters are all the rage in cultural politics. Anything that crosses the boundaries between the natural and the cultural, the human and the machinic – and, we might add, fantasy and reality – is hailed as politically progressive. Add to this blurring of gender and sexualities eluding classification and we seem to be in cultural-political utopia on earth. Cast in the long line of shadowy predatory/protective monsters (from the Golem, to Frankenstein, to the current literary obsession with angels), the cyborg seems to have been created for academic deconstructionists of the binaries of modern subjectivity, whose business it is to identify 'other' inspirational possibilities of psychologies no longer fettered to patriarcho-capitalism (cf. Lykke and Braidotti, 1996).

But it was not always like that. As Donna Haraway (1985) acknowledges, the cyborg is the brain-child of military technology, of labour substitution and deadly destruction. Often placed as the origin point for these debates (Hamilton, 1998), Haraway's intervention was an appeal to retain a(n albeit ironic) place in the socialist feminist imagination for the possibility that cyborgs could be sufficiently 'unfaithful' to their techno-military parents/masters to become our (politically) flexible friends. Her 'manifesto' appealed to technophobic feminists not to overlook the radical possibilities of instantaneous transglobal communication systems alongside the very real development of the 'informatics of domination'. She argued that the modes and relations of production of the new world order (multinational rule in the name of neoliberalism) call forth correspondingly different strategies of organizing. The world of cyborgs, she argues, intimates ways of waging politics that move us away from the stultifying hierarchies of oppression of identity politics that have confined feminists (and others) to either naïve and spurious commonalities or solipsistic essentialisms, and rather promotes unstable affinity groups or coalitions and partial, transient alliances of diverse political tendencies acting in relation to locally defined goals.

The problem is that elsewhere the irony of Haraway's vision seems to have washed out over time and reception, to be replaced in two ways. Either there is the breathless enthusiasm and smug self-absorption of cyberspace celebration. Or alternatively there is a wholesale rejection of engagement with cyber sociality fuelled also by a new feminist organicism and cultural fetishization of 'the natural'. Another binary is set up between those who love it, and those who do not; those who are willing to grant that cyberparaphernalia (in its various forms – the Internet, virtual reality, 'intelligent' prosthetics) might offer some benefits and those who hold onto their doom-laden suspicions and who are just waiting to be able to say ' I told you so'. Is it possible to stand outside this binary of (evangelical versus hostile) reaction to cybermania? Is the only choice between an uncritical subscription that ignores inequalities of access to, and relations of exploitation facilitated by, technology and a gloomy fatalism that disallows the possibility of change and fetters cultural-political analysis to a critique of not-so-late capitalism?

One way of restoring the irony is to return to treat it as artefact, as a cultural form that demands interrogation and evaluation. Such is one reading of 'cyberpsychology': not a warrant for, but a study of new psychological responses to, and varieties of, human–machine interfacings. The problem is, you have to get involved to understand (stand under/around, withstand), so (like any claim to 'objectivity') the space of disinterested evaluation is always liable to evaporate. Now that 'the uncanny' has become high chic, technobabble might shed its strangeness at any minute and become homely. After all, you have to lurk around in cyberspace in order to look at it. Such is the tense and contested moment of cyberpsychology, always vulnerable to recuperation into the bourgeois individualism of both dominant psychology and of the market for technological consumption, caught between fascination and repugnance, seduction and horror. For 'the monster, like the abject, is ambiguous; it both repels and attracts' (Creed, 1987: 65).

Just like children. Before/alongside the cultural fetish of the monster there was (always) the child. Perhaps they are twins (non-identical offspring of common cultural phantasies). Just as the cyborg operates at the triple levels of metaphor, fantasy, and literal being (Hamilton, 1998), so too does the child. Children, like cyborgs, are 'our future', but they tend to hook a retroactive telling of the future, foreclosed by the impulse to repeat that which was – the past – as a restorative gesture. The dominant image of the child, then, is compensatory, if also relational: the child is that which the adult is not, and social policies and agencies struggle to create for children the life circumstances 'we' lack (or think we have lacked). Clearly this can work politically in mixed (and not all reactionary) ways. Critics of the cultural chauvinism and imperialism of international economic development, for example, portray restorative impulses as preferable to the colonial-infantilizing model of rescue (of children or of 'developing' countries), since these allow for local self-definition of what is to be restored, and a sense of reconnection with past traditions rather than impositions of new (Gronemeyer, 1993).

Nevertheless, the conservative dynamic structured within a(n adult-centred and defined) recovery model (including the constructed character of notions of heritage and tradition) should not be underestimated. It is, however, worth recalling the banal fact that, notwithstanding its proclamations, cyberspace is far from free (and acquiring more toll charges by the second), and the question of whether the cyborg can shed its history sufficiently to write a new political script remains unclear.

Yet perhaps I am moving too fast, not only from cyborg to child (and from child to global economics), but also from the cyborg to the whole of cyberia. Continuities notwithstanding, the 'borg' part of the cyborg now sounds quaintly hardware amid the current discourse and market of liquidity. It recalls the chaotic wiring and monotone bleat of the Star Trek collective entity of two (TV series) generations past. But its inflexibility is not only anachronistic; it is horrifying, in one sweep threatening to annihilate both human existence and individuality. Their chant 'We are Borg, you will be assimilated, resistance is futile' conflates the two.

But this perhaps prompts other perspectives. For, first, while the cyborg exercises conventional boundaries of individuality, it scarcely threatens existence, except insofar as individual human agencies might use it as a weapon(s carrier). It certainly has changed conditions for material existence through automating tasks hitherto performed by humans (generating more automating tasks for others), so putting some out of a job and opening up for others the dubious flexibilities of home working. Nevertheless the conflation between social relations (notably of labour) and the particularities of (individual) subjectivity may fuse together structures that, while intimately interconnected, are not instantaneous productions. Anxieties about the cyborg seem to rest precisely within that tension between the two.

Second, if the cyborg is starting to be considered too 'low tech' to symbolize postmodern technoculture (cf. Hess, 1995), it may, as Hamilton (1998: 117) suggests, precisely thereby prove fruitful for 'those living in the low- and middle-tech gaps of our increasingly cyberized world'. For it is within those 'gaps' that the fantasies of children and cyborgs may be most ambivalent and therefore politically contested and contestable. It is also at the local and specific level of the literal and the material, as well as the metaphorical, that such links can be made.

It seems that the 'we' of the Borg is horrifying precisely because of the loss of modern individuality implied by cyber-robotic (read coercive-automatic) collectivity. The Borg personifies the most dismal nineteenth-century representation of 'group mind' and mobilizes all the corresponding disparagement for those (cultural, gender, class) groups that fail to conform to those norms of modern Western life, that is, to US-style bourgeois-imperial subjectivity. Yet in any discussion of the reception of cyborg culture, it is hard to resist an equivalently globalizing move, to assimilate all responses into a homogenous 'we', the globalized 'we' of Western consumption, that ignores differences of cultural-political location and corresponding perspective.

A natural break?

I am reminded here of reactions of the women's studies students I teach to Haraway's (1985) piece. I have come to expect that the class will be split between those fired up by the ideas and the wild sweep of the writing, and those alienated and driven to fall back on the popularist anti-intellectualism of 'Why do women write like this?' – a regular refrain on a course composed of women new to, or rebelling from, (and therefore all the more ambivalent about) higher education that we tutors struggle to reframe in terms of critical engagement with academic practice. Perhaps surprisingly, given the general cultural shift towards celebrating technological achievement, over the years the proportion of the class exhibiting the first (positive) reaction dwindled to almost none in 1998, forcing us to wonder why it is that we subject these students to this 'difficult' material. Yet I have rarely paused to wonder whether the return of the essentialist category 'woman' in their complaint is an elliptical response to, rather than refusal to engage with, such challenges.

Here we may have the seeds of an answer to the cultural divisions paradoxically ushered in by the cyborg as a harbinger of the new technological age. For just as fundamentalism is a response to modernity (mid-term and late), rather than a return to something that predated it (Yuval-Davis, 1997), so in feminist debates celebrations of (women's) 'nature' – whether of femininity, motherhood, menstruation or ethical-spiritual connectedness – arose in relation to a devaluation of cultural expressions of being a woman, and for some the change of social-political mind is insufficiently robust to merit giving them up so soon. Just as feminists were suspicious of claims to have decentred the humanist subject at the very moment when women were beginning to be accorded some of its privileges (for example, Jackson, 1992), so it may seem a little premature to surrender a fleshy, leaky vulnerable body before we have even fully come to term(s) (so to speak) with it.

Indeed, this may be part of the dangerous seduction of the cyborg to which these students are expressing resistance. For all the purported transcendence of gender, its androgyny, in the end the cyborg always seems to be *masculine*. Clearly as military instrument and in dominant cultural representation the cyborg is so, but that is not my primary concern here. (Still, the extent to which these legacies are detachable are very much at issue, see also Galison, 1994; Marsden, 1996.) Perhaps it is not surprising that the much vaunted androgyny of the cyborg always tends to resolve itself into masculinity, for such is the dynamic of the concept of androgyny – at least in its popular varieties. The story seems to be one of combining the 'best' bits of masculinity and femininity and assimilating them into a marketable and efficient (therefore culturally masculine) product. In this sense women managers – currently favoured for their kindly interpersonal style of, for example, doing 'outplacement counselling' in a way which defuses protest and progresses company interests 'with care' – exemplify the current gendered status of the cyborg (Itzin and Newman, 1995). As feminists have argued, the concept of androgyny, far from deconstructing the masculine/feminine polarity, reinscribes it (for example, Squire, 1989), just as the fashion image of the thin, boy-like, gamine woman works to standardize women as compact, space-efficient (young) men, and 'assertive' communication reiterates US bourgeois individualism (Crawford, 1998).

The impetus to allocate gender to cyborgs appears irresistible (and gender was indeed the key definer of quasi-human subjectivity in the Turing test), and yet by such means so many possibilities of subjectivity and sexuality are foreclosed. It seems a major and spurious concession for the cyborg of *Body of Glass* (Piercy, 1992) to have been scripted as 'male' – endowed with a penis, and in the end schooled into heterosexual desires and relationships. True, this figures as part of the plot, but so we enter here into the fantasy of *Making Mr Right*, (1987, dir. Seidelman – tellingly described by Halliwell as 'a slight comedy that soon runs out of anywhere to go' (Walker, 1997: 469)), a new take on the old story of woman moulding and changing a man to make him a suitable (sensitive) mate. So he becomes her creation; another tale of women's work to make relationships with men possible, tolerable. True, the loss of this relationship with Shira in *Body of Glass* is what endows the expiry of Piercy's cyborg Yod's sell-by and kill-by date with such tragedy – highlighting once again how the cyborg gains its 'human interest' through the affective relations it inspires (rather than is granted *ipso facto*). But this perhaps is one of the more accurate dilemmas of cyborg existence – how to transcend the primary purpose of being built as an instrument of military defence. Nevertheless all this could undoubtedly have been conveyed through a non-heterosexual relationship.

Far from fashioning new forms of subjectivity that escape traditional gender binaries, then, current representations of cyborgs – Creed's (1987) claim of their gendered conflation within the 'monstrous feminine' notwithstanding – currently seem to work more to reconstruct them anew. Does the trope of the child fare any better? The category of childhood, like that of the cyborg, carries no explicit gender marking, but despite the polymorphous perversity of infancy it too is structured according to gendered meanings. The realm of childhood as other, as outside (Western, 'high') culture, is largely feminized, while the productive (growing, thinking) child of developmental psychology is culturally masculine (Burman, 1994). The huge success of *Sophie's World* (Gaarder, 1996), a book describing philosophical problems in accessible terms through the device of explaining them to a little girl, offers pause for thought. Is the girl child now interpellated into rational expertise (corresponding with the widely publicized current educational success of girls relative to boys)? Or does this rather mark the resurgence of the old story of hidden depths and wisdom 'out of the mouths of babes'?

What both figures share is the opportunity to rehearse and reflect upon contemporary mores through practices of education. So Yod's questions within *Body of Glass* function in much the same way as children's naïve but unprejudiced queries figure in modern literature, that is to highlight customs and social structures, including their (racial, sexual, class) inequalities and injustices. At this moment the trope of cyborg and child converge. Indeed the same themes of the extent to which the hardware determines the history and fate of the entity are figuring as much now around children and humanity as with artificial intelligences. The rise of biotechnology not only makes cyborgs more 'conceivable' by the day, but also ushers in discourses of genetic determination of a piece with other fundamentalisms. If new generation cyborgs are increasingly expected to require extended periods of vulnerability and helplessness to accumulate the skills required for flexible and adaptive behaviour, then children are becoming less romanticized and 'othered', and more (socially and genetically) engineered. The selective abortion of girls is a sobering case in point.

Ambiguous beginnings

One of the more progressive features of the cyborg is said to be its anti-developmental character. While the child is recruited into the grand narratives of truth, science and reason through its location in modernity's racist and sexist chain of being, the cyborg – as a hybrid between human and machine – has no parents, no childhood, and no easy affiliation. Always the exception, the construction, the clay-built figure animated by (and then sometimes invested with) demonic appetites, the cyborg does not sit easily alongside the discourses of normalization and naturalization that give rise to developmental psychology's regulative activities. Shorn of the romance of the origin story, the primal scene, the cyborg is portrayed (by Haraway at least) as potentially freer to configure its political horizons in novel ways (although, significantly, for Piercy the primal scene of its creation and history preoccupied her cyborg's imagination). If the child codes for the humanist subject, is the cyborg its antimony?

This is an important political-rhetorical moment to stay with. Is the child irrevocably tied to the narrative of linear development that fixes the world in its current order? Is the cyborg somehow better placed to figure subjective possibilities that can be historically discontinuous with – or in Haraway's terms illegitimate and unfaithful to – the past of modern human relations of oppression? Would we emancipate ourselves from the crime of making the poor and needy shoulder the burden of development (and blaming them for our de-development of them) by jettisoning the child of the modern social imaginary? It is this child in whose name whole peoples were and are infantilized under colonial rule and which made them operate as justification for their 'civilization' (see for example, Cooter, 1992). It is this child whose 'rescue' reproduces Western fantasies of omnipotence and competence. This child is bartered for, traded in, and yet for whom wars stop to allow immunization because children are designated 'zones of peace'. Can the motif of the cyborg challenge the inexorability of the modern industrial narrative of progress that development – the embodied development of the child – inscribes?

Political ambiguities

I begin to wonder if notions of illegitimacy and infidelity are perhaps sufficiently modern (rather than postmodern) in morality to appeal to us 'low' and 'middle-tech' consumers who form the majority of the world's population. Amid the celebrations of the flux and flow of cyberdiscourse, these words stand out as residues of (currently widespread and accelerating) patriarchal control over women's sexuality and (re)production. They resonate with notions of (false) claims, of individual ownership and accountability to 'traditional' (religious/class) communities, of people as property. But they also allude to deep emotional attachments and social codes – of honour, loyalty and passion – that call for reconfiguation and reconciliation, rather than retribution, as a response to changing moralities and life-'styles'. They set up an arena of subjectivity that interpellates the cyborg as something we might be able to identify with, as the inadvertent rebel, or the innocently wronged; of a subjectivity born of a failed, rather than token, (parental, societal) commitment. In this sense the cyborg – in its isolation, its unique and freakish aspects – does invite some identification for the alienated (post)modern subject struggling to achieve ontological security.

But would this not be to recreate another modernist subject? Surely the politically progressive aspects of the cyborg demand that it should remain inscrutable, a projective surface that resolutely repels rather than absorbs fantasies. Surely the cyborg is a symptom, a process, rather than a new psychological model? How then to resist such personalizing, individualizing impulses? And in particular, how to prevent it fulfilling the same functions (of regulatory generalization and homogenization of differences) as those currently carried out by the trope of the child as ideal-typical subject. For it was precisely such moral-political tensions of cultural differences and sex/gender varieties that were eclipsed by the singularizing shift from children to 'the child', and that permitted the installation of the linear narrative of progress.

If, as Creed (1987) suggests, the abject is a domain of projected (cultural) fantasies, constructions of naturalized archetypes based on the historical position of women rather than a necessary intrapsychic structure, then one way forward may be to recognize those aspects as already existing features of modern Western subjectivity, as within, rather than beyond, this. What would it mean to take back the projections and empty the borderlands of the dominant cultural imaginary, that is also 'our' own, of such subjective investments? Is it possible to see the cyborg as bits of wire, tin and electronics and explore what (its as well as 'our') 'life' might be? Could 'we' start to explore the many other hybrid, monstrously ambiguous, living entities that already populate late modernity, who already constitute who 'we' are? For as Sandoval (1995) points out, the radical possibilities accorded cyborg consciousness are a specific reiteration of the technologies and methodologies of oppositional consciousness already produced by postcolonial critics and third world feminisms, of subalternity and alterity, of displacement and hybridity.

It seems that in order to maintain the generative and inspirational qualities of the cyborg it is paradoxically necessary to ward off the 'specializing' impulse to treat it as something new and qualitatively distinct from previous representations and incarnations of subjectivity. This involves resisting the capitalist dynamic that markets the cyborg as the new product that renders old brand models obsolete. For in allowing such a break 'the cyborg' is abstracted and deified, as much as was 'the child'. To retain the political force of Haraway's celebrated claim that she would rather be a cyborg than a goddess, then, I want to argue for staying with the material complexity and diversities of hybrid forms and tentative relations. In the end the cyborg is probably as politically unstable a metaphorical resource as any other, but if its physical and epistemological ambiguities can be used to work out some of our own (in all the diversity of who 'we' are), we might well get ourselves into better (and better conceived) political shape.

References

Aries, P. (1962) *Centuries of Childhood*. London: Cape.
Burman, E. (1994) *Deconstructing Developmental Psychology*. London: Routledge.
Cooter, R. (ed.) (1992) *In the Name of the Child*. London: Routledge.
Crawford, M. (1998) The reciprocity of psychology and popular culture, in E. Burman (ed.) *Deconstructing Feminist Psychology*. London: Sage.
Creed, B. (1987) 'Horror and the monstrous feminine: an imaginary abjection', *Screen*, **28**(1): 44–70.
Davis-Floyd, R. and Dumit, J. (eds) (1998) *Cyborg Babies: From Techno-sex to Techno-tots*. London: Routledge.
Gaarder, J. (1996) *Sophie's World*. London: Orion.
Galison, P. (1994) The ontology of the enemy: Norbert Weiner and the cybernetic vision', *Critical Inquiry*, **21**(1): 228–66.
Goldberg, B. (1997) 'Humouring the subject: theory, discourse and situated comedies'. Unpublished PhD thesis, The Manchester Metropolitan University.
Gronemeyer, M. (1993) 'Helping', in Sachs, W. (ed.) *The Development Dictionary*. London: Zed Press.
Hamilton, S. (1998) 'The cyborg, 11 years later: the not-so-surprising half-life of the Cyborg Manifesto', *Convergence*, **3**(2): 104–20.
Haraway, D. (1985) 'A manifesto for cyborgs: science, technology and socialist feminism in the 1980s', reproduced in Haraway, D. (1991) *Simians, Cyborgs and Women*. London: Verso.
Harris, A. (1987) 'The rationalisation of infancy', in Broughton, J. (ed.) *Critical Theories of Psychological Development*. New York: Plenum Press.
Hess, D. (1995) 'On low-tech cyborgs', in Gray, C.H., Figueroa-Sarriera, H.J. and Mentor, S. (eds) *The Cyborg Handbook*. London: Routledge.
Itzin, C. and Newman, J. (eds) (1995) *Gender, Culture and Organizational Change*. London: Routledge.
Jackson, S. (1992) 'The amazing deconstructing woman', *Trouble and Strife*, **25**: 25–31.
Kristeva, J. (1982) *Powers of Horror: An Essay on Abjection*. New York: Columbia University Press.

Lykke, N. and Braidotti, R. (eds) (1996) *Between Monsters, Goddesses and Cyborgs: Feminist Confrontations with Science, Medicine and Cyberspace.* London: Zed Books.

Marsden, J. (1996) 'Virtual sexes and feminist futures: the philosophy of cyberfeminism', *Radical Philosophy,* **78**: 6–16.

Piaget, J. (1933) 'Social evolution and the new education', *Education Tomorrow,* **4**: 3–25.

Piaget, J. (1957) 'The child and modern physics', *Scientific American,* **197**: 46–51.

Piercy, M. (1992) *Body of Glass.* London: Penguin.

Rutkowska, J. (1993) *The Computational Infant.* Hemel Hempstead: Harvester Wheatsheaf.

Sandoval, C. (1995) 'New sciences: cyborg feminism and the methodology of the oppressed', in Gray, C.H., Figueroa-Sarriera, H.J. and Mentor, S. (eds) *The Cyborg Handbook.* London: Routledge.

Squire, C. (1989) *Significant Differences: Feminisms in Psychology.* London: Routledge.

Steedman, C. (1996) *Strange Dislocations.* London: Virago.

Stone, L., Smith, H. and Murphy, L. (eds) (1973) *The Competent Infant.* New York: Basic Books.

Walker, J. (ed.) (1997) *Halliwell's Film and Video Guide,* 12th edn. London: HarperCollins.

Yuval-Davis, N. (1997) *Gender and Nation.* London: Sage

CHAPTER 11

Cyberpsychology and Cyborgs

DAN HEGGS

The impact and extension of computer technology continues unabated as schools and businesses are encouraged to get on-line and join the microserf bandwagon. At stake is the ability to access, and make available, information: 'Information has become our clothing, our food, our air and free access to it has become a basic human right' (Pesce, 1992). But as the computer revolution increases its influence and hold on everyday life social and cultural patterns swirl into place which connect with a variety of discourses that inhabit the pullulating technological matrix. Such technologies map the virtual territories that are being opened up and colonized. This mapping also throws into question the relationship that humans have with technology and therefore also remaps the lived world. For example: Weather satellites alter perceptions of weather systems, as land masses and hot and cold fronts offer visible plans far broader than the depiction of merely local effects. Such changes are not possible unless articulated through a technological paradigm (see Berland, 1996; Žižek, 1997).

A variety of approaches has been employed to examine the discourses of new technology and, as such, interest in its effects and consequences are not restricted to a single discipline. Links are forged between cultural theory and technoscience that map the extent of the technological matrix and its political effects. *Cyberpsychology* is one of the approaches. It rests uncomfortably, we hope, on a boundary. This allows it to engage with debates and wider issues within the matrix while acknowledging the long association that psychology, and particularly cognitive psychology, has with new technologies. In doing so, cyberpsychology, highlights 'some of the relationships between psychological knowledge and social control' (Gordo-López, 1995: 7).

Cyberpsychology looks to the emerging psycho-social spaces and virtual communities of the technological matrix as sites of possibility that aid the development of strategies and political critiques. It is therefore subversive and enabling, indicating points and means of resistance. The cyborg is a central image and concept within cyberpsychology. It is the site, the 'body', that can be made legible and can be thought of as the starting point for explorations of the relationships between humans and technology.

Interest in cyborgs has been fuelled by speculative science fiction narratives that offer the opportunity to return to the present: 'New forms of experience and social relationships are created in science fiction, and these new forms offer distinctive vantage points, different arrays of subject positions from which to view the present' (Parker, 1997: 190). Another related vantage point from which to view the present is the corpus of superhero narratives. The superhero genre often partakes of science fiction discourse but, for the most part, the stories are set in the present. In this instance superhero narratives offer an instructive means of comparison with cyborg imagery.

The American comic book has two main tributary sources. First, the popularity of dime novels in the first half of the twentieth century and, second, collections of comic strips used in marketing campaigns in the mid-1930s. The first issue of *Action Comics* (a DC Comics title) in June 1938 featured a brightly coloured figure in dramatic pose on its front cover. The character was Superman, and his popularity was to forge the success of the superhero genre. Many imitators soon followed in his speeding wake. One of these, a year later, was Batman. They are probably the best known comic characters, having had continuous success in comics and other media.

The focus in this chapter is on the construction of superhero and cyborg identity. I display similarities between superheroes and cyborgs as they appear in popular cultural representations, and demonstrate that the cyborg and superhero resist the consequences of boundary transgression and that the political affinities, so often desired of cyborgs, are open to naturalization, for example around the thematic of masculinity. However, when the emphasis is moved away from the analysis of identity to that of reporting *events* then the superhero and the cyborg can be reconfigured politically to enable various forms of domination and transgression to be examined from a number of alternative vantage points. In this way it is possible to develop strategies that examine and map the resistances and changes within emerging psycho-social spaces and develop a cyborg language that maps and inscribes more than just individual bodies.

What is a cyborg?

Theory and descriptions pertaining to cyborgs resonate uncomfortably with the salient features of many comic book heroes. The cyborg offers a critical approach to superheroes, but this is reciprocated as superheroes offer a critical approach to cyborgs. Before comparing cyborgs with superheroes it is necessary to outline some of their chief characteristics.

The term 'cyborg' (coined by Clynes and Kline, 1960) is a contraction of 'cybernetic organism' and a result of research into cybernetic systems. These are 'complex, feedback-controlled systems, responsive to the flows of matter and energy that pass or "dissipate" through them' (Marsden, 1996: 7). Research into such systems was important during and after the war for military and space research.

Haraway's (1985) germinal essay, 'A cyborg manifesto: science, technology and socialist-feminism in the late twentieth century' has, as Marsden (1996: 6) indicates, 'attained cult status in many branches of contemporary theory', and is important for its explicitly political description and definition of cyborg imagery.

A cyborg at its simplest is the conjunction of humans and technology. More frequently it refers to the extension or enhancement of the body through its fusion with technology. Cyborgs are therefore *hybrids* of human and machine, or machines and organisms. Cyborgs are not static or held to one form. Different types of prosthesis lead to a variety of cyborg types that relate to the environment through a technological paradigm which re-articulates notions of identity and subjectivity. This is one of the starting points for Haraway's exploration of cyborg affectivity. Cyborgs are more than the technological enhancement of human ability, but the site where the relationship between nature and culture are reworked.

Haraway's cyborg is a complex hybrid. It integrates more than a technological paradigm, connecting with a variety of competing discourses in order to reinvigorate feminist-socialist politics – hence the subtitle of the paper. The cyborg is the central figure in an attempt to write an ironic myth which also functions as a 'rhetorical strategy and political method', one Haraway 'would like to see more honoured within socialist-feminism' (1991: 149). It is a boundary creature resident in the hinterland between fact and fiction, and it partakes in science fiction discourse and lived experience. Haraway argues for the cyborg as a 'fiction mapping our social and bodily reality and as an imaginative resource suggesting some very fruitful couplings' (ibid.: 150). The cyborg therefore appears to function as a descriptive mechanism that aids critiques and suggests possibilities, but it is a great deal more than just 'an imaginative resource': 'The cyborg is our ontology; it gives us our politics' (ibid.). There is, as Marsden reminds us, something 'unashamedly utopian' about Haraway's cyborg vision (Marsden, 1996: 6). It does not revel in the dystopian visions of cyberpunk but prefers to consider the possibilities inherent to affinity and hybridity. An important aspect of Haraway's cyborg vision is the rejection of 'Western' origin stories.

The cyborg appears, and is politicized, at the points where boundaries are transgressed. Such transgressions are also acts of creation that occur outside Oedipal narratives: 'In a sense, the cyborg has no origin story in the Western sense' (Haraway, 1991: 150). Cyborgs are illegitimate, unimpressed by notions of organic wholeness and are 'oppositional, utopian, and completely without innocence' (ibid.: 151). They are, of course, the progeny of military research, of patriarchal capitalism and state socialism. This is not a handicap as there is no need to remain faithful to their fathers, who are 'inessential' (ibid.).

The cyborg myth written by Haraway, then, is a fiction, a seductive non-Oedipal narrative that functions as utopian cyberpunk and political manifesto. The cyborg characteristics she describes are desired characteristics. She is, in effect, defining a cyborg identity that has nothing to do with any actual lived empirical subjectivity, that refuses hierarchies and dualisms and posits a postgender world in which 'we are all chimeras, theorized and fabricated hybrids of machine and organism' (ibid.: 150). It is in the sidestepping of the Western origin story that the cyborg has its roots. I will now look at two characters whose origin stories are clearly based within Oedipal narratives in order to problematize some cyborg characteristics.

Superheroes and origin stories

One of the defining characteristics of superheroes is the *origin story*. Such stories provide explanations of the characters' powers, why they assumed hero identities and the nature of their campaigns. As such, they supply the characters with personal histories and psychological motivation and so render them meaningful. Origin stories, therefore, can be understood as myths of origin that are invoked to offer convincing accounts of superhero subjectivity. Probably the best known examples of superhero origin stories are those of Batman and Superman. The origin stories have been extensively used in the comic books to update the characters for new audiences (most notably in the 1986 revamp of *Superman: The Man of Steel*), to help the transition to other media, to transfer the characters to other times and settings (for example in the *Elseworld* series) and to explain the characters' actions in the face of adversity and possible (but never final) defeat. The origin stories are simple and easily précised. For Batman it is thus:

> As Bruce [Wayne] and his parents walked home from a movie, a nameless thug attacked them. Attempting to steal the mother's necklace, the hoodlum shot and killed both mother and father when the latter attempted to resist. A traumatised Bruce swore to take vengeance through a war on criminals... Seeking both disguise and psychological advantage he decided that 'I shall become a bat'. (Uricchio and Pearson, 1991: 194)

And for Superman:

> A brilliant scientist fails to persuade the ruling council of his planet's imminent demise. To save his son he places him in a rocket ship and blasts him toward a distant planet. The child is found by a Kansas farmer and his wife, who raise him as their own. As he grows he develops amazing abilities. He realises that he must put these powers to the benefit of mankind and so takes the role of Superman to be able to act anonymously and protect his identity. (Heggs, 1996: 3)

These two stories have underpinned the enduring nature of the characters. Over the period during which the characters have been fighting to preserve the public peace they have not aged. The origin story confers authenticity on the various versions of the characters and all take place in the present. The origin story therefore functions as a fountain of youth and bestows a form of textual immortality. There is obviously a history to the various versions of the characters, but each incarnation contains its own present and refers to its own past and future. There is therefore a spatial relationship between versions that resignifies the present of the narrative around common themes. For Walter Benjamin (1992: 91) 'storytelling is the art of repeating stories, and this art is lost when the stories are no longer retained'. The Superman and Batman origin stories have been endlessly repeated and in the process altered to fit the needs of the plotlines.

This is what Barthes (1977), referring to the 'myth', called the 'privation of history'. Each invocation of an origin story is drained of meaning and resignified. As the process is repeated 'history evaporates' leaving only a 'beautiful object'. Myths are, therefore, constructed, they 'cannot possibly evolve from the "nature" of things' (1977: 110). As the public becomes aware of these mythic stories, and as these stories are retold and elaborated upon, they are also *depoliticized*. In other words the constant repetition make politically constructed relationships appear to be natural. So, we might now even take it for granted that a young Bruce Wayne should grow up to take on the guise of a Batman, and that an alien baby should land in Kansas and eventually become Superman. Narrative coherence is therefore structured by the use of origin stories. By placing them into wider contexts the characters can be read alongside contemporary concerns and anxieties that are reflected and resisted within the texts. It is therefore possible to see how the narratives operate as a screen for the projection of fantasies and desires. These fantasies and desires are also found within other genres and disciplines, in this instance, cyborgs.

A closer look at one version of both origin stories will aid the critique and comparison with cyborgs. The example I have chosen is *World's Finest* (Gibbons and Rude, 1992). The story focuses on two orphanages in Gotham and Metropolis and the interest shown in them by Lex Luthor and the Joker, the best known adversaries of Batman and Superman. As the plot unfolds it becomes evident that Luthor intends to expand his business concerns in Gotham, while the Joker seizes the opportunity to holiday in Metropolis. Neither Superman nor Batman can cope with the series of disturbances caused by the visiting foe. An agreement is reached whereby the heroes swap cities in order to maintain the peace and thwart the plans of their antagonists. The origin stories are invoked early in the story, following an introduction to both cities and the problems faced therein.

There is a juxtaposition of the panels in the comic which visually demonstrates that the form of the stories are structurally equivalent, and also that the characters are opposites, positioned at either extreme of a superhero spectrum: 'Their primal, complementary qualities have given rise to the entire field [of comics] and, arguably, they define its parameters' (Gibbons, 1992: in introduction). The origin stories, as they are represented in this instance, show how the tragic loss of (biological) parents haunts the characters. An EEG-like framing of the panels indicates the increasing excitement and agitation connected with the recollection of the origin stories. These stories are shown to haunt the characters. The first frames of the origin story show concerned and caring parents, and the actions taken to protect the children. The first two panels of the second page show the moments in which the course of the characters' lives are irrevocably changed. The following panels contain the consequences of the freeze-framed irreversible moments. A small child is held in the arms of a woman while a man behind her fights to put out a fire; a young boy is led away by a policeman while another searches for a pen and readies his notebook. In the background of each panel is what has been lost by the characters, their biological parents. In the foreground there are indications of their future roles. Such dreams are disturbing, threatening; they awaken the characters, who react in different ways.

The origin stories, as outlined and described, are indicative of exactly the kind of 'Western' origin stories maligned by Haraway. A fall from grace, from originary fullness is illustrated to which the heroes yearn to return. Clark Kent and Bruce Wayne have been wrenched – more than separated – from the comfortable state of fullness. But where the cyborg 'skips the step of original unity, of identification with nature in the Western sense' (Haraway, 1991: 151), the superhero places a firm foot on the ladder's first rung. They are beholden to the Oedipal narrative, and donning a tight-fitting costume acts as a cover that allows Batman and Superman to operate at a distance from societal regulation. The origin stories of Batman and Superman are precisely that; they refer to the subjective origins of the heroes, not of the mild-mannered reporter or of the playboy millionaire. The origin stories may be thought of as *primal scene fantasies* (Laplanche and Pontalis, 1973). Such scenes are concerned with the origins of the subject (in this instance, of the superheroic individual) and refer to a past event that can be returned to and retroactively resignified in order to make sense of the subject's current situation. They are fantasies, and need not necessarily have occurred to be psychically effective. Each case is rooted in the Oedipal narrative.

In Freudian theory it is through the internalization of the Oedipal narrative that society is supported. The desire to kill the father leads to feelings of guilt, the inevitable effect of the Oedipus complex and development of superegoic structures. This sense of guilt is repressed and sealed within the unconscious. The constant return to the origin story is indicative of a compulsion to repeat 'and the regression it implies leads to the annihilation of the subject' (Penley, 1986: 81). Becoming Batman or Superman might, therefore, be seen as the visible symptom of guilt. The superhero identity therefore serves to protect, not the society in which it appears, but the individual against threats to a past fantasy state found in the 'family'.

Superman and Batman may, then, be thought of as boundary creatures but not as boundary transgressors. To transgress the boundary between human and non-human would require Superman and Batman to retire from their day jobs. Their opponents do not have this reservation, particularly those of the Batman. The Joker, for instance, rarely tries to hide the stigmata of his appearance. Batman and Superman serve the societies in which they act by protecting it, by combating threats to the status quo and this is supported by their close associations with institutional signs of public morality, Gotham City Police and *The Daily Planet*. To act within the boundary is to mark its limits and signal a resistance to its transgression. The origin stories depict a rupture in the natural order of things, based in a family structure, that opens a subjective space in which the super-hero identity can eventually be placed.

There is, then, a double bind that holds the hero identity in place. On the one hand, Clark Kent and Bruce Wayne need to transcend their physical limitations and to be freed to signify different relations on the margins of the societal order, in order to be able to protect the populace from danger. On the other hand, their rooted-ness in Oedipal narratives armours them with a rampant individuality that prevents them from transgressing the boundaries produced by societal norms. This rootedness pulls them back and prevents them from exploring the consequences of their actions or their need to continue acting. The actions of Batman and Superman armour the subjectivity of Bruce Wayne and Clark Kent. Guilt is transformed into trauma and the repetition of the origin story neutralizes the possibility for collective action. The prospect of a

utopian ending is negated before it can arise. The child-like innocence of the characters requires them to adopt a superheroic guise.
They are monstrous inflated humanist characters unable to acknowledge their own culpability and to face their own fears and desires.
They act to support the status quo, but in doing so also highlight,
for critical readers, forms of domination.

Superman and Batman offer images of a masculine ideal. Strong,
self-sufficient bodies acting independently in the world. The characters fit comfortably into the mould of the American monomyth (Lang
and Trimble, 1988) where individual solutions are preferred over
societal problems. However, the individual solutions on offer are
symptomatic of the pathology of Batman and Superman and their
desire to reinstate an impossible originary fullness.

Cyborgs and superheroes, or some problems with cyborg identity

Cyborgs are everywhere, populating cyberpunk and science fiction
texts, as well as within the lived experience of the social body. And as
the number of breaches between the human and the non-human
increases so does the importance of the cyborg as an imaginative
resource: 'This figure of the cyborg helps us bring together myths
and tools, representations and embodied realities, as a way of understanding postmodernity' (Gray et al., 1995: 2). This cyborg has the
marks of its hybridity written upon its body and it is rendered intelligible, or at least identifiable, by such inscriptions. Yet, as the figure
of the cyborg accumulates more and more prostheses and as the
number of possible combinations and configurations proliferates,
and connects with a wider variety of discourses and technologies, so
too does the image of the cyborg become increasingly complicated
and disputed.

Haraway highlighted the border transgression that marked the
point of emergence for the cyborg. However, the image placed at the
centre of her blasphemy is left undescribed while its properties are
defined and described. The cyborg occupies a cypher-like space of
possibility. Its qualities and characteristics are outlined but not
inscribed in physical bodies. The body of the cyborg is, therefore, also
a constructed concept, with theory functioning as a technological
implant that provides it with a political and descriptive valency. I
shall argue that a focus on cyborg identity, characterized by forms of

cybernetic implant, is open to naturalization and reclamation, particularly when the focus is placed on the individual body.

Clearly, many of the descriptions of cyborg identity have been inspired by popular culture representations. Such images of the cyborg, as seen in film and comics and novels, obviously are related to the theorized cyborg that inhabits some strands of academic discourse. They are, however, different in a number of ways. Rather than opening up utopian and political opportunities, characters such as the *Terminator* (dir. Cameron, 1984) and *RoboCop* (dir. Verhoeven, 1987) violently resist any such possibility. An outline of comic book counterparts will aid a critique of the construction of the film cyborg.

Within the panelled world of comic books there are increasing numbers of cyborgs that 'reveal much about how these characters are perceived. [They] represent the most prevalent medium in which many children and adults are forming their impressions of cyborgian culture' (Oehlert, 1995: 219). Comic books have long had a tradition of cyborg-like characters ranging from the Nazi-bashing adventures of *Captain America* during the Second World War to the industrialist Tony Stark acting as *Iron Man* (whose suit also helped him to live with his heart condition). However, with the dawning of a more distinct cyborg age the cyborg figure has become more clearly articulated within comic book narratives. Oehlert distinguishes between three main categories which refer to different levels of integration and of an increasing complexity. The first is called *simple controller* (simple implants or removable suits). Such systems augment natural abilities and 'would seem to be the equivalent of mental Waldos [prosthetically operated machines]' (ibid.: 224). The next category is that of the *bio-tech integrator*. These are non-removable systems of greater complexity. Characters have greater control over intimate and alterable implants. Whereas characters in the first category cannot reconfigure the functioning of their cyborg implants, characters in this category are able to do so. The final category is that of *genetic cyborgs*. This is where there is purposeful alteration of genetic code that leads to enhancement of abilities. Characters, such as Superman, do not fall into this category as no deliberate alteration has taken place.

This categorization, while it identifies three different possible varieties of cyborg prosthesis, does not consider the manner of the boundary transgression between the human and non-human and fails to examine the extent of the political ramifications of such hybrid identities. These are all high-tech cyborgs. Oehlert's categorization is based on research on cyborg soldiers, and it appears that

they do remain faithful to their fathers in a way that is not desired
by Haraway: 'The issue of humanity with comic book cyborgs then is
not if the machine will take over the human side of the equation but
what will the human half choose to do with his new abilities'
(Oehlert, 1995: 227). Such cyborg characters have a tendency to
violence, to dealing with problems in a personal and graphic style
that highlights an ambiguity of the comic book cyborg. The clear cut
moral divide between heroes and villains is blurred and is 'indicative
of our unease with these creations' (ibid.: 226).

An example of this follows from the exaggerated reports of Superman's death in 1993 in *The Return of Superman*. Four pretenders to his
crown appeared in Metropolis. The different versions of Superman
and the public's doubtful response to their presence over Metropolis
seems to indicate a general feeling of insecurity, one that is
connected to the truth of the Superman identity. The first is a clone
of the original Superman, the second an old Kryptonian weapon in
the shape of Superman, the third a man in a suit (not unlike the Iron
Man) and the last a cyborg Superman. While all of these characters
fit into the categories used by Oelhert, only the cyborg Superman –
who here does have his own origin story – is truly dangerous with
his face permanently cut away in a style reminiscent of scenes from
The Terminator and the ability to alter parts of his body at will and
combine with different machines. This 'Superman' intends to
destroy Metropolis, to ruin the reputation of the 'Man of Tomorrow'.
It would appear that in the Superman narratives fully integrated
polymorphing cyborgs are a threat (especially as they also have at
their command great war machines capable of destroying cities at a
stroke). The resurrected Superman, acting in concert with the
remaining supermen, defeats the cyborg and in so doing asserts the
legitimacy of the Superman role. With the defeat of the cyborg
Superman by the hand of the one true Superman affairs in Metropolis settle down to 'normal' once more.

The Return of Superman story arc can be read alongside fears and
anxieties connected to the dissipation of concrete subjects. A
discourse on identity is played out through the narratives whereby
'true' identities are being sought as guarantors of the truth of the
subject. The confirmation of Superman's return by Lois Lane rein-
states the figure of Superman as a master signifier that guarantees a
concrete subject against boundary transgressions and the disintegration of the subject. The only person upset by the return of Superman
is Lex Luthor, as Superman is a threat to his plans to dominate

Metropolis through his company LexCorp. Corporations and multinationals are the great evils of the cyborg comic book world, a concern shared with film cyborgs (see Oelhert, 1995: 228). The influence and power of the nation state is perceived as waning in comparison to the hegemony of corporate strategy who are the producers and controllers of cyborg technology, in film and comics at least (see Gray *et al.*, 1995). In the *Terminator* and *RoboCop* films the central characters struggle against the control exerted over them by the corporations Omni Consumer Product and Cyberdine Systems. There is a sense in which RoboCop and, to a lesser extent, Terminator rebel against the systems which produced, maintain and manipulate them. The only form of response, however, is one of extreme violence. The use of violence would then appear to be a defining trait for comic book and film cyborgs.

Making a stand against the impersonal corporation is, again, an attempt to assert a concrete identity and re-find a sense of wholeness. The armoured bodies of RoboCop and Terminator transgress the boundary between the human and the non-human and between the machine and organism but they are seemingly unaware and resistant to their cyborg nature. They seek identity rather than affinities, and the site where nature and culture should be reworked becomes a point of resistance. These characters are reminiscent of the *Freikorps* members described by Klaus Theweleit (1989) where bodies were armoured in leather 'to assert their solidity against the threat of fluid women' (Claudia Springer, quoted in Bukatman, 1993: 306). Now the bodies of cyborgs are armoured 'against a new age (political and technological)' (Bukatman, 1993: 306). Springer suggests that it is the passivity of the interaction with computers that cyborgs resist. The feminization of the technology, concealed and fluid systems, is a threat to forms of masculinity. Thus, through the battle with the morphing T-1000 in *Terminator 2: Judgment Day* (dir. Cameron, 1991) film 'the mechanical Terminator expunges the nightmare of masculine and industrial obsolescence' (Bukatman, 1993).

Film cyborgs integrate with technology precisely in order to inoculate themselves against the threat to fragmented identity. They can therefore resist the consequences of full integration with the machine and preserve a sense of self. Such hybrid identities are, then, immune to the spread of the matrix. The example from *The Return of Superman* highlights how superheroes can function as a defence against the threat of the dangerous cyborg; they protect the 'body' from invasion. Film cyborgs, on the other hand, stand in a similar position on the boundary but are immunized against the spread of implantation. In both cases, the threat may still be thought of as emanating from an unseen female body.

Here the cyborg is similar to the superhero, at least in its popular culture versions. Figures like *Terminator* and *RoboCop* are particularly conservative and violent, attempting to gain and regain a sense of identity and wholeness. However, in the next section I shall look at how the superhero might be reconfigured in a progressive manner.

Reconfiguring superheroes

The longevity and remarkable ability of Batman and Superman to remain popular and adapt to changing audiences and social situations while desperately trying to stay the same is an outcome of the effective use of the origin stories. Such adaptation and constant renewal is a form of reconfiguration. The characters are merely reflections of their former selves. However, as the storylines have become more complex with more fixed elements accruing to the narratives the characters have become increasingly conservative. For example, Siegel and Shuster's original 1930s Superman frequently confronted social issues in a way that is now unthinkable. As the 'champion of the oppressed' Superman made munitions manufacturers and mine owners face the consequences of their business actions. A process of naturalization has taken place that has rounded the politically and socially sensitive corners from the characters, but while the construction of identity within the Superman and Batman narratives is deeply conservative and reliant on an origin story in the 'Western' sense, there is still a sense in which such characters may be reactivated politically against the grain.

In 1986, for example, DC Comics published *Batman: The Dark Knight Returns*. This was a radical reworking of the Batman mythos written and pencilled by Frank Miller. The story starts when Bruce Wayne narrowly survives the explosion of the car he is racing and has pushed past the limits of its capabilities. The explosion is reported in a news report which also includes items on the current heat and crime waves and also the anniversary of the 'last recorded sighting of the Batman' (Miller, 1986: 3). From this news item we learn that Bruce Wayne has retired from the Batman role, that debate continues as to the morality of Batman's actions and that many young people 'consider him a myth' (Miller, 1986: 3). Obviously, Batman does not remain retired. As events unfold, we are shown Bruce Wayne struggling to repress the beast inside: 'You are nothing – a hollow shell, a rusty trap that cannot hold me' (ibid.: 17). Shortly after, Batman is seen once again in the streets of Gotham dealing with a gang of teenagers called the Mutants, coping with the reappearance of Two-Face and the Joker, and finally facing down Superman following the detonation of a nuclear bomb.

The 'cyberpunk rebirth' (Rushkoff, 1994: 233) of an aged Batman placed the geriatric hero into a media-saturated city where his actions are reported, interpreted and debated. However, other than being much older, Miller's version of the Batman is little different from earlier (and later) versions of the character. He still triumphs in the face of adversity and the origin story remains a core motivating force for the character. What is markedly different in *The Dark Knight Returns* is the narrative setting: 'He is the same Batman who fought criminals in earlier, simpler decades, who now, as an older man, is utterly unequipped for the challenges of Cyberia' (Rushkoff, 1994: 233). There are evident difficulties in overcoming the compulsion to repeat and the need of Bruce Wayne to act as the Batman. As Bukatman (1993: 307) puts it 'Miller has become the poet laureate of last-gasp cyborgism... his characters are always "returning" to their killing ways despite their perceived obsolescence.' Such a statement alludes to the cyborgian nature of this version of Batman and also implies that similar characters may be seen as anachronistic, displaced from a society they no longer understand and dealing with problems using the only method they know, violence. However, it is necessary for characters like Superman and Batman to obscure their age-old origins in order to retain an audience. But if the characters remain 'essentially' the same then how ought the use of the origin story be understood, especially for progressive political purposes? The invocation of origin stories function not to update the character but to realign the character to the needs of an updated narrative. A shift in emphasis away from the construction of identity to one that considers the actions and interactions of characters can enable the site of the superhero 'body' to be reconfigured politically. Explicit emphasis on events enables political critiques that would be overlooked if their focus is only on a fixed Batman 'identity'.

Reconfiguring cyborgs

The reconfiguration of cyborgs is more problematic than that of superheroes. There are a number of reasons for this that arise as a result of the cyborg being the 'always already' theorized body. This is to say that the figure of the cyborg draws together a hybrid body of theory that is politicized as it is enunciated. For example, Haraway's descriptive definition of cyborg characteristics reworks the hybridized body in a politically progressive direction and in doing so refuses less politically astute cyborg bodies political valency. However, the blasphemous image of the cyborg that Haraway promotes remains a hybrid of fact and fiction, of myth and lived experience. The cyborg figures I have examined clearly reside in the popular imagination. While such figures are cyborgian there is often a resistance, an armouring of the body against change. RoboCop and Terminator do not gain their ontology from their hybrid body forms. Rather they carry their prosthesis as stigmata, as signs of their suffering at the hands of the corporation. The armoured body marks its limits precisely and stalwartly defends it against all comers.

The cyborg in film sheds light on the fears and anxieties that surround the penetration of the body through new technologies. These particularly masculine fantasies are little different from the constructed superhero figures of comic books and film. Oehlert's categorization of cyborg types in comics ignored the similarities shared with other superhero types. In fact, the current plethora of cyborgs in comics might be best seen in line with the superhero genre's unerring ability to update narratives. In other words, the fascination with cyborgs reflects current preoccupations and fears in the same way that mutant and alien hero characters did in previous stages of the genesis of the superhero genre. As such, the characters might be best seen as part of a continuum that plots the changing visage of 'the hero of a thousand faces'. The cyborg hero-type in film and comics therefore resists the temptations of cultural change and collective action so that 'it is not society that is to guide and save the creative hero, but precisely the reverse' (Campbell, 1993: 391).

The focus here has been on the construction of identity of the superhero and so of the cyborg within popular-cultural texts. This focus has stressed the difficulty in side-stepping the initial identification with nature in the 'Western' sense and the difficulty in overcoming essentialist accounts of subjectivity. However, as I argued in the previous section, a shift in emphasis can rework the politically conservative figure against the grain. By placing the accent upon actions and events the emphasis is displaced onto the connections forged by cyborgs and so highlights forms of domination that would otherwise remain invisible.

The image of the cyborg described by Haraway functions as a tool, or more accurately as a theoretical prosthesis, as a nexus for accounts of changing notions of subjectivity and identity within postmodernity. However, it appears that there is a resistance to changing accounts of the construction of identity. What Haraway, and other 'cyborgologists', successfully highlight are the boundary breakdowns between human and machine and human and animal (see Pfeil, 1990: 93). When the accent is moved from the construction of identity to that of cyborg events then the monstrous cyborg unities enable 'the political struggle [to be seen] from both perspectives at once because each reveals dominations and possibilities unimaginable from the other vantage point' (Haraway, 1991: 154). The cyborg, as I have described it, suffers from single vision and only looks from one perspective. But it does allow others to gaze upon it and view political struggles from other perspectives.

My concern with Haraway's cyborg as a myth of political identity is that it too is naturalized and that, maybe, seeing from the point of view of the cyborg, is to suffer from the illusions of single vision. The cyborg figure is open to reclamation in a number of directions and this might also be to naturalize its political potency. A focus on identity is seductive and alluring. To become a cyborg is an exciting, consciously chosen, origin. But to look to cyborg events is to confront oppositions and be made to question the functioning of discourse as it appears in various situations.

Reconfiguring cyberpsychology

The use of cyborg imagery within cyberpsychology provides a potent myth which enables alternative perspectives to be highlighted. As I have stressed, however, this can lead to a set of oppositions being maintained between critical perspectives and the institutions such perspectives hope to disrupt. The identification of cyborg *events* functions to subvert this process and requires a transdisciplinary approach in order to explore the variety of aspects that impinge upon it. It allows affinities and different vantage points to be explored which may be overlooked when the emphasis is simply placed on the construction of identity.

References

Aronowitz, S., Martinsons, B. and Menser, M. (eds) (1996) *Techno science and Cyber Culture*. London: Routledge.

Barthes, R. ([1957]1977) *Mythologies*. London: Johnathan Cape.

Benjamin, W. ([1970]1992) *Illuminations*. London: Fontana Press

Berland, J. (1996) 'Mapping space: imaging technologies and the planetary body', in Aronowitz, S., Martinsons, B. and Menser, M. (eds) *Techno Science and Cyber Culture*. London: Routledge.

Bukatman, S. (1993) *Terminal Identity: The Virtual Subject in Postmodern Science Fiction*. Durham: Duke University Press.

Byrne. J, and Giordano, D. (1993) *Superman: The Man of Steel*. New York: DC Comics Inc.

Campbell, J. ([1949]1993) *The Hero of a Thousand Faces*. London: Fontana Press.

Clynes, M. and Kline, N. S. (1960) 'Cyborgs and space', *Astronautics*, Sept., 26–7, 74–5.

Fuchs, C. J. (1995) 'Death is irrelevant: cyborgs, reproduction and the future of male hysteria', in Gray, C.H., Figueroa-Sarriera, H.J. and Mentor, S. (eds), *The Cyborg Handbook*. London: Routledge.

Gibbons, D. (1992) 'Introduction', in Gibbons, D. and Rude, S. (eds) *World's Finest*. New York: DC Comics Inc.

Gibbons, D. and Rude, S. (1992) *World's Finest*. New York: DC Comics Inc.

Gordo-López, A. (1995) 'Cyberpsychology: an introduction', in Burman, E., Gordo-López, A. J., Macauley, R. and Parker, I. (eds) *Cyberpsychology: Conference, Interventions and Reflections*. Manchester: Discourse Unit.

Gray, C. H., Figueroa-Sarriera, H.J. and Mentor, S. (eds) (1995) *The Cyborg Handbook*. London: Routledge.

Haraway, D. (1985) 'A manifesto for cyborgs: science, technology and socialist-feminism in the late twentieth century', reproduced in Haraway, D. (1991).

Haraway, D. (1991) *Simians, Cyborgs and Women: The Reinvention of Nature*. London: Free Association Press.

Haraway, D. (1995) 'Cyborgs and symbionts: living together in the new world order', in Gray, C.H., Figueroa-Sarriera, H.J. and Mentor, S. (eds) *The Cyborg Handbook*. London: Routledge.

Heggs, D. (1996) 'Origin stories: psychology and popular culture'. Unpublished Presentation at the University of Valencia, Valencia.

Jurgens, D., Kesel, K., Simonson, L. *et al.* (1993) *The Return of Superman*. New York: DC Comics.

Lang and Trimble (1988) 'Whatever happened to the man of tomorrow? An examination of the American monomyth and the comic book superhero', *The Journal of Popular Culture*, **22**(3): 157–73.

Laplanche, J. and Pontalis, J. B. (1973) *The Language of Psychoanalysis*. London: Karnac.

Marsden, J. (1996) 'Virtual sexes and feminist futures: the philosophy of "cyberfeminism"', *Radical Philosophy*, **78**: 6–16.

Miller, F. (1986) *Batman: The Dark Knight Returns*. New York: DC Comics Inc.

Oehlert, O. (1995) 'From Captain America to Wolverine: cyborgs in comic books, alternative images of cybernetic heroes and villains', in Gray, C.H., Figueroa-Sarriera, H.J. and Mentor, S. (eds) *The Cyborg Handbook*. London: Routledge.

Parker, I. (1997) *Psychoanalytic Culture: Psychoanalytic Discourse in Western Society*. London: Sage.

Penley, C. (1986) 'Time travel, primal scene and the critical dystopia', *Camera Obscura*, **15**: 66–85.

Pesce, M. D. (1992) 'Final amputation: pathogenic ontology in cyberspace', gopher://alishaw.ucsb.edu:70/00/.speed/.s1.1/.articles/.pesce.txt

Pfeil, F. (1990) 'These disintegrations I'm looking forward to: science fiction from new wave to new age', in Pfeil, F. (ed.) *Another Tale to Tell: Politics and Narrative in Postmodern Culture*. London: Verso.

Raymond, E. S. (compiler) (1996) *The New Hacker's Dictionary*. Cambridge, MA: MIT Press.

Reynolds, R. (1992) *Superheroes*. London: Batsford.

Rushkoff, D. (1994) *Cyberia: Life in the Trenches of Cyberspace*. London: Flamingo

Theweleit, K. ([1977]1989) *Male Fantasies*, Volume 2. Cambridge: Polity Press.

Uricchio, W. and Pearson, E. (1991) 'I'm not fooled by that cheap disguise', in Pearson, E. and Uricchio, W. (eds) *The Many Lives of the Batman: Critical Approaches to a Superhero and his Media*. London: BFI Publishing.

Žižek, S. (1997) *The Plague of Fantasies*. London: Verso.

CHAPTER 12

Against Social Constructionist Cyborgian Territorializations

Francisco Javier Tirado

What do we know about cyborgs? We know that 'cyborg' is a neologism formed by the fusion of the terms 'cybernetics' and 'organism', coined by Clynes and Kline (1960). We know that cyborg is a metaphor (Haraway, 1991; Piscitelli, 1995; Wolmark, 1995), that it speaks of what we are becoming; it speaks of the transgression of boundaries and of a way of breaking through old limits; between the modern oppositions 'I/other', 'mind/body', 'culture/nature', 'man/woman', 'civilized/primitive', 'reality/appearance', 'whole/part', and so on. We also know that the cyborg can develop into a discipline of knowledge, such as cyberanthropology (Escobar, 1996).

But what do we *not* know about cyborgs? Although the cyborg brings transgression and is a notion which speaks of hybridization and crossbreeding rather than purity, we have hardly started to follow through the implications of this; we do not thoroughly hybridize, we are not transgressors of old academic disciplines or hegemonic conceptual positions. Instead, it seems we are moving in the opposite direction. We do this, for example, precisely when we create specific disciplines, as is the case of 'cyborg anthropology' or when we try to describe its imaginary quality and the means it uses to produce knowledge. It seems we that we seek the *isolation* of cyborgs as if they were discrete things rather than studying their insertion in our everyday experience. In this sense, we have hardly

202

done anything more than affirm that with this notion the categories of modernity break down. The main exception to this is the work of subversion epitomized by Donna Haraway (1991) within a feminist frame of reference. She has shown how most North American feminists assume profound dualisms between mind–body and animal–machine in social practices. For this reason, they have developed analytical tools that are no more than the mere reflection of the object of their critique.

The purpose of this chapter is twofold. First, I shall try to subvert the commonly used notion of cyborg. To this end, I will pose three questions:

1. What is a cyborg? Here I will argue that it is not a metaphor but a *becoming*.
2. Do cyborgs have a history? Here I will argue that they are ahistorical and more than being simply processes, they are *events*.
3. What are the consequences of cyborgs? Here I will recover Haraway's portrayal of cyborgs as our ontology and will try to develop it in order to extract from it as many consequences as possible.

I will defend the idea that cyborgs are 'folds upon folds', as opposed to the forms of 'folding' and 'unfolding' involved in classicism and modernity respectively. Second, I will use this re-encounter with the idea of the cyborg to propitiate a re-encounter with social constructionism. The encounter with this perspective seeks to alter, at least to criticize, and even perhaps to contaminate it. We will then be in a better position to develop a definition of the term 'cyberpsychology' and to comment on the possibilities this opens up.

Cyborgs revisited

The cyborg is often treated as a metaphor, but it also operates as a form of transgression. The problem with treating it merely as a metaphor is that the notion of metaphor itself belongs to the realm of analogy, and to representationist thinking. Representation entails the subordination of something original which does not reveal itself as such, and which only does so through an image.

As long as the cyborg is treated as a metaphor, then, it seems that it would be well nigh impossible to ask what it represents, what underlying object and relations give it meaning, how the foundation for such a metaphor was laid, and what synthesizes its presence. Thus, within the realm of analogy, the cyborg appears to us like the figure represented by the hybridization between humans and animals, or animal–humans and machines, or a network of organic, inorganic entities and interests, or things and beings in general. As long as the cyborg remains within representationist thinking, then, it will be subject to *limits*. It will always depend on the original object from which it takes its meaning. For Bergson (1957), the transgression offered by metaphor, in this case the cyborg, operates on the underlying idea that concepts are formed to exactly resemble solid bodies. Constant, stable and consistent, with distinct and distinguishable borders. Indeed, this is what our concepts are like in Western culture, and this is what our conceptualization of the individual, artefact, attitude, gender, and so on is like in contemporary psychology. But the cyborg is a figure, a concept which *defies* these distinct and uniform borders. It introduces an oscillation between frontiers, shaking around the edges, borders with mobility and flexibility. The effect of the cyborg as metaphor is to force us to picture concepts with images other than that of solid bodies.

The controlled transgression which metaphor normally produces has other implications for cyborgs. It means that they lose their potential for subversion as, in the end, they are homogenized and turned into a unique, identifiable species. The metaphor converts cyborgs into go-between beings and things, leading to the appearance of another seemingly solid entity, the cyborg. The cyborg is placed in an intermediary position as a third element, fenced in by the previous two, continually dependent on them and at a point held on the same plane as the others. And so, despite transgressing this idea that concepts are like solids, the cyborg ends up being turned into a simple meeting point between beings and things. From this it follows that the representation of the cyborg is possible, albeit as a transgressive blend, but it is still a representation nevertheless. This is good certainly, but not good enough.

Let us try to think of cyborgs in another way. Let us try to tear them from the ambit of the metaphor and, therefore, from the terrain of representation. In this way we can make them more subversive and corrosive, and avoid the ultimate homogenization that converts them and reifies them into a species apart, as another species for the inventory of knowledge. We can do this by going further along the path which Bergson's reasoning opened up.

The metaphor of the cyborg can be employed as part of a kind of critique which affords the possibility of intermediary concepts which oscillate, fluctuate between other limits, which are further apart but present nonetheless. Michel Serres (1980), following Bergson, calls this situation or possibility of intermediary or oscillating concepts the logic of what is liquid or fluid. Fluids oscillate, change, vary, but always within certain boundaries, wide but unsurmountable, so the ultimate transgression of these limits is never reached. To think that a cyborg is a metaphor can help us to think of it as being fluid, like a liquid element.

Is it possible to cross these last frontiers? It is possible if we continue with Serres' proposal. Let us abandon this object model of liquids and think of fire, specifically of a flame. The topology of a flame is extremely paradoxical. The edges of the flame vary at such a speed for us that it is impossible to say either if they are actually present or where they are. All of a sudden, the flame disappears, it moves somewhere else, or it represents itself right here, and it is no longer the same flame. It continues and discontinues. It is more than unstable and less than stable. It is not a flow, as it lacks any constant to give it order. It is random fluctuation, always the same flame but bearing no relation to what it was a moment ago. It dances unpredictably. It has no constant edges, frontiers or margins. The flame enables us to get away from representationist thinking.

But if 'cyborg' has broken beyond the limits of metaphor, what is it now? What shall we call it? How do we understand it? We could say it is a flame, that it is like a flame. But this alone is just an image without concept; we need a concept which might take root in this image and escape from that of solid and fluid.

The logic of the flame is taken up in the notion of 'becoming' put forward by Deleuze (1977, 1990, 1993) and Deleuze and Guattari (1977, 1980). What is becoming, or a becoming for these authors? Becoming is not evolution, it does not operate by filiation, likeness, relationship or inheritance. It engenders mutual transformation between heterogeneous entities, establishing meetings and relations between them. Becoming does not imitate, but establishes relations between multiplicities.

So what does becoming cyborg or a becoming cyborg involve? It means that, in the first place, cyborgs are not intersections, midpoints or meetings between beings and things, subjects or objects. They are not even fluid concepts among solid concepts. Becoming cyborg is a movement without pause, without brakes, with a random speed which traps beings, things, subjects and objects. It is a sudden event. It is a movement which never ceases, with different speeds and different intensities. As becoming, cyborgs are not identical to each neither are they self-identical; there are no two cyborgs the same, they vary in size and appearance. They are in networks which continually join up and then disappear. There is no space or empty moment in which they can be considered a simple mixture of flesh and metal, of life and artificial organ. The cyborg is a logic in its own right, a movement of endless incorporation.

Haraway (1991: 254) claims that we are cyborgs. I think it is more a question of claiming that we *become* cyborgs. The difference in approach is important. It would seem from Haraway's text that each one of us is a distinct, identifiable cyborg in time and space; we are always becoming different cyborgs. We become mixtures at the inter-section of animal and machine, perhaps, but also with specific various interests and ideologies. These mixtures are not constant but change repeatedly. It is an agonizing process, without origins or teleologies.

We become cyborgs then, and becoming cyborg includes the poss-ibility of participating on different planes simultaneously. The cyborg is a to-and-fro between things and beings, languages and meanings. There is a multitude of superimposed planes, a gyration in endless movement, and the logic of this action is a *becoming cyborg*.

Cyborgs are ahistorical

A corollary of the argument so far is that cyborgs do not have a history. Does a flame have a history? A flame lights up and goes out, nothing more. In the flame, there is no history, only change. The flame is lacking in a point or moment which contains anything permanent or which sets a standard for writing its history. The flame either exists or it does not, simply that.

There are sometimes attempts made to make a history of the notion of cyborg. In these cases, we come across three different situations. In the first, we find a work of the etymological type which runs aground, of course, in 1960 with the article by Clynes and Kline in which the neologism 'cyborg' is coined. In the second, an effort is made to give depth to this neologism, and cyborgs or records of them in literature and mythology are sought and found. Frankenstein or the Greek god Hephaestus are well-tried examples in such cases. As a third strategy, we find a blend of etymological work and literary criticism.

There are two conditions for the realization of history. It requires an object perfectly identifiable in space, univocal, and homogeneous in its components. It also needs to inscribe in this object a single temporality which begins to unfold from the present moment. But what happens when we have an object with limits unidentifiable in space? What happens when our object has a present in which it is formed and deformed from a heterogeneous multiplicity of entities? What happens when an analyst freezes a becoming cyborg in an attempt to understand it, only to find that it possesses a multitude of temporalities?

The cyborg *surpasses* the historical. This is not because cyborgs are outside or on the edge of time, but because they condense a multitude of temporalities. They condense all possible times; unforeseeable, accelerated, determined, related, dead, forgotten, continued, and so on. Also, such condensation is continuous, random; it varies, and depends on each new relation which is established or dies. To picture this, let us imagine a network of associations continually growing and diminishing, encompassing new elements and eliminating them, moving, and shrinking. This situation does not allow us to describe either lineal genesis or continuous evolution. Rather than history or histories, we should be in the business of *cartography* and *topology* if we really want to get closer to cyborgs. If cyborgs are a collage of alien parts, it is then absurd to think about an origin in their identity. So how may we write the history of something containing a multitude of alien, unrelated temporalities?

It is not enough to say that cyborgs are a process because to know the process is to describe it in its temporal trajectory, to risk attributing that sedimented temporal process with an essence of some kind. Cyborgs are without essence. They are completely different one from another and have heterogeneity built into them. So, more than a process, cyborgs are an *event*. They refer to the singularity of their appearance or disappearance, singular emergencies; they do not represent the successive figures of a same meaning or use; they do not obey any pre-established logic or unwavering teleology. In a way, cyborgs are just a perpetual present, without a past that might be distinguished, without a future to dream of. Events are always different; difference is what is gathered up in events. They contain a law of absolute singularity, the knowledge of which is all we can aspire to, without any possibility of generalization. The cyborg is more a question of description of context than a history of succession.

Archaeology: the cyborg form

If, as Haraway (1991) claims, cyborgs are our ontology, we do need to know what form they take and how they came about. To this end, I shall turn to the archaeological approaches developed by Foucault (1966) in *The Order of Things*. Archaeology aims to establish that basic unit which at a given moment lays down the conditions which organize the order of things, the relation between beings and things, the possibilities of knowledge, of what can and cannot be said. Archaeology seeks to establish conditions of possibility in the same terrain of knowledge:

> One thing in any case is certain: man is neither the oldest nor the most constant problem that has been posed for human knowledge... In fact, among all the mutations that have affected knowledge of things and their order... only one alone, that which began a century and a half ago and is now perhaps drawing to a close has made it possible for the figure of man to appear... man is an invention of recent date. And one perhaps nearing its end. If those arrangements were to disappear as they appeared, if some event of which we can at the moment do no more than sense the possibility – without knowing either what its form will be or what it promises – were to cause them to crumble, as the ground of Classical thought did, at the end of the eighteenth century, then one can certainly wager that man would be erased, like a face drawn in sand at the edge of the sea. (Foucault, 1966: 386-387)

The 'man' to which Foucault refers here, or the man-form speaking in the terrain of knowledge, has not always existed. We maintain that term 'man' here quite deliberately, for this category is something that the cyborg will disrupt later. Let us see how, from the archaeology of man as a figure of knowledge and all that it implies, we may gain access to the cyborg as an ontological figure.

As Serres (1980) and Deleuze (1986) maintain, classical thought is notable for its passion and the central role it gives to the idea of the infinite. The most significant texts of the seventeenth century make reference to orders of infinitude: the infinite in size, the infinite for its own sake, the infinite within limits. Classical thought forever pursues and is lost in the infinite. Forever committed to this pursuit, it ends up without a centre or territory, it strives to establish a finite place among all these infinites so as to set about putting them in order. With this infinite, the individual in their everyday existence is limited, and cannot account for these infinite powers which transcend and surpass it. The encounter, the resulting compound of finitude and infinitude gives rise to the god-form (Deleuze, 1986). The sciences which emerge in this age are general disciplines because everything that is general indicates an order of infinitude, it approaches the infinite. Thus, for instance, there is no biology but natural history, no political economy but analysis of wealth, and instead of philology or linguistics, general grammar. To refer to the operations of this knowledge and in harmony with the task of representation, Foucault (1966) uses the word 'unfolding'. Classical thought explains reality by unfolding it, unfolding is the operation which leads to the infinite. Unfolding is the operator of classical knowledge, it is the movement which carries the finite towards the infinite, and man towards God.

Modernity presents a mutation in classical knowledge and the order of things. The god-form is substituted by the man-form. The individual, finite, measurable, comes into contact or relation with an exterior which is no longer infinite, but finite too. That which is exterior to man is as finite as he is. What has happened in this exterior? What is it that made it change? For Foucault, the answer can be given in archaeological terms. At the end of the eighteenth and into the nineteenth century, historicism enters into things, isolating them and defining them in line with its own coherence. It imposes on them a new form of order, the form of order implicit in the logic of time; that is, finitude. In their mere becoming, things find their principle of intelligibility. The individual's contact will not now be made with God, but with semi-transcendental categories such as life, work and language (Foucault, 1966). This is a triple root of finitude which will originate biology, political economy and language. This substitution of the original infinitude for finitude will be called the Kantian revolution. Instead of generalization in knowledge, there is comparison. For Foucault, knowledge folds over onto finitude which is the finitude of man himself. The world folds over onto the man-form. This form becomes the epicentre and the reference point of all knowledge. Biology, political economy and language will search for their foundation in this figure: 'It is rigorously contemporary of man, as an epistemic bond, the paradox which governs all modern philosophy: to look for foundation in a finite being' (Wahl, 1975: 73).

Has this man-form now died, been erased, as Foucault claims? And if this is the case, what new form has emerged? Can we continue the archaeological explanations which Foucault brought to an end with the man-form to make explicit how this new form emerges? The dispositions of knowledge of things and their order which gave birth to the man-form or man, of our sciences, have *disappeared*. In their place a new figure is emerging, a substitute which is the *cyborg-form*. The characterization of such a new ontology, however, has not been explored, and we believe that this is fundamental with regard to understanding the possibilities for thinking of and conceiving the reality offered by this figure.

The relation between the individual in their everyday existence and their exterior has changed. The cyborg-form has emerged from the relation of individual with an exterior which is unlimited-finite. This form is neither god nor man. Nor is it the mere transgression of limits. It is the ability or possibility to act, to exist and to be on different planes simultaneously. It is the capacity to be defined in different ways through multiple positions, chains of genetic codes folded over on top of one another, the potential relations of silicon, information stored in cybernetic machines, the contours of the sentence and the dispersion of words in postmodern literature. Human subjects and conceptual or material objects among those living can now no longer be conceived in singularities isolated from the dynamic, correlative, multipartite systems within which they appear. The fold upon fold expresses something of the way the cyborg-form is more than a figure and a network, but is a logic of continual incorporations of things, beings and structures, in totalities which emerge, develop, and repeatedly fold over on themselves to the point of saturation and redundancy.

Let us now revisit social constructionism in order to contaminate its basic boundary markers, to infect its clean, clear limits.

Social constructionism revisited

Authors such as Michael (1996) have started to demand of social constructionism that it incorporate the role of the non-social and the non-human in it. According to Michael, the reasons which impel us not to exclude the non-human and the non-social from our descriptions and explanations are aesthetic, historical, and political. Social constructionism has shown itself to be highly sensitive to the linguistic resources which operate in the production of meaning from what surrounds us. These, in their turn, are systematically located in spaces as diffuse and abstract as those ambits called 'culture', 'ideology', or 'language'; spaces which are populated by ideas and thoughts, and empty of walls, doors, dogs, computers, fish. The effect of all this is to make the social omnipresent.

Michael's claim seems to me to be sound. However, in its form, it fails to convince me. Simply incorporating the non-social and the non-human in our explanations has two effects. The first is to leave intact the dichotomy between the social and the non-social. The second is a corollary of the first. We leave the notion of the social present in social constructionism intact. This is still a relationship, now between humans and non-humans, but a relationship all the same, and a process.

Why should we question that the social be a process? Is it not the case that when social constructionism conceived of the social as process, it broke away from thinking which understood the social to be fact, objective, external to the individual and beyond time and the historical? When Gergen (1994: 49) writes that 'the terms and forms by which we achieve understanding of the world and ourselves are social artifacts, products of historically and culturally situated interchanges among people', is he not subverting traditional social psychology? He is, but he is also still trapping the social in time, in the hegemony or tyranny of the temporal.

There are two elements to the confinement of the social – of 'territorialisation' in Deleuzian terminology, or 'stratification' in that of Foucault – in time. On the one hand, social reality is historical, subjected to the vicissitudes of, and keeping step with the historical, and nowadays it seems unquestionable that:

> Society constitutes a human production which is modified through time... social phenomena, social practices, social structures have memory, and 'what they are' at a given moment is inextricable from the history of their production... to say that social reality is intrinsically historical is to say that it results to a great extent from the cultural peculiarities of the traditions, the way of life that a society has gradually built up throughout its development. (Ibáñez, 1994: 229)

By the same token, the social is a process. As I said earlier, the procedural is inextricably linked to time. This is the case to such an extent that one of the meanings of the word process is that of the passage of time. Process is the action of continuing a series of things which have no end.

This means that the true mechanism of intelligibility of the objects of social constructionism is time, or history. The social as process is conceived of as a set of phases or moments which unfold in time. For instance, racism is that set of actions which, unfolded, lead to discrimination. However, it is time which allows us to gather and agglutinate them in a meaningful unit. Time gives a logic to, or unites along a line, the dispersion marked out by these practices of violence. Furthermore, however, racism is limited as a phenomenon which appears in a particular culture and in a specific historical period. Here we have the double encapsulation of the social by time: it labels a process and thereby employs the trope of homogeneity. This double confinement of the social has an important effect. It makes 'the social' seem like the designation of something coherent, univocal, homogeneous and identical in its appearance and recognition. The social as a process is a species, recognizable in its manifestations, identifiable.

Knorr-Cetina (1995: 75) seems to be pointing to something similar to this:

> Sociology considers many of its categories as 'primitives' – as categories constitutive of daily life and applicable to any arrangement of human subjects. Categories such as actor, action, interaction, social, social structure and organisation, are such primitives. Can we watch human beings 'do' things with each other and yet not call this behavior interaction? Is it conceivable that a group of people who live together in a village is not a social group? Is not anything people do as long as they do it within collective arrangements by definition social?

Let us make this author's questions our own, and add one more to the list: Is it possible to break, alter or contaminate this notion of the social? Can we escape from it? Let us do a simple exercise: try to think of the social from the cyborg angle.

Let us think of two people – for example; a scientist in a subatomic-particle laboratory and her husband at the supermarket. Here we have two individuals in very specific and different circumstances. If I were a social constructionist, I would accept that identity is no more than the theory we use to understand ourselves, or which others use and which is subject to contextual variations. To say something about our scientist in her laboratory, I had only to observe how she relates to her colleagues, how she speaks, what she speaks about, how she defines herself, how she is defined, what she writes. In her husband's case, things are not so simple. The supermarket seems a tricky context to talk about social identity, but I would, nevertheless, end up resorting to standards, norms, lessons, the sort of relationship he has with the cashier and the other customers, and I could also say something about how his identity is constituted in the supermarket.

The point I wish to arrive at with this, perhaps excessively cari-catural, example is to show that the social is the result of an exercise in abstraction in which I set off a process of vacuum production. In it, I take the actors out of their most immediate material context and transport them to a plane in which only they, their relationships with other humans and pre-defined elements such as language, norms, and so on exist. I do not suppose that the shopping trolley, the Geiger counter, or the microscope can tell me anything about their identities. In the final analysis, the word context boils down to certain ques-tions: When is she in the laboratory? When is he at the supermarket? Who do they see, who do they talk to? Why do they talk about that in a supermarket? How do they write? How do they talk?

Do we wish to think of the social in another way? Can we say of these individuals that they are cyborgs? Not *a priori*. It does not seem appropriate. However, if a cyborg is not just a metaphor, we may answer affirmatively. They *become cyborgs*. She becomes cyborg in her laboratory. He becomes cyborg at the supermarket. Why? In the lab-oratory, she establishes relationships with non-human entities (the microscope, the electron-accelerator, Einstein as myth, radioactivity, and so on) which have no place in the usual explanations of the social sciences. Moreover, these relationships have standards of meaning, possess symbolism and are not merely automatic actions. Thus, she can treat the Geigercounter as an actor in a social network whereas she can relate to her assistant as if they were not human.

All the myriad relationships with their meaning and symbolism support, give foundation to, and guide her actions and behaviour in this context. In the laboratory, she forms part of a network through which things and beings are organized and related. The operations carried out in this network are continually crossing the limits which classical thinking sets between humans and non-humans, the cultural and the natural. For this reason, I claim that she becomes cyborg. In order to understand her, to get closer to her in this context, I cannot make the *a priori* abstraction of only considering relevant in it the relationships that she makes with human beings, that she has a set standard which guides them, and that the non-human are only things for her. A similar thing would happen with her husband at the supermarket.

Each becoming cyborg is an event and not a process. To approach these becomings, it is not enough for us to relate their history. It is not enough for us to make a narration, with a beginning, middle and end. We would be better off making a map, charting the set of relationships of which she is a part, and observing the variations in this map. Does all this mean that there is a need to give up the notion of the social? Not necessarily. We can consider that the social is not a presupposition but an effect, a product which may emerge or not. When it appears, it is thanks to the becoming cyborg which incorporates it as just another element. The social may appear in distinct forms, particular ways of materializing and particular ways of being given meaning. These are going to depend on a framework, on a map which distributes relationships and actions. This distribution respects none of the limits that the social sciences have assumed until now as *a prioris* of their thinking.

If there are no hidden planes organizing daily life in the laboratory, but only a becoming cyborg, and that in this becoming our scientist and the things and beings which interact with her acquire their identity, then we are dealing with ontological reorganizations – with a framework of ontological activity. And ontology or ontological activity is politics.

Becoming cyborg is a becoming political

Gergen (1994) claims that social constructionism is marked by a refusal to speak of things ontological, but this proves to be an untenable position. When Ibáñez (1994) sets an agenda for the new critical social psychology, he includes a section dedicated to the ontological presuppositions of this tendency. He has seen that when it is stated that social reality is historical, that it has a historical nature, a movement into the ontological terrain is made. Surely this statement is about the historical becoming of social practices a theorization about the logic of things, about their being and, then, about ontology?

What has to be highlighted, however briefly, is that it is not a matter of discovering foundational discourses, but of elaborating them, even knowing them to be untrue. It is a question of the use value that these discourses have. Given that a plane called 'out there' as opposed to another called 'in here' does not exist, but that these and their differentiation are constructed and that this elaboration has consequences, we may try to exploit this construction's possibilities.

On this point I follow López Petit (1994) in maintaining that ontology is not an ideological and obfuscatory instrument. Ontology is a
space of confrontation, a political space. Examples to support this
statement are to be found in the work of Deleuze or Negri, where
ontology is more of a toolbox for experimentation than an attempted
explanation of reality, of things just the way they are. Ontology
affords us new ways of thinking of what surrounds us, of organizing,
of understanding.

As Haraway (1991: 254) states, 'The cyborg is our ontology, it gives
us our politics'. Cyborgs allow us to redefine and continually alter
the limits of our world, of our everyday existence. Ontology is no
longer the space of the thinking of 'being' which philosophy used to
manage; now it belongs to the everyday becoming of cyborgs.

As opposed to ontological silence, it is necessary to call for an
excess of ontological discourse. I claimed earlier that cyborgs are a
'fold on a fold', this form or idea enables us to approach this excess,
this piling up and accumulation of differences and entities set against
each other which are integrated in one unit. Becoming cyborg
continually removes order in so far as it transgresses all limits or
unceasingly reconstitutes them. Order in its own dynamics is unre-
lentingly removed in this becoming. We need a different logic to that
of frontiers to try to approach an everyday existence populated by
becoming cyborg. This search is in itself a political action. The becoming cyborg is a 'fold upon fold'. It forces us, therefore, to confront the
multiple and the varied, the fragmentary and the unfinished, the
nomadic and the hybrid.

The forms of cyberpsychology

In conclusion, I would like to explain how I imagine the forms of
cyberpsychology. Above all, I believe that it cannot be a doctrine, a
school or a method. I imagine cyberpsychology as a project that is
always open, without doctrinal or methodological limits. I imagine
it as a critical analytic tool, as a way of reading that which
currently surround us. This manner of reading has an express
political commitment.

I imagine a cyberpsychology that does not substitute ontology
with a refusal to speak but which searches for the polyphony of
creations, of ontological inventions. If cyberpsychology is a critical
tool, I imagine it incorporating within its reflection what has always

been the great otherness of social thought, technology, to be more precise, that which is not human; the events that populate our days spread out in networks, in chains made up of human and non-human assemblies. Nature and society, or society and technology are not concepts that operate as a starting point in order to explain our day to day, on the contrary, they are points of arrival. Purification exercises where human action is separated from that which is not human and where the mechanisms of intelligibility are separated from these actions. Cyberpsychology would not recognize artificial limits between the subjective world of politics–culture–morality and the objective world of science–technology–nature. We live in a present with a different logic to the one expressed by this dichotomy, we could call it the logic of assembly. Neither human subjects, nor conceptual or material objects can be considered in their singularity or isolation from the networks and dynamic systems within which they appear. All things and all individuals arise, develop and disappear by joining together or by being incorporated in other structures that arise, develop and disintegrate.

Finally, I imagine cyberpsychology as vagrant knowledge which, at the same time, is not lacking in objects. I imagine it as an analysis of a changing, heteromorphological present, populated with a multitude of sensitive data that do not cease to be produced, fractual, unassimilable. I do not imagine it as a renunciation of the study of that which surrounds us, as an abandonment to the mere flow of data and experience. I imagine cyberpsychology made by a fragile, uncertain being, shifting in like manner to the terrain upon which it moves. Approximate and momentary, without firmly capturing its object, without drowning it in final explanations. In particular, I imagine a knowledge made up of 'mini-concepts', previously made up of ancient words with new meanings, ancient words in original combinations. I imagine a knowledge of dispersed remnants, more or less achieved, provisional.

References

Bergson, H. ([1957]1977) *Memoria y vida*. Madrid: Alianza Editorial.
Clynes, M. and Kline, N. S. (1960) Cyborgs and space. *Astronautics*, Sept., 26–7, 74–5.
Deleuze, G. ([1977]1980) *Diálogos con Claire Parnet*. Valencia: Pre-Textos.
Deleuze, G. ([1986]1987) *Foucault*. Barcelona: Edicions 62.
Deleuze, G. ([1990]1995) *Conversaciones*. Valencia: Pre-Textos.

Deleuze, G. ([1993]1996) *Crítica y Clínica*. Barcelona: Anagrama.

Deleuze, G. and Guattari, F. ([1972]1977) *El AntiEdipo*. Barcelona: Paidós.

Deleuze, G. and Guattari, F. ([1980]1988) *Mil Mesetas*. Valencia: Pre-Textos.

Escobar, A. (1996) 'Welcome to Cyberia: notes on the anthropology of cyberculture', in Sardar, Z. and Ravetz, J. R. (eds) *Cyberfutures: Culture and Patterns on the Information Highway*. London: Pluto Press.

Foucault, M. ([1961]1991) *Historia de la locura*. Madrid: Fondo de Cultura Económica.

Foucault, M. ([1963]1989) *El Nacimiento de la Clínica*. Madrid: Siglo XXI de España editores.

Foucault, M. ([1966]1970) *The Order of Things*. London: Tavistock.

Gergen, K. J. (1994) *Realities and Relationships*. Cambridge: Harvard University Press.

Haraway, D. ([1991]1995) *Ciencia, Cyborgs y Mujeres*. Madrid: Cátedra.

Ibáñez, T. (1994) *Psicología Social Construccionista*. Guadalajara: Universidad de Guadalajara.

Knorr-Cetina, K. (1995) *Epistemic Cultures*. Chicago: Chicago University Press.

López Petit, S. (1994) *Entre el Ser y el Poder*. Madrid: Siglo XXI de España Editores.

Michael, M. (1996) *Constructing Identities*. London: Sage.

Piscitelli, A. (1995) *Ciberculturas*. Barcelona: Paidós.

Serres, M. ([1980]1991) *El paso del Noroeste*. Madrid: Debate.

Wahl, F. (1975) *Qu'est-ce que le Structuralisme?* Paris: Seuil.

Wolmark, J. (1995) 'Cyborg bodies and problems of representation', in Burman, E. A., Gordo-López, Macauley, J. R. and Parker, I. (eds) *Cyberpsychology: Conference, Interventions and Reflections*. Manchester: Discourse Unit

PART FOUR

Commentaries

CHAPTER 13

The Cyber and the Subjective

S TEVE J ONES

It has been often mentioned that technologies shape our images of ourselves, but little has been made of how our selves shape technology. Once science overcame superstition, the explanatory narratives humans used to make sense of life processes mirrored the scientific narratives explaining nature. Holy fires and vital life forces gave way in the Enlightenment to complex narratives concerning mechanics, physics and biology. Industry operated on the basis of hydraulics, and science estimated that the human body operated as a machine, that various connections of pipes, tubes, motors, governors, made life possible. Genetics forms the foundation for the life sciences at present, and our computer technologies' binary codes mimic DNA.

What has happened to our human narratives, though? Do they, too, mimic the digitized, fragmented bits to which we have become accustomed by science? Postmodern discourse as a form of human and social narrative would seem to suggest that in fact we have adopted a kind of digital, or at least digitized, viewpoint. Postmodernism has much to offer as we try to determine who we are in the late twentieth century, approaching a new millennium. But as postmodern philosophers would probably readily admit, it is but one of many explanatory schemes. Perhaps that will be the legacy of digitization: as the bit has standardized the format by which the media of communication operate, it has also levelled the value of the content mediated. At least it has inscribed valuation within the subjective, for if, as Nicholas Negroponte (1995) and other 'digerati' are wont to point out, 'bits are bits,' then it is only what individuals do with bits that matters. If we understand humans in a fashion similar to the way we understand digital being, might we not also level the value of our selves, or at least imagine into being a hypersubjective realm in which mediation of the self through communication is the *sine qua non* of networked technologies?

As other chapters in this volume remind us, our most recent technologies are indeed particularly ones of the self. They conflate the narratives we construct about who we are with ones we construct about who we are in relation to technology, rather than in relation to one another. One might even say that these are not only technologies of the self, but selfish technologies. The affective dimension of network technologies is difficult to assay, but is of great importance. The contributors to this volume have done a masterful job of mapping out that terrain, alerting us to the tasks that lay ahead as we come to grips with new subjectivities.

A note about the subjective: I am an interloper into the discussion of cyberpsychology. My training is in the study of communication and in cultural and critical studies. Any scholars in the social sciences and humanities, however, ignoring the consequences of network technologies for their work, do so at their peril. The issue is not merely whether the Internet, for instance, can disseminate information more rapidly, whether on-line journals are a suitable arena for publication, or whether educational technology will displace traditional teaching methods. An overarching issue is the manner in which these technologies implicate the objects and subjects of scholarship, along with scholars themselves, in new webs of significance and meaning that impart new frameworks to our experiences and encounters. In addition to encapsulating us in any variety of Foucauldian panopticons, like some global Hawthorne effect, network technologies affect our thinking and behaviour as much because of the attention we pay the technology (and ourselves embedded in it) as because of anything else.

Additionally, we must attend to the very definitions of selfhood as these technologies engage us more than imaginatively in realms other than the ones we physically occupy. Marshall McLuhan's (1964) characterization of the media of communication as 'extensions of man' was meant to make sense in the realm of the senses. The Internet, however, is in these terms extrasensory. It less extends our senses and more extends our selves. The discussion in these pages of cyborgs and bodies is relevant and important. We must continue that discussion and consider the nature of software agents and bots to best understand the social system being envisioned and engaged in these networks. In addition to asking who we are when we are online, and who we are when we are off-line, what heuristic power may derive from asking who we are when we are, simply, not present? Does telepresence fundamentally alter not only the nature of both presence and selfhood but also the nature of absence?

The critical nature of these chapters is of great importance, too. We must move critical discourse about cyberculture to the forefront of our debates about network technologies. And when we do so we must keep at bay nostalgia, not for the past, but for the future. Behind much of what has been written about cyberculture lies a series of 'if onlys' that at best make its authors seem presumptuous, and at worst reveal an uncritical perspective. One is reminded of a type of Country and Western song with the refrain, 'We could have had it all'. Predictions of the future are as much about the past as they are about our imagination, and, as James Carey (1998) pointed out by borrowing from David Abrahamson (cited in Carey), 'the only thing certain about the future is that we know nothing about it'.

What is needed, I believe, is an interpretive turn to our discussions of cyberculture. Let us ask of ourselves: for whom are our words meant? For the psycho-technological complex in its entirety? For the individuals engaged in it in innumerable ways? For ourselves, the disciplines of which we are a part and/or for (not necessarily because of) the experiences we have had of technology? As we write, debate, speak about these matters, do we repress what we explain? Do we explain it away? Do we explain it into being? In what ways do we make meanings even as we understand those extant? Vannevar Bush's (1945) fortunate phrase in the title of one of his essays, 'As We May Think', inspired not only the artefact we term the Internet, and its hypertextual character, but the meaningful and deep structures of thought with which it is overlaid. The network of networks mimics human thought, but at a level beyond the individual it mimics culture itself. Post-structuralists should recognize the Internet's character as an articulative process and not only a technology. In Lewis Mumford's (1934) terms, it is the *technics* of the Internet that are of greatest importance. The Internet more than any other modern technology embeds technics in reference to social relations. Consequently, our inquiries and interventions into cyberculture are, as Stuart Hall (personal communication) said in relation to cultural studies, deadly serious intellectual work. And cyberculture appears to be a particularly resonant site for such work. Will the work we do also have serious material, cultural effects on cyberculture in turn? The Internet particularly has roots in academia, and we should be attentive to that rootedness as we examine both its past and its future.

In regard to articulation, the Internet's meaning, as meanings within and among culture(s) generally, is not simply in its structures, nor is it in its users, although at any one given time it is located specifically there. Rather, its meaning is in the connecting between and among nodes, accreting and dispersing, (virtually) ahistorically, or so the technology makes it seem to us. The Internet, and thus cyberculture (although I do not equate those but only refer to them in the same sentence to note their for-better-or-worse constant conflation and necessary interdependence) are technology-as-process rather than technology-as-product.

Within a technology-as-process where and how does one locate the self? Judging from the chapters in this book (although this is the least of its contributions), the relationships between society and self are in flux, and self (itself) is in flux. Self has always been multiple, as most recently and popularly noted by Verve singer Richard Ashcroft declaring 'I'm a million different people from one day to the next,' although he goes on to note that he 'can't change the mould' he's in. A pertinent question, then: who has made the mould? Is it indeed a human construction at all, or a technological one, or a combination of those? In what ways is cyberculture a mould, a cyberstructure, as a technology-as-process, perhaps one akin to a coral reef that grows, is eaten away, regrows? An example: Most of us have a variety of voices we use on the telephone. One voice is for friends, another for family, still another for telemarketers, and so on. Those are typically voices we do not use in person, or at least we are not conscious of using them. Did the telephone split our selves via our voice? Was the potential for such a split there already? Does networked communication fragment us similarly, along lines of identity forged by email address, IP node, Internet tool, or something else altogether?

Answers to these questions have typically engaged issues of culture, technology and communication, and in turn those issues fall upward to analyses of the human relation to space and time. The chapters in this book do as well, to an extent. But they also focus on subjectivity in a way that must force us to a more substantive discourse of what space and time mean in relation to communication. Marshall McLuhan (1964), Harold Innis (1972) and James Carey (1989) have greatly added to our understanding of space and time in relation to communication. This volume's contributors in their own way further that work and allow us to bring subjectivity into these discourses. We have thus far had a tendency to apply subjectivity only at those times when we need to explain how and why digital media, quintessentially linear, bounded, discrete forms, seem anything but linear, bounded and discrete. How has it come to be that these technological forms seem analogue, continuous and relative? Is it their speed? Is it that time is not linear, not flowing, but discrete, and that our perceptual processing provides sufficient closure, as it does when we hear a CD, or use a telephone, for example, and hear sounds made up of millions of discrete bits that form analogue sound?

I ask these questions because they have been much on my mind lately, as I have tried to make sense of the transition from one type of society to another, from one forged by the Industrial Revolution to one inscribed by bits and lasers. It took decades to make sense of the transition from an agrarian to an industrial society, and it will likely take decades to make sense of the one from an industrial society to a networked one. The upheavals the first transition brought to the surface were vast, and in many cases dangerous. Whether the ones we are now experiencing are, or will be, dangerous, we cannot yet know. That they are vast, however, is certain. We are beginning, however, to chase down that vastness, perhaps like William Cowper's philologists 'who chase/A panting syllable through time and space/Start it at home, and hunt it in the dark' (1968: 691). Illumination follows.

References

Bush, V. (1945) 'As we may think', *Atlantic Monthly*, 162(7): 33–40.

Carey, J.W. (1989) *Communication as Culture*. Boston: Unwin-Hyman.

Carey, J.W. (1998) 'The Internet and the end of the national communication system: Uncertain predictions of an uncertain future', *Journalism and Mass Communication Quarterly*, 75(1): 28–34.

Cowper, W. (1968[1785]) *Verse and Letters*. Cambridge, MA: Harvard University Press.

Innis, H.A. (1964) *The Bias of Communication*. Toronto: University of Toronto Press.

Innis, H.A. (1972) *Empire and Communications*. Toronto: University of Toronto Press.

McLuhan, M. (1964) *Understanding Media: The Extensions of Man*. New York: McGraw-Hill.

Mumford, L. (1934) *Technics and Civilization*. New York: Harcourt Brace.

Negroponte, N. (1995) *Being Digital*. New York: Knopf.

CHAPTER 14

Are Media Cyborgs?

VIRGINIA NIGHTINGALE

In the following comment on the changing (and anti-communicative) character of global culture, the late Michel de Certeau suggested that the shift to flows of 'people, things and ideas' as the organizing mode of culture is changing the structure and balance of our social and cultural worlds:

> Communication is the central myth of our societies split between the development of circulation and atomisation. On the one hand, emphasis is placed on everything that circulates (people, things, and ideas), on travels, on modes of transport, and on schools and the media, these two great interchanges of ideas and images. On the other hand our social organisation endlessly scatters and fragments groups, individuals, and traditions; it collapses the inner logic that used to structure former ways of thinking, a use of relations, a language of everyday life, and the memory that used to inhabit gestures and speech. As the information that is distributed throughout social space increases, the relations among the practitioners of this space tend to decrease. Communication thus becomes the paradox and the system of the juncture of what informs and what relays: distribution of communication increases, but its reality diminishes. At the core of these tensions is located the place and that which pertains to locality. (Certeau 1997: 91)

Certeau envisaged a relation between flow and culture such that as flow processes accelerate, the infrastructure of the old culture atomizes into smaller and smaller units. Its logic collapses, and so do its traditions and social relations. The survival advantage, whether material, social, cultural or spiritual, shifts to the capacity for flexibility with which cultural units can assemble, disassemble and reassemble again, no matter whether the assembling is assisted by post-Fordist commodity production or human reproductive technologies.

Certeau anticipated that the stress and tension which results from the pace of flows and from the fragmentation of social relations under such pressure places greater emphasis than ever before on 'locality' as the sites where flow 'fall-out', both good and bad, is likely to become evident and where strategies and tactics of resistance will occur. If I can be forgiven an analogy, this is a *Feng Shui* culture, where *chi* energy threatens to overwhelm locality unless controlled or deflected by tactics such as reflections, sound, barriers, screens, mazes and traps. It leads to the development of strategies for capturing the power of the *chi* in order to access its energy for human ends, and it seems to me that work produced for this volume, *Cyberpsychology*, starts this process as the beginning of a strategic engagement with the most powerful flow humanity has yet encountered – cyberspace.

Clearly, there are likely to be both benefits and potential psychological harms in social, technological and specifically cybercultural changes of this order, and it is to the mapping of such impacts that this anthology speaks. *Cyberpsychology* presents theorization and analysis of the psychological fall-out from the cultural shift to 'flow' (or 'circulation') as the increasingly dominating organizing principle of our culture. Where traditional psychology was predicated on assumptions of the body as the origin of the drive and on the self as the author of a life, *Cyberpsychology* contemplates the possibility of extra-corporeal origins and non-Oedipal psycho-geneses. It explores, as Gordo-López and Parker point out in the introduction to Part One, the nature of 'cyberpsychological modes of corporeality and subjectivity' and the possibilities for submission and repression, resistance and subversion in the cyber-environment.

Anthropomorphism and totemism as cyborg models

Nevertheless, my first reaction to *Cyberpsychology* is to wonder at the extensive anthropomorphism that permeates the discussion of cyborgs and patterns the developing agenda that will eventually be identified as 'cyberpsychology'. Somewhat strangely to me the regular punctuation of the readings with Haraway's judgement – 'we are cyborgs' – serves, in the 'cyberpsychology' context, to reinforce the imagining of cyborg agency as an elaboration of human agency, and of cyborg bodies as hybridized human bodies. Rereading Haraway, I cannot accept that this is an adequate apprehension of her position. Haraway seems to me to be affirming the present proliferation and hybridization of cyborgs as a continuation of our phylogenetic dependence on technological and social intelligence – intelligences that Mithen claims have evolved with humans from pre-human times (Mithen 1996). In fact the discourse on the cyborg seems to place too much emphasis on only one of the two extremely early modes of thought (anthropomorphism and totemism) which have assisted human cultures in the prediction of the archetypal flow – nature.

Mithen usefully reminds us that anthropomorphism and totemism mirror each other as ways of conceiving nature and as precursors to controlling it. But in my reading of *Cyberpsychology* there is very little elaboration of the totemic cyborg and rather too much elaboration of the anthropomorphic cyborg.

The anthropomorphization of the cyborg worries me because it obstructs my contemplation of an alternative, totemic vision of the cyborg. My cyborg 'vision' is informed, I shamelessly admit, by my interest in readership, audience and fan cultures, and from this perspective I see no *a priori* requirement that a cyborg must possess physical form or bodily parts in the way that both humans and the anthropomorphized cyborg do. This issue became most strongly focused for me when reading Sey's thoughtful and erudite comments (Chapter 2) on the delusions of ageing hackers that humanity is about to be replaced by a cyborg superrace. Sey claims instead that 'the body provides the limit not only to experience, but to knowledge and power also'. I completely agree, because I imagine the possibility that some extremely interesting cyborgs are dependent on transitory appropriations of human bodies and other physical and psychological properties of humans for their existence. They are humanoid rather than human-like. These electronic chimeras borrow human qualities by enticing humans into their flowing. They cathect human bodies to provide them with energy; they amass human bodies to command power. Without human service these cyborgs cease to exist; they evaporate almost without trace. Henri Léfèbvre (1991: 116–7) defined flows as the energies which surround living organisms – capable of both threatening and supporting life. Media flows begin by supporting life. They facilitate in various ways our primordial fascinations with both sociality and technology. But with human power and psychology behind them, media flows are also capable of threatening life in a variety of ways, which is why a cyberpsychology capable of understanding them is so important.

My 'cyborgs' contrast most dramatically with Heggs' (Chapter 11) superheroes and cyborgs. Heggs imagines an augmented equivalence between human and cyborgian agency. He suggests that at the very least the two agentic psychogeneses are comparable and therein instructive of each other. He presents a very interesting argument that the non-Oedipal psychogenesis of the cyborg threatens the world with a cyborgian predetermination to act as programmed, to act totally egocentrically, since the cyborg is perversely narcissistic and lacks the capacity to take another's perspective. The cybernetic organism as human person 'gone wrong' simply shines more brightly and blinks alternately as human/non-human consciousness and human/non-human body. The figure of this non-human cyberorganism is valuable, as Heggs indicates, for allowing humans to imagine another perspective (and its alterity). The imagining of accidental hybridization is the raw material of science fiction horror (see Heggs' account of *The Fly*), but here Heggs considers the accidental cooptation of insect agency and biological imperatives, while I remain haunted by images of spectral vectors and electronic Sirens.

My question, 'Are media cyborgs?', was prompted by a statement from Sey's essay and an example he used to explain it. Sey makes the following point. With the vast proliferation of technological systems beyond the initially crucial confines of the industrial relation between body and machine, we can discern that the ostensible disappearance of technology from the body, which might seem to mark a move into postmodernity, in fact emerges as the disappearance of the body into technology. Technological systems, that is, have extended to form the context of our experience of time and space, duration and extension.

This statement suggested for me an even more radical understanding of 'audience' than that I proposed in my book, *Studying Audiences* (Nightingale, 1996). In particular it concretized a vision of media as cyborgs, and I immediately began to imagine example on example of places where people disappear 'into' media – video game play; TV viewing; net surfing; radio listening. This is the chilling reality explored in Alexander Besher's 'novel of virtual reality' *RIM* (Bescher, 1994) where children are lost in virtual reality, their bodies suspended, comatose in the real world until rescued by an unlikely veteran of virtual environments. With other media, such 'disappearances' are characteristically temporary and, usually but not always, voluntary excursions into an alternative experience of extension and duration from that of everyday life – but they have in various pre-electronic forms (from rock art to reading) always been a characteristic of human culture.

But then a few paragraphs down, I noticed that Sey expressed the view that it is 'sport' that has changed as a result of technology that allows 'the sedentary and distanced viewer to become either a wishful voyeur or a postmodern technographic scientist "manqué"'. The example disconcerted me because in this case I strongly believe that neither sport nor the viewer has changed fundamentally. The viewers' expectations of what they consider they should be able to see and of how they should be able to see it *have* changed. Viewers expect the deployment and exploitation of technology, but that exploitation is not changing sport. It is changing the meaning of participation and engagement in sport on the one hand, and the expectations of the quality of the information brought to the contemplation of such participation and engagement on the other. In some cases sub-varieties of the particular sport may be developed to meet the requirements of media broadcasting (as in the development of one-day cricket) but fundamentally 'sport' has not changed.

Sport is, as Sey understands, a very interesting example. Sporting events are major socio-cultural fixtures. They pre-date the electronic media and are one of the contexts where contemporary totemism continues to be practised. Football teams in my home town, Sydney, are called Tigers, Bulldogs, Sharks, Sea Eagles, Eels – the list goes on. Broadcasting has added to the sporting event its parallel broadcast form and inadvertently created a level of competition between attendance at the broadcast form and the live form. The intensity of the competition is attested by the introduction of regulations and agreements about broadcasting rights which limit the synchronic presentation of sports broadcasts with the live event. Much more could be said about this, especially if social problems linked to off-course betting for horseracing and box-office takings for cricket and football games were more fully analysed.

The new twist in sports broadcasting is that it is now possible for the sporting field and its advertising to be altered for the broadcast image – advertisements for cigarette companies using billboards and hoardings on the field may become advertisements for entirely different products in the broadcast event. A potentially boring broadcast of a less than world-class local event can now be enhanced by the interweaving of other cultural forms (perhaps animation or comedy). Imagine for example the case of a home goal in a soccer match – suddenly it is possible to play mini-cartoons in the outfield which joke at the player's expense or which rehearse the win presaged by such a mistake for either or each team. If viewers pay per view and select their team broadcast, even more intense programming is possible, with in-jokes and all pretence of impartiality by the commentators dispatched. Of one thing there can be no doubt, the direction this change takes will be to increase the intensity of the viewing experience for both live and broadcast events, to lure more people into the flow because without people there would be no broadcast. And yet the live event and the broadcast event remain necessary to each other. The broadcast event annexes not only the players, referees and linesmen, it also annexes the crowd – its look, its voice, its mood, its energy and vital essence, not to mention its buying power and its non-verbal commentary on the game. The broadcast event annexes these characteristics of humans and replays them as television entertainment, in the context of televisual flow, where the bodily amassing of a second (viewer) crowd completes the cyberphenomenon.

The cyborg hybrid lurking here is a variety of broadcast television entertainment. It is TV sports broadcasting. To be more precise, the cyborg is the phenomenon produced by the combined interaction of the technology, the viewers and the owners, financiers, broadcasters, producers, ratings agencies, technicians and all participants in television – that is by human labour and human technologies. The agency of this television cyborg is unidirectional – towards self-maintenance and self-enhancement. It is based on the model of totemism, and it works with a logic of flow, feigns political and cultural weakness in order to encourage the largest possible number of people to lend it their bodies for the longest possible period of time. But one of its most interesting characteristics, and the reason why I raise it in the context of a discussion of cyberpsychology, is its capacity to develop a psychology of engagement that is parasitic of human psychology.

Media psychologies

Each medium of communication is dependent on human bodies, some media (usually commercial media) develop their own psychological pitch or seduction – and yet we have been very slow to look closely at the psychologies of electronic media (radio and television) when compared with the volumes written on the psychologies of print, film and the photographic image. 'Selling' psychologies have dominated these mass broadcasting terrains and this probably explains the lack of interest they hold for most academic researchers who prefer the more complex media psychology challenges of the novel or the film. The virulence of radio psychology was brought home to me recently when collaborating on a conference paper with my colleague, Jackie Cook (Nightingale and Cook, 1997). Cook's research on talk-back radio had revealed the capacity of the highest rating talk-back radio hosts to 'sex' the space of radio talk by deploying a hypermasculinity augmented by the production codes of radio. She demonstrates that the host cultivates seduction and 'dirty talk' from women callers, but challenges or 'calls out' male callers, 'beating them up' with bad language and unfair abuse to parade his dominant position. The talk-back host does not hesitate to mercilessly exercise his control of the studio and the production crew to censor callers. He uses gift giving (of sponsor-donated gifts) to repay favours or to hide his guilty conscience. His 'bad behaviour' attracts callers like bees to a honey pot!

Such behaviour is not confined to radio. A very similar spatial sexing is described in *Wired!* as the style of the late Tom Mandel, moderator of several, and contributor to most, *Well* conferences over a period of ten years (*Wired!* May 1997). Mandel's sexualization and monstering of explorers in the cyberspaces created by *The Well* had an effect similar to that of the radio host – it kept people involved as participants and as voyeurs, and demonstrated a commercial potential for the Web as an entertainment medium.

So are media psychologies part of cyberpsychology? The seductive hypermasculine environment of radio developed not only to hook listeners but also to sell the capitalist 'gift' of commodities. Cook's research examines how a production team and a fan club coordinate the listening and buying activity that maintains the programme, and a technology of control operates to maintain the radio space as an active one. Psychological strategies and techniques which exploit the frustrated sociality of frequently aged and isolated people are deployed to this end. Similarly the broadcast sports event, another environment promoting the advantages and power of the male, extols the virtues of male competitive strategies and muscular development. It parades the sociality of the crowd and in doing so hints at the managerial expertise of male power.

Certeau considered flows to be contemporary and culturally destructive phenomena. Henri Léfèbvre considered 'space' – whether physical or mental, concrete or abstract – and the production of 'space' to be the key cultural product, and he defined 'flows' as the energies which surround living organisms – capable of both threatening and supporting life. He considered flows to be the 'spatio-temporal rhythms of nature as transposed by a social practice' (Léfèbvre, 1991: 117); composed of 'raw materials and energy' (ibid.: 85). For Léfèbvre, flows could be contrasted with 'those realities which some geographers call 'networks' and which are subordinated to the frameworks of politics' (ibid.: 116). Media are obviously flows, and flows which are capable of supporting life. In fact they mostly facilitate life by offering opportunities for sociality in the spaces they colonize from absolute space:

> Absolute space cannot be understood in terms of a collection of sites and signs; to view it thus is to misapprehend it in the most fundamental way. Rather, it is indeed a space, at once and indistinguishably mental and social, which comprehends the entire existence of the group... and it must be so understood. In a space of this kind there is no 'environment', nor properly speaking, any 'site' distinct from the overall texture. (Léfèbvre, 1995: 240)

Léfèbvre (1995: 234 ff.) explains the concept, absolute space, by pointing to the relationship between town and countryside, a populated space of use patterning, irreducible to the blank abstraction of corporate representations. His description is usefully extended to the pioneering of cyberspace as a new media space and to the current attempts to transform it into a selling space. A gendered characterization of the processes of engagement between town (website) and countryside (cyberspace), produces a symbiosis, following Léfèbvre, which results in an initially unsexed space of power and sacredness. In the context of websites and experiences of surfing the Internet, this engagement ostensibly remains 'outside' physicality, in a realm of disembodiment where there is no 'environment', only a 'texture' fabricated from the very interaction of websites with cyberspace. This 'dislocated' relation however, by its very claim to extra-terrestrial or terra nullius mythical states, becomes primordial and primogenitive. Both maternal and paternal, absolute (cyber)space becomes the antithesis of both, and in this absoluteness, invokes the sacred. The sense of the sacred is evident in the names chosen and in the fates befalling the more notorious Internet communities – for example 'The Well' and 'Heaven's Gate' – examples of the political and the religious identifications and intrigues which characterize Internet communities, and of the beginning of a totemism based on life source analogies of the ineffable. The sterility and emptiness of the unformed website is characteristic of the evacuated yet sublime character of cyberspace, and perhaps explains the determination with which the Heaven's Gate cult quit this earth-bound life and decided to seek permanent dissolution of their psyches in the mythical homeland behind the Hale-Bopp comet.

Reflection: exhibitionism and harassment

I once re-read the current week's crop of Internet stories. The focus was on net exhibitionism – Lorraine Chew replaced, or joined, Jennifer Ringley in living her life for her Web camera and the entertainment of the thousands who visit her website each day; Ty Taylor and Michelle Parma finally conceded that their loss of virginity is totally unrelated to their plans to have sex on the Internet; and the mother who gave birth to her fourth child on the Internet was arrested for writing false cheques (Sevrens, 1998). Such life transition phenomena, rites of passage – birth, defloration, initiation – remind me of the totemic identifications such transitions often accompany. Their expensiveness for the participants is obvious in the arrest for fraud, unsolicited surveillance and other forms of harassment that stalk the unwary at every turn in this cyberfrontier.

Web panics about Internet rape and the unregulated preying of pornography and pederasty groups on unsuspecting young Web users are quickly outpaced by new panics about e-commerce and credit card fraud. In this discourse the press replays a popular litany of media anxieties, sometimes in and sometimes out of sync with the complex philosophical, psychoanalytic and socio-cultural reflection of the chapters in *Cyberpsychology*. *Cyberpsychology*, by contrast, focuses on the 'conditions' of cyberpsychology and at times seems troubled more by the ontological status of cyberpsychology itself than interested in its phenomenology and scientific development. Is it succumbing to or recoiling from the insistent, creeping and perverse narcissism of the cyberworld?

References

Bescher, A. (1994) *RIM: A Novel of Virtual Reality*. New York: HarperCollins.

Certeau, M. de (1997) *The Capture of Speech and Other Political Writings* (Conley, T., trans.). Minneapolis and London: University of Minnesota Press.

Haraway, D. (1991) 'A cyborg manifesto', in *Simians, Cyborgs, and Women*. New York: Routledge.

Léfèbvre, H. (1991) *The Production of Space*, trans. (Nicholson-Smith, D., trans.). London and Cambridge, MA: Blackwell.

Mithen, S. (1996) *The Prehistory of the Mind: A Search for the Origins of Art, Religion and Science*. London: Orion Books/Phoenix.

Nightingale, V. (1996) *Studying Audiences: The Shock of the Real*. London: Routledge.

Nightingale, V. and Cook, J. (1997) 'Hard buys and soft sells. Unpublished paper presented to IAMCR Mexico Conference, July.

Sevrens, J. (1998) 'Lust for fame', *The Weekend Australian*, August 29–30.

Wired! (1997) 'Push! Kiss your browser goodbye: the radical future beyond the Web'. Editorial (March 12–23).

Index